Synge and Anglo-Irish Drama

Synge and
Anglo-Irish Drama

*

ALAN PRICE

NEW YORK / RUSSELL & RUSSELL

FIRST PUBLISHED IN 1961 BY
METHUEN & CO. LTD., LONDON
© 1961 BY ALAN PRICE
REISSUED, 1972, BY RUSSELL & RUSSELL
A DIVISION OF ATHENEUM PUBLISHERS, INC.
BY ARRANGEMENT WITH BARBARA PRICE
L. C. CATALOG CARD NO: 70-173554
PRINTED IN THE UNITED STATES OF AMERICA

TO
BARBARA

Contents

A Brief Chronological Table

1871   16th April, J. M. Synge born in Rathfarnham, a suburb of Dublin; son of a barrister who died in 1872.

Synge delicate, educated in private schools and at home.

Fond of nature-study and of walking in the country.

Mother a firm evangelical Christian. Synge became agnostic.

1888 to 1892   Read languages at Trinity College, Dublin, and graduated with B.A., Second Class. Main interests: music (played violin in concerts), natural history, literature.

1891   Yeats, George Moore and Edward Martyn meet.

1892   National Literary Society founded in Dublin.

1893   Stopford Brooke lectures on 'The Need and Use of Getting Irish Literature into the English Tongue'.

Douglas Hyde forms Gaelic League and publishes *Love Songs of Connacht*.

1893 to 1898   Synge spends much time in Germany and Paris, and spring or summer near Dublin. Studies Gaelic, French and Italian at Sorbonne. In love with Cherry Matheson; she refuses his offer of marriage in 1896.

1894   Yeats's *Land of Heart's Desire* performed in London.

1896   21st December, Synge meets Yeats in Paris.

1897   Synge's hair falling out, a lump on his neck, the first manifestations of lymphatic sarcoma; a surgical operation.

1897   Synge making various attempts at writing, doing some book-reviewing.

1898   May–June, Synge's first visit to the Aran Islands.

Yeats and Lady Gregory meet and discuss plays.

1899   Irish Literary Theatre founded, under the auspices of the National Literary Society; promoted by Yeats and Martyn, aided by Lady Gregory and Moore.

First productions of Literary Theatre in Dublin: *The Countess Cathleen* by Yeats and *The Heather Field* by Martyn. Further productions each year until 1901 when Martyn and Moore withdraw and Fay Brothers join with Yeats.

1898 to 1902   Synge spends summer of each year on the Aran Islands, and the rest of the time mainly in Paris.

1902   'A.E.' joins Yeats and Lady Gregory and Fays, and the Irish National Theatre Society is founded. Plays by several authors produced. Synge begins to take an active part in the movement and gives up his Paris room.

1902 to 1909   Synge spends most of his time around Dublin, writing and working at the Abbey Theatre, and making occasional visits to the West of Ireland and one or two trips to England.

1903   First production of *The Shadow of the Glen*.

1904   First production of *Riders to the Sea*.

Abbey Theatre founded with the aid of Miss Horniman, and Irish drama thrives.

1905   First production of *The Well of the Saints*.

Synge becoming known on the Continent.

Synge makes a trip with Jack B. Yeats through the Congested Districts, then by himself to Kerry and the Blasket Islands.

Some actors secede from the Abbey and form the Theatre of Ireland with Martyn as president.

1906 First production of *Deirdre* by Yeats.

Synge in love with actress Molly Allgood (Maire O'Neill), and becomes engaged to her.

1907 First production of *The Playboy of the Western World*.

Riots at the Abbey. *The Playboy* a marked success in London.

The Aran Islands published.

1908 Fays leave the Abbey.

Synge operated on: impossible to remove the tumour.

1909 24th March, Synge dies.

First production of *The Tinker's Wedding*, in London.

First production of *The Shewing-up of Blanco Posnet*, after a struggle with Dublin Castle officials who tried to ban it.

1910 First production of *Deirdre of the Sorrows*, at the Abbey.

First edition of the Collected Works of Synge published.

Synge and Anglo-Irish Drama

CHAPTER ONE

Introductory

English Literature has been enriched immeasurably by writers who have been born or bred, or have spent an important part of their lives, in countries where English is the main language but which have traditions differing from the specifically English tradition. Of these countries Ireland is perhaps the one which has made the greatest contribution through such writers. This is particularly evident in the writing of the past sixty years, and no thorough understanding of contemporary achievement and trends in the novel, drama and poetry is possible without a study of the works of Joyce, Shaw, O'Casey, Synge and Yeats. Nor, in many respects, is such study neglected; there is already a considerable body of comment and criticism of all kinds on Joyce, Shaw and Yeats; on O'Casey, who is not of their stature and whose work, maybe, is not yet finished, there is accordingly not so much, but on Synge, who died in 1909 and whose writings may be seen in perspective, there is little. It cannot be said that he does not merit further consideration, for Una Ellis-Fermor points out:[1]

> In the American and English theatre and university world it has long been recognized that the work of Yeats, Lady Gregory, Synge and the group of men that supported and followed them at the Abbey Theatre must take its place in the world's drama, in that drama which contains already Euripides, Shakespeare and Molière.

Yet this recognition has not resulted in the production of any book devoted to a full treatment of Synge which gives an adequate appreciation and evaluation of his writings. I do not here presume altogether to supply this deficiency. I intend to examine and expound one aspect of Synge's work in the hope that I may thus help towards a fuller understanding of his genius. This aspect is the tension between dream and actuality, and it is central in Synge.

To place this appropriately something must first be said regarding the context of Synge's achievement – his relations with the Irish literary renaissance, the circumstances and pressures affecting his writings and the trends of opinion about them.

A Survey of Criticism of Synge

During Synge's life his work produced much controversy and many articles[2] but little criticism of more than ephemeral interest, apart from the utterances of Yeats. A spate of comment, partly hostile but mainly laudatory, came after Synge's death, and by 1916 many of the books and articles on Synge had been written. Nearly all of these deal with Synge's place in the revived Irish drama, and are introductions to his dramatic work as a whole or to some aspect of it. Francis Bickley's *J. M. Synge and the Irish Dramatic Movement* (1912) is a competent preliminary survey, giving a sketch of the literary scene, biographical information, an outline of the plays and some shrewd and appreciative comments upon them. P. P. Howe, in *J. M. Synge* (1912), following similar lines but making a more sustained and serious examination, particularly of character, is both enthusiastic and sane, and offers criticism which can still illuminate. Sensibly he keeps within his limits and makes few judgements about the Irish elements in Synge. Instead, with marked literary taste, he begins to link Synge with English writers. Sometimes he glosses over difficulties but is usually perceptive, and although his book is an appreciative expository study rather than a critical study and contains too much outlining of the actions of Synge's plays or mere recapitulation of his writings with insufficient assessment of them, it is probably what was intended and what was most needed at the time. Maurice Bourgeois's contribution too was timely. He presented 'a biographical and sociological, rather than a purely literary, interpretation of Synge's life-work'. His analysis of the Continental influences on Synge is authoritative, and his conclusion that these 'as compared with the solid Irish substance of Synge's genius are practically negligible'[3] is noteworthy. With a biographical approach and a belief that literature is mainly a form of self-expression, he claims that in Synge 'the personal element gave richness, depth and intensity to his blending of Continental art with Irish observation, and that it is by far the most important element of the three . . . his plays are Ireland; they are mankind; above all, they are Synge'.[4] True though much of this may be, Bourgeois's literary discrimination is not usually so impressive as his scholarship; he can descend to such dubious minutiae as the estimation of the number of blank-verse lines in *The Playboy* and *Deirdre*, he is rarely inside or at one with Synge's writings and his judgements on them are a bit superficial or literal-minded. Nevertheless, his book, a product of astounding industry, is a large storehouse of information and still remains useful. Synge's writings were soon engaging the attention of the philologist and their linguistic worth was shown by their use as the main material for A. G. van Hamel's scholarly study 'On Anglo-Irish Syntax' (1912).[5] Synge's name spread further, and during the Abbey Players' turbulent American tour in 1911 Lady Gregory reported that 'Synge's plays and others' in the Abbey list were 'being used in the course of English literature' at Yale and that 'professors and students wanted to see them'.[6] A sign of this widening interest was Cornelius Weygandt's *Irish Plays and Playrights* (1913) which, zealous and well-informed, provided the first tolerably full account of the new drama. About Synge he is stimulating and just; he indicates that Synge's characters are 'all natively Irish' and at the same time 'so human that they are prototypes of men and women the world over';[7] and he points to one outstanding truth – that the ultimate effect of Synge's writings, with their savagery, irony and sorrow, is exaltation and nourishment of spirit. The profound effect that Synge could have upon a fellow-writer with no predilections for the Irish can be seen in John Masefield's homage to him.[8] Masefield's description of Synge's appearance and behaviour in social gatherings is most striking: 'his face was pale, his cheeks drawn, rather seamed and old-looking, his voice was very guttural and quick, with a kind of lively bitterness in it . . . grave and courteous, he seemed to be listening to life's case before passing judgement'. The unsentimental feeling that both Masefield and Synge had for the hard, vigorous life of 'unaccommodated man' (the sailor or the tramp) facing the elements, may have helped to bring them together and enabled Masefield to outline Synge's methods of composition and to record such insights as Synge's declaration, after pondering on Shakespeare's line 'As any she belied with false compare', that 'no good writer can ever be translated',[9] and his reflection after speaking about past happy days that 'Nature brings not back the mastodon, nor we those times'.[10] Equally acceptable is Ma•efield's conclusion that 'Synge's mind is perhaps a little like Shakespeare's'.[11]

Englishmen, a Frenchman, a German and an American having published their appraisals of Synge and related writers, the Irish set forth their accounts. That of Lady Gregory is singularly interesting coming from one who was near the centre of creative power most of the time and thus giving insight into such varied matters as costume-making and play presentation, collaboration in play-writing, theatre finance and publicity, the fight with Dublin Castle about *The Shewing-up of Blanco Posnet* and the amazing riots over Synge's plays in Ireland and America. Without presuming to understand Synge a lot she admired his writings greatly, although unfortunately she recorded nothing but a few general remarks about them. Likewise her *Journals*, useful though they are for the background of drama, particularly that of O'Casey, say nothing material about Synge, and it is clear that her contribution lay not so much in literary theory and evaluation as in resourceful play-making and business management, in harmonizing personal relationships and in devoted support of Yeats. Having nothing like so close an experience of everyday Irish actualities as had Synge's colleagues Lady Gregory and Padraic Colum, but with a larger and better cultivated mind, George Moore provides a more cosmopolitan approach in *Hail and Farewell* (1911–14). Rather vain and derisory, unfair, gossipy though he sometimes is, Moore writes engagingly with wit and discernment, and, with all his carelessness about details, he occasionally unfolds truth. After sundry gibes at Yeats he memorably acknowledges Yeats's position as the prime creator of the revived Irish drama; he proclaims *The Playboy* a masterpiece from its opening lines, and he distinguishes deftly between Lady Gregory's and Synge's use of Anglo-Irish idiom, showing the superiority in naturalness and imaginative vitality of Synge's. Resembling Yeats and Synge in recognizing the necessity for returning to Ireland, Moore remarkably grasped the importance of the Aran Islands, though his scepticism as to whether the man and the moment would meet there and genius flower was ironically proved wrong. More exactly detailed and systematic is E. A. Boyd's *Ireland's Literary Renaissance* (1916). This provides an intelligent and comprehensive survey, demonstrating aptly the distinctiveness of Anglo-Irish literature from both Gaelic and English literature, the eminence of Synge and the genuineness of his idiom. Relishing the best, Boyd was quick to deplore the spate of superficial peasant plays written to a formula and a movement towards naturalism after 1909, since they represented a sorry departure from the vital principles of the dramatic movement. His *Contemporary Drama of Ireland* (1918), though placing Synge 'amongst the great dramatists of the world', is a rather hurried, unexceptionable reiteration of parts of his earlier and more penetrating book. Generally, Boyd's work reveals considerable understanding and discrimination and is not superseded by later histories; Malone is clearly indebted to him.

By about 1916 the first phase of criticism of Synge was complete. Almost entirely favourable to him, it was mainly concerned to describe his writings fully, to provide information about the circumstances of his life and work, and to relate these to the times and, in particular, to the literary revival. While his characteristic literary excellencies were expounded and a place in world literature claimed for him, the most important aim was to vindicate Synge against his accusers by establishing that he was genuinely Irish and that his writings were a valid expression of peasant life. Nearly all of this was well done, and a firm basis for the fuller appreciation of Synge and some of the more profitable lines for future investigation and discussion were laid down.

Between 1916 and 1929 little criticism of note was written on Synge, apart from Hugh I'A. Fausset's fine essay 'Synge and Tragedy',[12] and although O'Casey emerged spectacularly there was a slackening of interest in Synge and Irish drama, a result, perhaps, of such diverse happenings as the armed conflicts in Ireland, the temporary fading of the English susceptibility to Irish charm, America's withdrawal from Europe, the cosmopolitan fashion for jazz and clever cynicism, and a preponderance of naturalism together with a cautious policy at the Abbey Theatre which meant that it was no longer so progressive a force in world drama as it had been in its earlier poetic phase.

That it had never really been of much consequence was being said by three writers, from Northern Ireland significantly enough. Easily the finest and most temperate of them, Forrest Reid in the course of his *W. B. Yeats* (1915) had said incidentally that Synge was an artist 'but certainly not a great writer. His sympathies lay too exclusively with what is exceptional for that', and the vital

sentiments of admiration and pity were almost completely absent
from his 'intense, hard, narrow, bizarre talent'.[13] This unsubstan-
tiated slight was echoed by other essayists reacting against the
first enthusiasm for Synge. One, Robert Lynd in *Old and New
Masters* (1919), deploring the 'obsessions and idolatries of the
Synge cult', asserts that Synge could not create character, 'his
genius was a genius of decoration, not of psychology', and that
in *The Playboy* and after, Synge's style became vicious, 'a thing of
tricks and conventions';[14]

> Synge was an extraordinary man of genius, but he was not an
> extraordinarily great man of genius. He is not the peer of
> Shakespeare: he is not the peer of Shelley: he is the peer,
> say, of Stevenson. His was a byway not a high-road, of genius.
> That is why he has an immensely more enthusiastic following
> among clever people than among simple people.

Here the inconsistencies, the facile identification with 'ordinary
sensible folk' against 'intellectuals', the confident generalizations
unsupported by analysis of texts are the signs of the periodical
essayist exploiting his 'personality' and regarding literature more
as a cultivated accomplishment than as a prime source of human
values. A similar outlook, expressed with a more crude, colourful
and plausible vehemence, is embodied in St John Ervine's strictures upon Synge. Ervine had been Director of the Abbey
for some stormy months in 1916 which led to open conflict between him and the actors and ended in his resignation. His subsequent onslaughts upon the Abbey's most famous dramatist are
typical of a critic whose aptitude for bludgeoning surpasses his
taste and intelligence and who speaks of 'the odour of the char-
nel-house . . . the sewer-revelations of Mr James Joyce, who
may fitly be described as Rabelais after a nervous breakdown'.[15]
As certain patriots, mawkish about Ireland, called Synge's reality
cynicism, so Ervine, apt, in Lawrence's phrase, 'to do dirt on
life', called Synge's richness sentimentality: 'Synge was a faker of
peasant speech. . . . It is high time that all the tosh that was for-
merly spouted about Synge, and still is by sentimentalists late for
the fair, was stopped.' As a man Synge was weak, 'spiritually
ineffective and totally unable to stand up to life' and although he
'brought a desirable element of bitterness and acrid beauty into
the sticky mess of self-satisfaction and sentimentalism which is

known as Irish Literature' he lacked staying-power and 'died of sheer inability to assert himself'. He was a man of 'small twisted talent, an odd intruder into the realm of letters whose work smelt too strongly of the medicine bottle'.[16] On the rare occasions when Ervine pauses in his unwholesome generalities and approaches the actuality of Synge's words he displays the same rank obtuseness; in *Riders to the Sea* Maurya's language is 'entirely unrepresentative of the speech that Maurya was likely to use',[17] and generally Synge's dialogue is 'contrived stuff, withdrawn from reality and made into a pattern, pretty enough, but, after a time, tiresome and tedious'.[18] In brief, Synge fails because his dialogue is not naturalistic, not a close reproduction of what people say in everyday life; yet Ervine goes on properly to censure Coward for writing dialogue undistinguishable from ordinary speech and then quotes a lyrical passage from *Romeo and Juliet* to show the inadequacies of Galsworthy's naturalistic dialogue.[19] Clearly these attacks on Synge, so void of textual analysis, of sensitivity and coherence, are worthless as literary criticism, though they have some interest as representing the hostility to literature of the prosaic 'man of the theatre', and views that gained some currency during the nineteen-twenties and are not even today quite dead.

A related though less violent feeling that too much was being made of the twentieth-century literary revival, to the detriment of older writers, was expressed in H. A. Law's *Anglo-Irish Literature* (1926). He denied the generally accepted view that Anglo-Irish literature did not really begin until the second half of the nineteenth century, and he pointed to Swift, Goldsmith, Burke, the Edgeworths and others. In contrast to Corkery who saw these writers as tainted with Ascendancy attitudes and who cut down to a bare one or two the genuine Anglo-Irish writers, Law included as much as possible under his heading and so when at last he came to Abbey drama and Synge he added nothing fresh or noteworthy.

In 1926 Padraic Colum remarked: 'Not all has been said about Synge's plays and few poems, but little remains to be said about them at this day and hour; later, new and then newer, values will be set upon them.'[20] Colum himself makes a distinct contribution to future Synge studies. As a friend and fellow-dramatist of Synge he is able to give a personal account of moments such as the first night of *The Shadow of the Glen* or to evoke the period like this:[20]

> Outside Trinity College, I met W. B. Yeats; he was in a state of exaltation, like one who has seen something very grave and very revealing. 'Synge is dead,' he said to me. I met Padraic Pearse walking gravely with his head bent, thinking, I suppose, of his school. I told him that Synge was dead. 'It's too bad,' he said and he was silent for a while.

Coming from a man steeped in peasant life, Colum's observations on Anglo-Irish idiom and on the authenticity of Synge's use of it and of his portrayal of Irish people, are notable, particularly as Colum had no vested interest to serve, having gone with the group that split from the Abbey in 1905 and formed the rival Theatre of Ireland. His book, with its unaffected manner, sympathetic observation and faithful records of country stories, anecdotes and characters resembles and corroborates Synge's. Without being profound or fully developed Colum's literary judgements are shrewd and illuminating and his final affirmation is admirable: 'John Synge's work augments the spirit by revealing to us the national virtue'.[21]

Little contribution to a more adequate regard for Irish drama and for Synge was made by Dawson Byrne in *The Story of Ireland's National Theatre: The Abbey Theatre, Dublin* (1929), a rather simple-minded recital of mainly well-known information, with scanty reference to other critics and with a bare modicum of taste and penetration. The English elements were minimized and the Irish accentuated (no photographs of Yeats, Lady Gregory, Miss Horniman or Synge were printed but one of the author was) and though a fresh and welcome account was supplied of the work of the actors, Byrne seemed unable to get much beyond national prejudice. It is this factor which mars *Synge and Anglo-Irish Literature* (1931) by Daniel Corkery. A Gaelic scholar with knowledge, though partial, of several literatures, and a writer of novels, verse and plays (his *The Labour Leader* at the Abbey in 1919 won praise), Corkery might have produced the most important book on Synge instead of the most provoking. He makes a comprehensive and acute examination of Synge's work from a consistent viewpoint and with a clearly defined aim, and he increases in a singular way one's appreciation of Synge's achievement and one's awareness of Synge's relationship with the people and the land of Ireland. Unfortunately Corkery's viewpoint – that of a fervent nationalist – and his aim – to show that Synge's strength came from Ireland and his shortcomings from England – distort his work, his misconceptions outnumbering his insights. He has a notion of an ideal Catholic Irish peasant and he is inclined to praise Synge when he embodies this ideal in his work, and to condemn him when he does not. His final impression about Synge, that there was considerable power which went largely to waste because of racial and religious bias, is really much more true of Corkery than of Synge.

The slack period in the appreciation of Synge, the usual reaction following initial admiration, was ending. 1929 marked the Silver Jubilee of the founding of the Abbey, and to celebrate this and to place in order and perspective the theatre's achievements to date, appeared A. E. Malone's *The Irish Drama*. Knowledgeable about world drama and having seen every play staged at the Abbey, he competently delineated the features of his subject and its attendant social, political and cultural circumstances, maintaining a nice balance between the various aspects, and produced what is still the standard work. In Malone there is a firm and intelligent attitude and some acute and interesting judgements are made, but as the historical element naturally predominates there is little scope for any notable addition to the assessment of Synge. Obviously less concerned with literature than with sociology was Herbert Frenzel in *John Millington Synge's Work as a contribution to Irish Folk-Lore and to the Psychology of Primitive Tribes* (1932), yet his monograph is another instance of Synge's integrity and of the use of examining him in detail. A bit more material to help this was provided in the *Journal and Letters of Stephen MacKenna* (1936). Synge and MacKenna were close friends, particularly in 'the distressingly hard up' Paris days, and they always 'had in common an ironic humour and a passionate interest in the problem of style'.[22] MacKenna never knew 'a man with so passionate, so pedantic a value for truth as Synge. He didn't so much judge the lie intellectually or morally as simply hate it – as one hates a bad smell or a filthy taste.'[23] And the 'sorrowfullest thing' MacKenna ever felt about death was Synge's tone and look as he confessed his pain at the thought 'that while he lay there cloistered the seasons would come and go and he know nothing of it at all'.[24]

But beyond these evocations, and prompting Synge into writing one or two noteworthy letters, MacKenna did not go, most unfortunately, for he was a remarkable man having rare opportunities for supplying a fuller interpretation of Synge. Nothing noticeably fresh or penetrating was offered in Stephen Gwynn's *Irish Literature and Drama* (1936), a tolerable survey, useful in places, but cautious and pedestrian about Synge and the Abbey. Gwynn has a preference for the cosy and conventional and he shows his limitations in saying that James Stephens had 'a genius less crabbed than Synge's – happier, luckier, destined to larger fulfilment'.[25] Nevertheless, his unspecialized 'popular' treatment was a further sign of widening interest. And this was made more apparent and developed on a higher level by the Abbey Theatre Festival in 1938 when a number of men distinguished in Irish literature gave lectures which were published as *The Irish Theatre* (1939), edited by Lennox Robinson. About Synge Frank O'Connor spoke brightly and appreciatively though his hasty assertion that at one or two crucial points Synge failed to motivate his characters does not bear examination. He affirms the true Irish quality of Synge and shows how close Yeats, Lady Gregory and Synge were in their artistic asceticism and in their opposition to middle-class commercialism with its 'knowingness', machinery and stereotypes, and in the theatre its 'loud-speakers, wind machines, properties, scenery, cycloramas, and lighting sets'.[26] Corkery too went wrong here in demanding that the artist should be a representative of abstractions, 'a parliamentary deputy of literature',[26] O'Connor says, and goes on neatly and wittily to show how mistaken Corkery was in blaming Synge for not suiting his writings to someone else's formula.

By this time Synge was becoming generally accepted and studied in the academic world, his literary antecedents and relations were being examined and articles and theses written. Too often in these plodding industry obscures judgement, and one published, *The Sources of Synge* (1939) by A. D. Estill, illustrates a very limited kind of scholarship, providing an assembly of facts (nearly all of which already existed in Bourgeois) and making no attempt to use them. Then at last in 1939 a scholar, aware of fundamental values and at home in several literatures, paid her tribute in an excellent critical survey, *The Irish Dramatic Movement*. Una Ellis-Fermor, acknowledging, as all of us non-Irish must do, that

Synge's countrymen have produced unique and indispensable
criticism, shows nevertheless that an outsider can do something
vital in that 'interpretation that must be made of all national art
sooner or later, as it passes from the national to the international,
from the exquisite flowering of a generation to that which belongs
to the ages and to all mankind'.[27] She does her part in this process
well, lifting the discussion far above the restrictive antagonisms of
a Corkery or an Ervine, setting Irish drama in relation to the rest
of world drama, bringing out what has often been overlooked –
the prime importance of poetry in drama, and in her chapter on
Synge displaying his sanity, his grasp of fantasy and folk-myth,
and the distinctive balance in him of nature-mystic and dramatic
poet.

This academic interest in Synge was accompanied by widening
general interest, as shown by the various productions of his plays
on the radio and on the professional and amateur stages and,
during the nineteen-forties, by that sure sign of a writer's becoming established, the appearance of his writings in cheap popular editions such as the *Everyman*, *Penguin* and *Guild*. A remarkable feature of the war years was the upsurge of enthusiasm for the
arts. This was further strengthened and guided by several agen-
cies, both public and private, and among these was a series of
concise P.E.N. books about writers vital to our culture, that
contained, notably, *John Millington Synge* (1941) by L. A. G.
Strong. With convincing zest Strong sketches Synge's salient
features, maintaining proper proportions and just emphases,
blending generalizations with pointed practical criticism, and ful-
filling his aim of supplying reasons for enjoying Synge's writings.
With fresh perception he draws attention to the pregnancy of
Synge's literary judgements and to Synge's 'clear vision of the
state of poetry and the measures needed for its cure' which 'has
influenced almost all his successors in Ireland, including Yeats,
whose *Responsibilities* shows strongly the impress of his friend's
mind'.[28]

Synge's stock was rising. Reviewers of the standing of V. S.
Pritchett and important poets and critics such as W. Empson
and T. S. Eliot were referring appreciatively to Synge to develop
or illustrate their various arguments, the assumption being that he
was becoming established as one whose writings could be cited
as valid pieces of evidence in the structure of literary criticism.

By 1948, Synge, without being 'fashionable' was 'a minor European classic' Gratton Freyer decisively affirmed in his 'The Little World of J. M. Synge',[29] perhaps the best recent concise account of Synge. Intelligent and cultivated, Freyer puts the interest where it now must be, not in Ireland some decades ago, but in the world 'for all time', and he neatly makes useful links between Synge and other European writers such as Cervantes and Lawrence. He grasps some of the essentials about Synge, his absorption in peasant life, his 'unusual capacity for emotional sympathy with the humblest of characters', his singular use of the simile for wit and description, and his ability to create a fresh flow of emotions 'experienced as though for the first time on earth', which, contrasted with 'the normal world of to-day, in which all our emotions and opinions are carefully labelled and pigeon-holed, evokes in the average spectator first astonishment, and then a sense of relief: a species of catharsis'.

Articles reiterating more or less adequately the accepted viewpoints about Synge continued to appear, and so too did histories of Irish drama. Peter Kavanagh's *The Irish Theatre* (1946) deals with pre-twentieth-century drama; his later book, a disappointing response to growing American interest, is *The Story of the Abbey Theatre* (1950). This contains some fresh material and admirable photographs but contributes hardly anything on any level, being inexact, uncharitable and smacking of journalese. It rightly sees Yeats as the master builder of the Abbey but is astoundingly blind to his quality, and in continually asserting that his main aim was to 'shock the public and teach them a lesson'[30] makes him appear a charlatan. Kavanagh says that Yeats put on *The Playboy* to strike 'more violently than ever'[31] and O'Casey's *The Plough and the Stars* to assault further because 'an audience, like a woman, is most attractive when it is beaten into humility'.[32] Equally appalling are Kavanagh's dismissal of Synge in a few slipshod sentences for writing 'a flamboyant dialect of English interspersed with numerous swearwords',[30] and the conclusion that O'Casey was 'a typical peasant' and the first to put 'on the stage an Irish dialect which was not only authentic, but artistic'.[33] No examination of the plays is made, most other writers about them are ignored, and the main source is the insensitive and unjust *Diary of a Dublin Playgoer* by Joseph Holloway. A slighter example of the gross misconceptions still abroad, of the persistence in the parochial mind of postures discredited long ago, is Owen Quinn's 'No Garland for John Synge' (1950).[34] This article crudely repeats some of Corkery's strictures and adds such fatuities as that Synge used his imagination too much and the 'English language is unsuited to the subtlety of the Irish mind'. To bury personal likes and dislikes, not to appreciate or criticize the Abbey but to provide a history of it was Lennox Robinson's aim in *Ireland's Abbey Theatre* (1951). Although this supplements rather than supersedes other histories it contains some information previously unavailable, mainly about the material side of the theatre – administration, finance, dates and casts of performances – and about the appearance and habits of some Abbey personalities. The usually undervalued Miss A. E. Horniman is praised, and her generosity which alone provided the fabric of the Abbey is suitably acknowledged. Generally this is a not very well organized source book, of more interest to the historian than to the literary critic, though he might be able to use a few facts here and there to deepen our response to one or two plays. In the course of reviewing this book and finding it 'in the main slovenly and uncritical', Roger McHugh affirmed,[35] what had become fairly clear, that 'the best literary criticism of our modern writers in English has been written mainly by writers outside Ireland'. The truth of this was further substantiated by the chapter on Synge in Raymond Williams's *Drama from Ibsen to Eliot* (1952). With a deep and reasoned conviction of the primacy in drama of poetry, Williams sensitively examines the texture of Synge's dialogue and shows how Synge creates out of naturalistic elements plays which have the unrestricted potency of poetic drama, plays which, while being brilliantly successful entertainment are also thoroughly serious in their pervading moral intention and are thus akin to the drama of Jonson and Molière. Williams is an austere critic who finds not much to admire in twentieth-century drama; his verdict is therefore all the more noteworthy:[36]

> Synge is undoubtedly the most remarkable English-speaking prose dramatist of the century, in the same way, and for much the same reasons, that the Abbey Theatre is the most remarkable development in the theatrical history of these islands for some three centuries. Certain aspects of his work, as of the Irish dramatic movement as a whole, offer some of the best

material we have for a study of the place of drama in the total culture of a modern society.

During the nineteen-fifties the current of Synge criticism flowed strong and broad; he, together with the Irish theatre, was a favourite subject for writers of academic theses,[37] and more publications about him appeared in several parts of the world. In Kansas E. R. Taylor in *The Modern Irish Writers* (1954) industriously set forth a lot of comment and opinion on recent Irish writers mainly by themselves. Here again the aim and interest reside almost wholly in the assembling of material instead of in the more arduous task of using or assessing it purposefully, and so nothing is added to our view of Synge. Little new was said in a worthy, somewhat verbose, article 'Synge and National Drama' (1954) by Brother A. C. O'Connor, F.S.C., of the Catholic University of the Philippines, but his main point should be noted:

> Synge bequeathed to the heritage of world literature an enduring expression of national life. . . . His themes rise out of the local situation and the conflicts are shaped by the local temperament, yet Synge selected human conflicts that were basic to life, the motivation and characterization are always plausible and interesting to those unacquainted with the locale. Thus, his plays are at once a vivid and fascinating reflection of a national life and excellent examples of the dramatic artistry that will hold the interest of any audience.

This, coming from such a source, is indicative of the acceptance of Synge as a writer of international repute even by those whose basic beliefs are different from his and who accordingly might have assailed him fifty years ago.

Other nations are also adding their quota. Raymond Williams said perceptively: 'Synge's plays need evaluation as *texts*, with a temporary suspension of interest in the wider cultural issues, save only those which the texts themselves raise',[38] and from the Swedish Uppsala Irish Studies (partly subsidized by the Irish government) has come an example of this approach, *Ibsen and the Beginnings of Anglo-Irish Drama: 1. John M. Synge* (1951) by Jan Setterquist. Undeterred by Synge's proclaimed dislike for Ibsen, Setterquist sets out to see if there are any links between the two dramatists, and he does find a few resemblances, as well as some dissimilarities. It is noticeable, however, that the links, such as they are, are mainly in matters of theme and not in treatment and technique, and this diminishes the value of the study, since, in poetic drama at least, treatment is more important than theme, and Synge did not, like many in his day, censure Ibsen's themes, but his treatment. Other recent examples of this more specialized examination of a particular aspect of Synge are Irving D. Suss's article 'The *Playboy* Riots' (1952)[39] in which Freudian psychology is intelligently used to uncover the forces that erupted against Synge, and Dennis Donoghue's 'Study of *Riders to the Sea*' (1955)[40] which imaginatively perceives in the play a basic tension between Religion and the Sea, which, at the end with its echoes of Christ's Passion, is dissolved into Christian Acceptance. How a close and sensitive study of texts (the method of the 'new criticism' in which Donoghue is adept) can correct superficial and hostile impressions may be seen further in Donoghue's article on *The Tinker's Wedding*, 'Too Immoral for Dublin' (1955).[41] He shows that those who censure this play on moral grounds or on its 'lack of characterization' are wide of the mark; in fact, the play is 'solidly grounded on an important social premise' – that the beliefs of the tinkers are bound up with the natural world instead of institutional religion – and the comedy derives from the 'ironic reversals' embodied in the interplay of the orthodoxy of the priest with the 'orthodoxy' of the tinkers 'on certain questions of morality and social living'.

The literary qualities of the Irish movement, and not its politics or social circumstances, are now, fortunately, to the fore, and Herbert Howarth in *The Irish Writers 1880–1940* (1958) while studying Moore, Lady Gregory, Yeats, 'A.E.', Synge and Joyce in relation to Irish nationalism, and showing especially the effects of Parnell's fall and of the Parnell legend, has a large perspective and is sane and not partisan. Displaying some of the better features of literary scholarship and criticism, he shows the links between Parnell's aristocratic spirit and Yeats's, and he finds the same crude and bitter frustrations in the mob that attacked Yeats and Synge as in the mob that overthrew Parnell. The word 'shift' that sparked-off the *Playboy* riots 'had a history behind it; the anti-Parnellites had waved a shift in the villages in 1891 to stand for Kitty O'Shea and adultery and to drive the Chief away', and it became 'a banner of freedom of expression for the next

generation'. Howarth praises the singular energy of Synge and
his skill in concentrating so much into his plays and economically
shaping each to its proper end, and he notes that Europe accepted
Synge speedily and warmly – even if Ireland could not – and that
Sir Walter Raleigh affirmed Synge to be superior to Shaw and one
who combined truth and poetry in dealing with Ireland. Probably
Howarth's most original contribution is his appreciation of the
pungent earthiness, the wholesome sexuality, partly under the
surface in Synge but exuberantly exposed in Joyce and the later
Yeats. Joyce, Howarth indicates, admired and learned from Synge,
and through such masterly devices as that of Sara Tansey's smell-
ing Christy's boot was stimulated to develop his amazing comedy
of filth; Synge and Joyce 'married comedy and poetry so that the
comedy is in touch with what mourns in man'. Howarth is intelligent and informed, particularly about American books and articles
– though he makes little mention of Irish critics – and throughout
he assumes that the writings of Synge are now an established part
of the heritage of the English-speaking world and are therefore
of importance to everyone with a serious interest in it.

In addition to being, at least in its first and greatest decade, a
poet's theatre, the Abbey was also a great actor's theatre. The
Allgood sisters, Maire Walker, Fred O'Donovan, the Fay
Brothers, Barry Fitzgerald, J. M. Kerrigan, F. J. McCormick,
Arthur Sinclair and others, by the rare excellence of their acting
not only played an indispensable part in establishing the Abbey
but also later achieved high reputations on the stage and in films
in America and Britain. This timely coming together of dramatic
and acting genius was little short of wonderful; each fitted in so
well, the plays of Yeats and Synge giving the best vehicle for the
players, and they in turn giving performances which swiftly made
palpable the distinction of the plays. The players, however, have
received comparatively little attention, a result, perhaps, of the
fact that acting is an evanescent art and therefore difficult to
discuss at length. Nevertheless, some record of them was needed,
and this has now been made in *The Abbey Theatre* (1958) by
Gerard Fay, himself once an Abbey actor, and the son of the
Frank Fay whose speaking of the language of Yeats and Synge was
so admirable. Frank Fay, a clerk, shared with his brother, W. G.
Fay, an electrician, a passion for the theatre, and by 1900 they
had built up flourishing dramatic societies in Dublin. Then Frank

Fay independently envisaged a national theatre and put forth his ideas in *The United Irishman* in a series of articles including reviews of the earliest productions of Yeats's Irish Literary Theatre. These brought him to the notice of Yeats, and the two exchanged correspondence about drama, finding that they had much in common. They agreed in disliking the commercial theatre and saw that the best hope lay in poetic drama about Irish life and legend, acted by Irish people. Accordingly, when the first three-year trial period of the literary theatre closed and Edward Martyn and George Moore withdrew, Yeats, together with Lady Gregory and 'A.E.', in 1902 joined with the Fay brothers and their company, and the most distinguished phase of Irish drama began. It is the story of this fruitful partnership between poet and actor and its attendant circumstances and implications that Gerard Fay engagingly tells. He quotes aptly from contemporary newspapers and provides some new material about details of production and the attacks on the Abbey and especially about the actors, their techniques and their speaking of Synge's idiom, and the tensions that inevitably grew in such a tight-packed group and the splinterings away that ensued. Without attempting any fresh judgement of Synge he affirms that Synge was a genius and a fine comrade, and shows from Synge's letters to Frank Fay how keen an interest Synge took in the day-to-day workings of the Abbey and how well Synge dealt with attempts by some actors to alter his lines, he being always 'ready to avoid hurting people's feelings needlessly' but refusing to falsify what he believed to be true for anybody. Altogether, Fay's book, though not a complete history of the Abbey – it virtually ends after the departure of the Fays in 1908 – is worthy and well illustrated, and it also offers a modicum of material for the interpretative critic.

Valuable for similar reasons is *J. M. Synge* (1959) by David H. Greene and Edward M. Stephens, the first fully authorized biography. It rightly does not seek to make interpretations or judgements about Synge's writings (except, of course, the obvious assumption that he is an outstanding writer) but provides ample material which in the hands of a competent critic may be used to produce more adequate evaluations. The lack of a comprehensive and reliable biography of Synge has been increasingly felt as his fame grew and those who knew him dropped away. Compared with the information available about most important twentieth-

century writers that about Synge has been scanty, and tales such
as that he spent two or three years after 1893 wandering around
Europe 'playing his fiddle to Italian sailors and listening to stories
in the Bavarian woods' or that Molly Allgood acted parts of
Deirdre for him as he lay upon his death-bed, were repeated for
lack of anything else. Synge saved a mass of material – papers,
manuscripts of published and unpublished writings, diaries, letters,
notebooks – but at his death it came into the possession of his
brother, Edward Synge, who kept it private. In 1939 the material
passed to Synge's nephew, Edward M. Stephens, who had been
very close to Synge. Stephens, a barrister and civil servant, began
to write a biography in his spare time, but, getting into difficulties,
in 1953 sought the help of an American professor, David H.
Greene, whom he had met in 1939 in Dublin when Greene was
'writing a Harvard doctoral dissertation on Synge'. In 1955
Stephens died, and the Synge material was made available to
Greene. It is this, together with the further information that
Greene assiduously collected in Ireland from surviving records,
relatives and friends of Synge, that forms the substance of the
biography. Greene acknowledges his debt to Stephens and others
but he makes it clear that the story of Synge's life, the interpretations and conclusions about it, and the actual writing, are all his
own. His too must be the credit for a job well done.

He sensibly allows the story to tell itself, as far as possible,
in the words of the people concerned. Hence, one understands
more at first hand about Synge's personal life; the influence of his
evangelical mother, his aptitude, despite his reserve, for making
friends (he swiftly and unknowingly impressed so eminent a man
as A. N. Whitehead), his methods of working, his place in the
Abbey, his attitudes (quite the reverse of superficial) to politics
and social questions, and his relationships with women, especially
with his fiancée, Molly Allgood. About his views on literature
there is much less. Some observations, quite worth having, are
newly recorded which supplement rather than change his position set forth elsewhere. It is now quite clear, though, that Synge
was a most rigorous critic of himself, never quitting 'the intolerable wrestle with words and meanings', and casting out whatever
did not reach his austere standards. Consequently he wrote very
much more than he published, and a mass of literary material by
him exists, from which Greene quotes appropriately. It appears

to be inferior stuff, yet more might have been said about it by Greene, just as fuller descriptions of Synge's diaries and forty notebooks might have been given. There is still then something that we should like to know about Synge; what he thought about James Joyce or why he waited seventeen months before following Yeats's compelling advice to go to the Aran Islands. Nevertheless, this biography, superseding all previous accounts, should stand for some time as a prime source for the study of Synge and drama.

Finally, it is reasonable to declare, in view of the symbolical handing-over of the Synge material from Ireland to America and of the publication of it in the definitive biography, that Synge is now, fifty years after his death, no longer to be thought of in terms of a particular time and place but is securely the possession of the world and has attained the status of a classic. Because of this, and because, as Synge said, 'the deeds of a man's lifetime are impersonal and concrete, might have been done by anyone, while art is the expression of the abstract beauty of the person', it is to the writings themselves that we should go more and more.

This completes the survey of the criticism of Synge, apart from the utterances of Yeats, which, because of their importance and of their relationship to Synge's views about literature, are dealt with in Chapter Two.

It is obvious that much good work has been done on Synge. Background and biographical information, histories of Irish drama and of related social and political trends and pressures, accounts of the Abbey and its personalities, of methods of play-making, production and acting, studies of Synge's relation to these and of aspects of his writings have now been sufficiently supplied. What is still required is literary criticism which will use and synthesize this material to increase our appreciation of Synge's writings. There have been only three considerable books of literary criticism of Synge, and the most recent of these – Corkery's – appeared over thirty years ago. Since then many shorter critical studies have appeared but no larger work focusing them and adding something of note, and the time now seems ripe, particularly as a definitive biography has arrived, for a full-length critical study.

The existing comment on Synge, worthy as much of it is, suffers, as a whole, from two shortcomings. First, it is partisan

and parochial. Commentators have tended to be unduly concerned with politics and religion; and consequently discussion
has ranged around matters irrelevant to the understanding of
Synge as an artist. Furthermore, no sustained attempt has been
made to see Synge apart from his place in the Abbey Theatre and
to approach him as one might approach the dramatists of other
nations. Second, critics have applied to Synge the assumptions of
early twentieth-century naturalism, and criticism has been mainly
an examination of characters as 'real human beings' and of points
of stage technique. This kind of criticism is essential, but, as the
trends in Shakespeare criticism during the past forty years show,
it is not the only kind which can yield valuable results. A close
examination of the texture of a poetic play is likewise necessary,
and this has hardly been supplied by previous critics, although
they have praised the poetic quality of Synge's dialogue. It is not
assumed that this book will compensate for these shortcomings,
but in it an attempt will be made both to see Synge's writings as
part of English literature and also to examine the plays in the
light of the knowledge that the poetic dramatist often operates on
more than one level of significance simultaneously and that he
uses symbol and allegory in addition to character and situation.

The attempt will take the form of an examination of a coherent
theme which runs through all Synge's writings. The theme may be
called the tension between dream and actuality. It occurs in various shapes, but they are all aspects of a basic tension between
life and death, between an intuitive, imaginative outlook and a
materialistic, mercenary outlook, between grace and physical
progress, between loveliness and desolation. Mingled with this
tension is an ever present and deep awareness both of close
links between Man and the natural world and also of the mutability of life and beauty.

Disturbances in the Irish Theatre

No reference was made in the previous section to the fierce assaults
upon Synge during his lifetime. This is because they are not, in
any sense, literary comment or criticism that merits consideration.
Yet, since they have a part, however deplorable, in the pattern,
and since they materially expressed or affected the attitude of the
audience to which the dramatist, whose art depends on colla-

boration, is peculiarly sensitive, something should be said about them.

The row over *The Playboy of the Western World* in 1907 is perhaps the most famous and well documented row in theatre history. But it was by no means the first or the last to occur at the Abbey. Even before the production of the Irish Literary Theatre's first play, Yeats's *Countess Cathleen*, in 1899, hostility was aroused and the formula outlined for subsequent abuse, misrepresentation and bigotry. The play concerns the selling of souls for food, and Edward Martyn, a strict Irish Catholic, feared that it was heretical. This being confirmed by a priest, Martyn sought to withdraw his financial backing. Yeats, striving to pacify Martyn and also to restrain Moore, who was raging at ecclesiastical interference with art, submitted the play to two Roman Catholic theologians, an Irish Jesuit, Father Finlay, and an English literary canon, the Reverend Dr Barry. Its intention being good, both approved the play, and Martyn was satisfied; rightly so, for the play honours saintly self-sacrifice. But then the play was crudely attacked in an anonymous pamphlet, *Souls for Gold*, written by Frank Hugh O'Donnell, an enemy to Yeats; and Cardinal Logue, without having read the play, told his flock to boycott it. Controversy in the press stirred up more antagonism, trouble was threatened and students at University College exhorted to attend and protest against the 'insult to their faith' if the play was presented. Yeats at once cut out the few phrases and actions which might have caused some offence and called in the police. *Countess Cathleen* was thus, somewhat inauspiciously for a national movement, put on under the protection of foreign-controlled police, but they preserved order, and although there were hostile hootings on each of the five nights, the play was well received in the theatre and generally reviewed favourably by the press in Ireland and England. Yet the more narrow nationalists, having convinced themselves that Yeats and his company were British agents intent on discrediting Ireland and Catholicism, continued to murmur. Their resentment became intensified on the production of Synge's first play, *The Shadow of the Glen*, in 1903. Again trouble started before the first night. One of the leading actors, Dudley Digges, refused to play in it and left the company, together with one of the best actresses, Maire Quinn, who later became his wife. *The Irish Independent* described the play as perverse and unwholesome, and an article in *The United Irishman* by J. B. Yeats, the poet's father, praising the play for exposing the 'Irish institution, the loveless marriage', while true, did not recommend the play to the vast majority who saw nothing but good in things Irish. Accordingly, although there was silence during the first performance of the play, it was found disconcerting, and boos and hisses mingled with the applause at the end. Next day the nationalist press attacked. Their main charge was that the play libelled Irish womanhood, it emanated not from the Aran Islands or Wicklow but from the decadent cynicism of Paris and London and was a corrupt version of a pagan farce. That it was really nothing of the kind but rather an image of actualities observable in Ireland and elsewhere, Yeats and others were able to show, but this did not prevent the resignation of Maud Gonne, who had been so queenly a Cathleen Ni Houlihan, or the continuance for some days of press attacks, or their outbreak again when the play was revived a year later. Hence Synge became a marked man, and although no exception was taken to *Riders to the Sea*, and *The Well of the Saints* was largely ignored, explosive feelings were accumulated, ready to be touched off by *The Playboy*. This major storm cleared the air, though in 1908 Lennox Robinson's first play, *The Clancy Name*, was assailed on grounds other than literary, and there were politically inspired disturbances at the presentation of Conal O'Riordan's *The Piper*, a valid, though obvious, satire upon Irish mentality. By 1911 the storm reached the United States of America with the arrival of the Abbey company and the mobilization against them of Irish nationalism there. The almost incredible happenings of the tour in a dozen eastern cities, the tumult in theatres and at public meetings, the frantic allegations in pulpits, newspapers and pamphlets, the arrest and trial of the company in Philadelphia and their release through the work of their firm friend, the lawyer, John Quinn, are all told inimitably by Lady Gregory. Their foes were, of course, quite unamenable to reason, and as void of any concern for drama as they were fervent in their belief that they were defending sacred Irish life and religion against vilification. In fact, vilification was their weapon, particularly against *The Playboy*; their tone is typified in the pamphlet distributed by the Aloysius Truth Society:[42]

Nothing but hell-inspired ingenuity and a satanic hatred of the

Irish people and their religion could suggest, construct, and influence the production of such plays. On God's earth the beastly creatures of the plays never existed.

Such are the productions which, hissed from Dublin, hawked around England by the 'Irish Players' for the delectation of those who wished to see Irishmen shown unfit for self-government, are now offered to the people of Washington. Will Washington tolerate the lie?

The opposition was persistent and unpredictable, but fortunately there were enough sensible people in America to counter the fanatics and to provide appreciative audiences for the plays. The tour was a marked success; Lady Gregory, ignoring lurid threats against her life, emerged as a fine organizer and public speaker; the players worked devotedly, and they all returned in triumph to Dublin with more fame and money than they had ever had. Tours of America in 1913 produced hardly any opposition and much diminished financial returns. During subsequent years, hostilities took other and graver forms, and it was not until 1926 that trouble occurred again at the Abbey. Then the first production of Sean O'Casey's *The Plough and the Stars* led to a row not much less intense than that over *The Playboy*. Once more there were frenzied public arguments, struggles in the theatre, police protection, and once more Yeats nobly faced the mob, and declared:

I thought you had got tired of all this which commenced about fifteen years ago. But you have disgraced yourselves again. Is this to be an ever-recurring celebration of the arrival of Irish genius? Synge first and then O'Casey. The news of the happenings of the last few minutes will go from country to country. Dublin has once more rocked the cradle of a reputation. From such a scene in this theatre went forth the fame of Synge. Equally the fame of O'Casey is born here tonight.

Since then there has been little disturbance, perhaps because of a lack of genius and the Abbey's decline, and the most recent protest, in 1947, was a civilized one, by Valentin Iremonger, poet and civil servant, against the management's policy and its disregard for the 'fine glory' of Yeats's tradition.

Greatest in this tradition, Yeats always proclaimed, was Synge, yet it is possible that he would not have been really recognized without Yeats's whole-hearted advocacy of him. This was most apparent during *The Playboy* riots of 1907 when Yeats risked all that he had built up, and withstanding severe pressure, not only from extremists but from men such as Stephen Gwynn, refused to compromise. It was a matter of principle, a vital test-case of artistic integrity against nationalistic expediency, and by upholding *The Playboy* Yeats won the case against mob-censorship, just as later in 1909 by producing *The Shewing-up of Blanco Posnet* he won the case against official censorship. Thus, although Bourgeois goes too far in saying[43] 'that had the Directors yielded to the hostility of the audience, and withdrawn the play, Synge would be utterly unknown nowadays, except to the curious student of Literature's by-ways', his conclusion is correct:

> It is difficult to over-estimate the service Mr Yeats rendered Irish letters at large, and Synge's fame in particular, by staunchly supporting him and indefatigably explaining his play to the public during the memorable week – an act of highly meritorious generosity and self-sacrifice.

And Boyd agrees:[44]

> It would be impossible to exaggerate the credit due to W. B. Yeats in this matter. A more timid mind would have shrunk from the odium of defying those who had, on the whole, befriended the work of the Dramatic Revival; a lesser personality would not have risked himself to forward the claims of the only writer whose fame could conflict with his own.

From the beginning Yeats saw that *The Playboy* was both a masterpiece and also a potential source of trouble, but he did not falter. Players objected (as they had done before) to certain words and phrases, and Synge, who was superintending rehearsals, was prevailed upon to allow some cuts. Assuming that these were sufficient, Yeats went to fulfil a lecture engagement in Scotland on the first night of *The Playboy*, but events then led Synge to give Lady Gregory leave 'in consultation with the players' to take 'out many phrases which, though in the printed book, have never since that first production been spoken' on the Abbey stage. During rehearsals unusual secrecy was observed, and Joseph Holloway being refused admittance snooped around and got the notion that the play was 'in praise of murder' and that there would be organized opposition to it. Before the curtain went up on Saturday, 26 January 1907, Synge was in a fever of excitement, and some of the cast were 'in a most deplorable state of uncertainty', despite 'a great screwing up of courage'. It turned out, though, that the first two acts were received in brooding quiet and with some applause; and Lady Gregory sent a telegram to Yeats reading 'Play great success', but it was followed at the end by another reading 'Audience broke up in disorder at the word shift'.

Apart from *The Irish Times*, which regretted that the author's indiscretions and undiluted realism had brought 'a brilliant success to an inglorious conclusion', the Monday newspapers were almost uniformly hostile; the play was 'squalid and offensive', 'vile and inhuman', written in 'the foulest language, a barbarous jargon of elaborate and incessant cursing' expressive of 'calumny gone raving mad'. Saturday's protests were insignificant compared with the stamping, shouting, singing and fighting of Monday night, which made the actors inaudible and led to police intervention and arrests. Lady Gregory and the company bravely refused to give in; Synge, sick in body and spirit, his nerves raw, could do little, and all were relieved when Yeats arrived on Tuesday morning and took charge. Through the Press he defied the 'commonplace and ignorant people' bent on destroying the Abbey, asserted the artist's right to consider no judgement but that of his imagination or of his peers, and called in the police, and, as part, at least, of the hostility was palpably organized, Lady Gregory's nephew arranged for parties of students from the pro-English Trinity College to support the play and to counter the opposition. On the Tuesday and Wednesday nights the packed house erupted in grotesque riot. The actors, again unheard, mimed, pausing only to dodge missiles or to repel assaults on the stage; songs and slogans were bawled about; shrieks, caterwaulings, threats and curses crepitated; trumpets blared; feet hammered and sticks clattered on the floor and seats; and up and down the aisles and over the seats, town fought with gown, and the police toiled incessantly to secure order. This marked the tornado peak. On the Thursday and Friday nights the audience was relatively passive, if not amiable, and there were only two or three arrests: Holloway's reaction was probably representative of the less illiterate of the objectors:[45] 'The police-protected drama by the dramatist of the dung heap attached to the Abbey got a fair hearing tonight and was voted by those around me very poor dull dramatic stuff.' On Saturday the police were 'as thick as blackberries in September', and so, in a charged atmosphere, the opposition in brooding frustration endured, while the fair gathering of non-partisans more or less enjoyed, the first uninterrupted performance of the play since the opening night.

Having kept the play on for seven nights and shown that he was not to be coerced, Yeats held a public debate in the Abbey on Monday, 4 February, and a huge mob, undeterred by an admission charge of one shilling and sixpence, crammed in. They were hostile and threatening, but Yeats, unruffled and defiant, in immaculate evening clothes, made 'one of the most courageous utterances of his life'. Mary Colum, then a student, 'never witnessed a human being fight as Yeats fought that night, nor knew another with so many weapons in his armoury'.[46] He was ably seconded by his father whose gibe 'Island of Saints – plaster saints' became famous, but Synge was absent, ill in bed, and those few who tried to support him could hardly make themselves heard in the pandemonium. Inevitably, much more heat than light was generated, and fastidiously surveying the scene Lady Gregory felt sorry that they 'had ever let such a set inside the theatre', but next day she was glad because they had shown that they were 'not repenting or apologizing'. Yeats too felt that something had been gained: a clumsy tyranny had been exposed, and, weary of it, decent people, especially the young, would refuse to 'crouch upon the one roost and quack or cry in the one flock' in obedience to bigoted little clubs and societies. In this he was sanguine; true, The Playboy did mark a turning-point and never again did clamour of such intensity occur in an Irish theatre, the play has become a classic, performances of it produce nothing but applause, and a recording of it on two long-playing discs by the Abbey Players is sold all over the world. Still, for some time after, antagonism and fierce argument persisted, fanned by the newspapers who had revelled for days, describing in lurid detail the scenes at the Abbey, printing equally lurid opinions about them, and reporting the resultant court cases and fines. Hence a sizable amount of material, variously factual and legendary, has accumulated about this memorable episode.

Speculation about the root causes of it is also abundant.

Among these were personal jealousies, references to feminine underwear and an uninhibited use of strong language and of sacred names. Much more potent was the notion that *The Playboy* constituted a vile defamation designed to depict the Irish as being unfit for Home Rule. At that critical moment in history no doubts about the shining worth of the Irish were to be entertained. Indeed, some people were deluded enough to hold that Ireland was uniquely virtuous and that any depravity came from England (the very whores were chiefly imported and found custom only among the English soldiery). Hence any attack on Ireland was bound to be unjustified and malicious, and her virtue was to be defended by any means. This assumption was brilliantly demolished by Shaw:[47]

> John Synge wrote a wonderful play called *The Playboy of the Western World*, which is now a classic. This play was not about an Irish peculiarity, but about a universal weakness of mankind: the habit of admiring bold scoundrels. . . . Well, this silly Dublin Clan-na-Gael suddenly struck out the brilliant idea that to satirize the follies of humanity is to insult the Irish nation, because the Irish nation is, in fact, the human race and has no follies, and stands there pure and beautiful and saintly to be eternally oppressed by England and collected for by the Clan.

The less simple-minded of the nationalists privately allowed that Ireland had a share of vice but asserted that at that crucial phase no one should publicly admit its existence. They were not altogether philistines and had some appreciation for literature, but they felt that it should bend itself to the political service of the nation. For them literature was basically a means, not an end. There was thus a clash between two groups of dedicated not unintelligent people representing two opposed views about the use of literature; nationalists, such as Arthur Griffith and Maud Gonne, who believed that their vision of a united, independent nation should take precedence over the artist's vision, and writers, such as Yeats and Synge, who saw that the best way of serving their country was not by writing propaganda, however fine, but by creating native literature that would win the admiration of discriminating people throughout the world.

Finally, there was probably one further, less obvious but hardly less potent, cause. It was very perceptively indicated by P. D.

Kenny in *The Irish Times* on 30 January 1907 and it has since been discussed by Irving D. Suss.[48] The cause of the riot was not the falsity of *The Playboy* but its truth.

> The merciless accuracy of Synge's revelation is more than we can bear. Our eyes tremble at it. The words chosen are, like the things they express, direct and dreadful, by themselves intolerable to conventional taste, yet full of vital beauty in their truth to the conditions of life, to the character they depict, and to the sympathies they suggest. It is as if we looked into a mirror for the first time, and found ourselves hideous. We fear to face the thing. We shrink at the word for it. We scream.

Christy Mahon overcoming 'the father figure' did what many Irishmen desired to do but could not; even to admit the desire to themselves was intolerable, and so they rose to stifle its dramatic representation. To them, outwardly conforming to, but inwardly chafing at, the overseeing power of church and parent, the strict sexual code and late marriage, Christy was a symbol, but since to accept it would be to destroy the social fabric they had to uphold, they sought instead to destroy the symbol.

> In this social context the self-liberation of the Playboy by violence was a picture of the hidden dream of the Irishman brought into the light of day. There was no intervening censor, no concealing dream-work to distort the wish and make it acceptable to the consciousness. Freud's reality principle operated in the mass, and there was a violent effort to suppress the feeling that the play generated and made recognizable. The countless reasons that Irishmen have adduced for *The Playboy* riots were only further efforts to deny a subconscious desire that conflicted with the accepted pattern of every-day life.

The Authenticity of Synge

It is probably appropriate at this stage to say something more generally about the authenticity of Synge's presentation of Irish life, and to dispose finally of the fallacy that he misrepresented it. How this fallacy has arisen it is hard to see. There is no evidence to breed it, it has never been expounded or rationalized, and it consists merely of assertion repeated from time to time, blindly, in the face of solid fact to the contrary. To the stock objection that Synge created figures untrue to Irish life and to human nature generally, it can be replied that his plays are firmly based on his experiences of Irish life, and that these experiences were not peculiar to Synge but were shared by many people and recorded by some. Moreover, the authority of Aristotle could be invoked to show that an artist is not to be confined to what is or has been, he may create what should be; for a work of art is a self-contained whole with its own laws. Synge, like every artist, has the right to expect from his audience 'that willing suspension of disbelief that constitutes poetic faith', so long as his work connects in some purposeful way with life as we fancy it to be. The artist often prefers a probable or plausible impossibility to an improbable or unconvincing possibility, and he may suggest truths of a more serious and universal kind than those of the historian who is limited to the particular fact.

Nevertheless there is no lack of particular facts about Irish life in Synge. He was proud of his Irishness, and all his writings and his life show his abiding interest in ordinary folk. Among them he found and loved much 'that has edge, that is salt in the mouth, that is rough to the hand, that heightens the emotions by contest, that stings into life the sense of tragedy'.[49] And his prose works, *The Aran Islands* and *In Wicklow, West Kerry and Connemara*, are, among other things, profound and sympathetic studies of the people of rural Ireland, particularly of the west coast islanders, the poor, the tramps and tinkers, and the unemployed. No one has impugned the truth of these accounts, they are usually highly praised, and even Corkery, so bitterly zealous in asserting that Synge's Ascendancy ties tainted the Irish quality of his drama, confirms Colum's praise of Synge and allows that Synge speaks as an informed patriot, a true lover of Ireland in these two prose books. And it is in them that we find the sources of his plays – the stuff of his actions, characters, incidents, atmosphere, idiom – and also evidence for the existence of pagan attitudes alongside Christian formulas, of distinctive habits and customs, differing from those of more settled communities, among the folk he met. Estill, examining Synge's sources, finds them in Irish life, and declares that Synge gives 'a true picture of Irish life'. In addition, the more controversial of Synge's plays are, ironically enough, those most closely linked with observed actualities. The well-established Lynchehaun case of the man concealed from the police by the Aran islanders, and the tale of the Connaught man who killed his father with the blow of a spade and was also saved by them, have several reliable parallels,[50] though, apart from them, the story of The Playboy, 'in its essence, is probable, given the psychic state of the locality'.[50] Moreover, the central incident of the much-abused The Tinker's Wedding comes straight out of contemporary Irish life, as Greene says,[50] and has a parallel in Douglas Hyde's Religious Songs of Connacht.

These were among the facts Synge used but they were facts most unpalatable, at the climax of Ireland's struggle for independence, to those nationalists who were trying to demolish the old stock image of the stage Irishman and to replace it by a new image, more accurate and more commendable. This was a very necessary and laudable process, and in it Yeats and Synge and other artists were at one with the nationalists. In John Bull's Other Island Shaw amusingly and effectively debunks the stage Irishman. Broadbent, like many Englishmen susceptible to Irish charm and blarney, is taken in by Tim Haffigan, until Doyle, really an Irishman, exposes Haffigan, and tells Broadbent 'all this business is got up in England to fool you . . . . No Irishman ever talks like that in Ireland.' But it is impossible to get a correct image of a nation; we are all individuals and only approximate to the national ikon. And the nationalists were doing little more than substituting a new stock image that probably flattered the Irish people for an old stock image that certainly libelled them. Yeats saw this, and how both these stock notions were shattered by the rich reality of Synge's art which 'bids us touch and taste and hear and see the world, and shrinks from what Blake calls mathematic form, from every abstract thing, from all that is of brain only, from all that is not a fountain jetting from the entire hopes, memories, and sensations of the body'.[51] Again Yeats observes:

The antagonist of imaginative writing in Ireland is not a habit of scientific observation but our interest in matters of opinion. A misgoverned country seeking a remedy by agitation puts an especial value upon opinion, and even those who are not conscious of any interest in the country are influenced by the general habit. All fine literature is the disinterested contemplation or expression of life, but hardly any Irish writer can liberate his mind sufficiently from questions of practical reform for this contemplation[52] . . . after a while in a land that has given itself to agitation overmuch, abstract thoughts are raised up between man's minds and Nature . . . and they cry down natural impulses with the morbid persistence of minds unsettled by some fixed idea . . . a secret feeling that what is so unreal needs continual defence makes them bitter and restless.[53]

It is against the erection of an inaccurate and arid notion between people and the life-giving reality which art can offer, that Yeats and Synge and all artists must protest. For they know that the stock image can pervert the mind and make it unwilling, or unable, to apprehend anything that does not permit of smooth over-simplification. Hence Synge upset numbers of his fellow-countrymen. His dramatic figures, very different both from the old stock image of the stage Irishman and also from the new stock image of the Catholic Irish peasant, are dramatic representations of the reality he saw around him, and since that reality contained groups of people, who, although sometimes nominally Christians, lived according to certain non-Christian customs, he did not condemn it, but used it. Moreover, our experience in Ireland, in England, or elsewhere, should show us that the figures of Synge have recognizable human characteristics: if Mary Byrne is unlifelike, then so is Falstaff, for she, though lesser in degree, is similar in kind to him.

The authenticity of Synge's vision of Ireland can also be confirmed from so nationalistic and unimpeachable a source as Padraic Colum's *The Road Round Ireland*. This, with its perceptive love of Irish life, has some of the qualities of Synge's prose works and supplements and supports them remarkably. Coming from good peasant stock, Colum understands the folk, and, like Synge, has the ability to draw from them tales, opinions and vivid speech, and to record these, and to reflect upon them fruitfully, in an unaffected style. He knew Synge well, and his verdict on him is noteworthy:[54]

Synge is the one dramatist of modern times, as far as I know, who is able to bring a landscape before his audience through the speech of people in his plays. . . . His plays were denounced as being alien to Irish life and to the Irish mind. Those who denounced them in these terms were wrong, and they were wrong because they knew nothing about the Gaelic tradition as it has been expressed in the poetry of the seventeenth and eighteenth centuries. . . . Synge is in line with this tradition . . . he was kin to these Gaelic poets in spirit . . . his work augments the spirit by discovering and revealing to us the national virtue. He was fortunate in that he found on these roads men and women, who, however disreputable, had in them something of the national virtue; who had something of the same outlook on life as he had, and who had a speech through which elemental humour and poetry could once more be expressed. . . . *The Playboy of the Western World* dramatizes what is most characteristic in Gaelic life – the Gaelic delight in vivid personality.

Again like Synge, Colum noted the influence of natural environment upon character, found in the west 'an extravagance of movement, of gesture, of words',[55] praised the intelligence, zest for learning, and graciousness of the Kerry people, then added:[55]

They have grave faults. They are mighty drinkers, and when drunk they can lapse into savagery. And they are noted for being untrustworthy witnesses in a court of law. . . . The Kerry people regard the law as something to be evaded and circumvented; it will probably be a long time before they get away from this attitude.

That Synge and Colum were not alone in finding Irish rural life instinctive and boisterous, and sometimes savage, is established by the writings of Irishmen such as O'Sullivan and O Crohan, whose autobiographies[56] are generally considered to be remarkably valuable. In his Introduction to O'Sullivan's *Twenty Years A-Growing* (1933) E. M. Forster calls the book an 'account of a primitive civilization which Synge too has described very sympathetically'. And the translators from the original Irish say that they use 'the Irish dialect of English as being nearest to the original and following the example of Synge, who of all writers in English had the deepest understanding of the Irish-speaking peasantry'. O'Sullivan speaks of fighting at a wedding: 'Nothing but disputing and shouting and drink flying in the air . . . blood flying to the rafters,' and, later, after the fair and sports: 'away with them all to the public house. . . . They were calling for gallons, one after another, till they were blind drunk

... soon songs began about the house and everyone raging-red with drink, as is the habit at such times.' O Crohan tells how the islanders repelled the police and bailiffs coming to eject them by bombarding them with stones, and how at a wedding 'the people of the parish came near to destroying one another . . . six of them had to be sent to hospital'; and he tells of:

> a marvellous woman who finished the bailiffs and the drivers who used to come day after day ruining the poor, who had nothing to live on but the famine. A bailiff climbed on the roof of her house and started knocking it down on her and on to her flock of feeble children. She seized a pair of new shears and opened them – a point this way, the other that. A stout woman and a mad woman. The bailiff never noticed anything till he felt the point of the shears stuck right in his behind. It wasn't the roof of the house that came through the hole this time, but a spurt of blood. That's the last bailiff we've seen.

O Crohan also tells of the exceedingly rough games of hurley they played at Christmas and other festival times, which left most of the population more or less maimed for several days afterwards. Synge's account is also valid from the viewpoint of the anthropologist. Von Herbert Frenzel, having made a study of this matter, describes and illustrates Synge's cordial sympathy with the peasants, and declares:[57]

> a great part of the mind of the Irish peasant and above all of the inhabitants of these isolated islands [i.e. Aran and Blaskets] is still linked to a world of magic ideas, which contrasts with his Christian belief. . . .
>
> The belief in fairies is firmly established in Gaelic-speaking sections, and the Celtic peasant would as soon give up his religion as his belief in the sidhe.

Finally, Forrest Reid characterizes the work of Synge as Irish,[58] O'Connor affirms that Synge's plays are a vivid and fascinating reflection of national life,[59] Una Ellis-Fermor sees Synge as one of the few to carry on unbroken the tradition of ancient Irish[60] poetry, Boyd judges that recent Anglo-Irish literature is a genuine expression of the Irish race and that Synge is most distinguished in intimately understanding 'a primitive yet highly sensitive race whose joys and sorrows we feel to be his own',[61] and Greene concludes:[62]

> Synge's work more than that of any of his contemporaries comes closer to achieving the assimilation of the Gaelic past which the Irish Renaissance stood for. Whether he was dramatizing a tragic fact or incident of violence in contemporary Irish life, exploring the applications of ancient folk tale or heroic myth, or merely describing in unpretentious language the daily life of the tinker, the farmer or the fisherman, he was interpreting the traditional life of Ireland. It is to him more than to any other Irishman writing in English that we go for an insight into this life.

The above extracts are a representative part of the solid body of evidence that exists to prove that Synge's work is based upon reality.

Synge's Irishness, his part in Irish life and literature, having been indisputably established, it now remains to bring out his universal quality, to show his part in English literature, just as one might, while agreeing that Eugene O'Neill, Tennessee Williams and Arthur Miller are truly American, be interested in their value in relation to English drama. A good deal of Synge's unique power resides in his ability to synthesize, to create in the same figure both individual states (true to Irish life) and also universal kinds (true to human nature generally). It is an activity of imagination in the fullest sense of Coleridge's classic definition – the fusing of the general with the concrete; the idea with the image; the individual with the representative. And for this great work Synge had to use poetry – 'a more than usual state of emotion, with more than usual order; judgement ever awake and steady self-possession, with enthusiasm and feeling profound or vehement' – a prose surface naturalism would have left him dated and insular, as it has left nearly all his contemporaries and imitators.

CHAPTER TWO

Literary Ideas and Craft

Synge's Idiom

There is no need further to trace here the antecedents and the development of the Irish dramatic movement, but something should be said about the genesis of the Anglo-Irish idiom which Synge has made famous and about his distinctive use of it, his imagery and cadences, the texture of his language.

For seven hundred years English has been spoken in Ireland, both by the English conquerors or settlers and also by the Irish alongside their native Gaelic. Over the years the use of English has varied considerably; during the thirteenth century it gained ground, it declined in the fourteenth and fifteenth centuries, picked up towards the end of this period, then came near to being replaced by Gaelic in the sixteenth century. And all the time English was being more or less influenced by Gaelic. The traditional Gaelic way of life was mainly destroyed or driven underground by the events of the seventeenth century, the English and Scottish plantations, the Acts of Settlement of Cromwell and of William and Mary, and the ensuing harsh Penal Codes. Though oppressed, the Irish held on firmly to their religion and to their culture, keeping alive the elements of Irish literature, history and legend chiefly in the minds of country folk and through the Hedge Schools. But it became increasingly clear that ignorance of English put the native Irish at a grave disadvantage. To alleviate their position materially, to seek political and economic emancipation, it seemed essential for the Irish to speak the language of their rulers, and so from about the middle of the eighteenth century more and more of them began to learn English. This spread of English throughout Ireland was encouraged by the Catholic Church, the great Daniel O'Connell and various patriotic groups, by the ending of the Penal Laws in 1782, the national endeavours of the Dublin parliament, the founding of schools in which the

35

medium of instruction was English, the emancipation of Catholics
in 1829, and finally by the necessity of English to the emigrant.
Hence by the mid-nineteenth century English was the main
language of the Irish, though some of them in remote areas still
retained their Gaelic also. It is this kind of English, deriving from
the Irish Protestant Ascendancy, mixed with older Tudor Anglo-
Irish survivals, learned and modified by a population with a Gaelic
speech-basis, which is the material of Synge's plays and the language of Ireland today.

The first expressions in English of national sentiments by Irish
writers were appearing by the beginning of the nineteenth century in the form of popular anonymous ballads or songs about
politics or contemporary happenings, and in the poems of Thomas
Moore. These were followed by the poetry of *The Nation*, the
essays of Thomas Davis and the writings of J. C. Mangan and
Sir Samuel Ferguson, all of which were patriotic and formative.
By the eighteen-forties the new language had been sufficiently
assimilated for the peasant William Carleton to express in it,
strikingly if sometimes verbosely, the condition and aspirations of
many poor Irish people. Yet these writers, though worthy, were
stylistically too much under the sway of English literature and
they showed insufficient awareness of the Gaelic tradition. The
glories of this were at last memorably set forth by Standish
O'Grady in his great *History of Ireland* (1878-80), which is
generally regarded as the fountain of the literary revival. A genuine Irish literature in English, embracing the most vital features
of the Irish tradition and of contemporary Irish life, was now
within reach, and soon to be shaped most finely through the
grasp of Yeats and Synge. Stopford Brooke in his influential lecture on 'The Need and Use of Getting Irish Literature into the
English Tongue' (1893) made manifest the right of Anglo-Irish
literature to be regarded as the successor of Gaelic, and the
most potent modern embodiment of the Celtic spirit and tradition.
He demonstrated

> the importance of the work of translation and popularization
> by which the legendary and historical past could be brought
> before the public. He defined the most essential tasks, as the
> translation of the Gaelic texts, the moulding of the various
> mythological and historical cycles into an imaginative unity,

after the fashion of Malory, the treatment in verse of isolated episodes and tales relating to the heroes of the supernatural and heroic world, and, finally, the collection of the folk-stories of Ireland. In these four branches he predicted that the sources of a literary renascence would be found. The results which are now traceable to the efforts of O'Grady, Sigerson and Hyde are proofs of the wisdom of Stopford Brooke's recommendations.[63]

The most famous of these men, Douglas Hyde, devoting his life to the renaissance of Irish culture, not only founded the Gaelic League to rehabilitate the almost extinct Gaelic tongue in 1893, but also revealed the worth of the Anglo-Irish idiom. A crude and absurd form of this idiom had been used by dramatists like Dion Boucicault and by novelists like Samuel Lover and Charles Lever, in their portrayal of the stock image of an Irishman. Hyde realized that his idiom could be used for serious purposes, and in 1893 with the publication of *Love Songs of Connacht* he demonstrated some of its merits and possibilities for the first time. These songs had been handed down orally in Gaelic, and Hyde collected them from the lips of the peasants, and recorded each song in two versions, one Gaelic and one English. For some of the versions in English he used a kind of conventional rhymed verse which is not interesting, but in others he used the Anglo-Irish idiom. The superiority of the latter is apparent:[64]

> *Did I stand on the bald top of Nefin*
> *And my hundred-times loved one with me,*
> *We should nestle together as safe in*
> *Its shade as the birds on a tree.*
> *From your lips such a music is shaken,*
> *When you speak it awakens my pain,*
> *And my eyelids by sleep are forsaken,*
> *And I seek for my slumber in vain.*

If I were to be on the brow of Nefin and my hundred loves by my side, it is pleasantly we would sleep together like the little bird upon the bough. It is your melodious wordy little mouth that increased my pain, and a quiet sleep I cannot get until I shall die, alas.

O had you seen her moving,
My love who was so cruel
She was a star-bright jewel
For dispersing fog and mist.

If you were to see the star of knowledge, And she coming in the mouth of the road, You would say it was a jewel at a distance from you, Who would raise fog and enchantment.

This Anglo-Irish idiom is a form of English modified by Gaelic habits of thought, speech, imagery and syntax; the words and meanings are English but the word-order corresponds to the word-order of Gaelic. Of this idiom Yeats says:[65]

The English idiom of the Irish-thinking people of the West which Hyde has begun to use . . . is the only good English spoken by any large number of Irish people today, and we must found good literature on a living speech. . . . English men of letters found themselves on the English Bible . . . the idiom of the people of the West mingles so much of the vocabulary of the Bible with turns of phrase that have come out of Gaelic.

Yeats, Lady Gregory and Synge were unacquainted in 1893, yet each separately recognized that this idiom was a potentially fresh and powerful means of literary expression, 'a new region for the mind to wander in'.[65] Lady Gregory, who spent many years promoting the welfare of the peasants on her estate in the West and learning their language and folk-lore and collecting folk-tales, used the Anglo-Irish idiom in her two books[66] designed to make the heroic legends of Ireland more widely known. In his Preface to the first of these, Yeats said:

I think this book is the best that has come out of Ireland in my time. Perhaps I should say that it is the best book that has ever come out of Ireland; for the stories which it tells are a chief part of Ireland's gift to the imagination of the world – and it tells them perfectly for the first time. . . . Lady Gregory has discovered a speech as beautiful as that of Morris, and a living speech into the bargain. As she moved about among her people she learned to love that beautiful speech of those who think in Irish, and to understand that it is as true a dialect of English as the dialect that Burns wrote in. It is some hundreds of years old, and age gives a language authority. One finds in it the vocabulary of the translators of the Bible, joined to an idiom which makes it tender, compassionate, and complaisant, like the Irish language itself.

Although Yeats is probably praising Lady Gregory too highly, her work in the Anglo-Irish idiom on the heroic sagas did make the legends accessible and enjoyable to people previously ignorant of them, and the two books became a great storehouse from which were drawn the materials for some of Lady Gregory's own *Irish Folk History Plays*, for Yeats's sequence of Cuchulain plays, for his, 'A.E.' 's and Synge's three dramatic versions of the Deirdre story, and for his and George Moore's *Diarmuid and Grania*. Synge knew Hyde's work, and he had been thinking about the Anglo-Irish idiom and writing it – part of an article published in November 1898 and later incorporated in *The Aran Islands* is in this idiom – so he was attracted by Lady Gregory's work; she says:[67]

> The rich abundant speech of the people was a delight to Synge. When my *Cuchulain of Muirthemne* came out, he said to Mr Yeats he had been amazed to find in it the dialect he had been trying to master. He wrote to me: 'Your *Cuchulain* is a part of my daily bread.' I say this with a little pride, for I was the first to use the Irish idiom as it is spoken with intention and belief in it. Dr Hyde indeed has used it with fine effect in his *Love Songs of Connacht*, but alas, gave it up afterwards, in deference to some Dublin editor.

Lady Gregory's enthusiasm has led her into a (pardonable) error, for the abandonment of Anglo-Irish in favour of Gaelic by Hyde does not prove that he no longer believed in it; he probably thought that he could do more good by concentrating on the revival of Gaelic and leaving Anglo-Irish to writers like Lady Gregory and Synge. In any case he was the first to use the idiom effectively, and he well deserves Boyd's warm tribute, summed up by Colum thus:[68] 'Hyde suggested a new literary medium; out of which developed the poetic dialogue of Synge's plays and the narrative of Lady Gregory's stories'. Synge too, while appreciatively reviewing[69] Lady Gregory's *Cuchulain*, held that Hyde used the idiom first, though as there had been a movement for over twenty years towards an appreciation of the country people and their language both Hyde's and Lady Gregory's efforts were the result of an evolution rather than a personal idea. Later, so firm a supporter of Lady Gregory as Lennox Robinson said that Synge was 'the first to discover what a lovely medium it was to write in.' [70] Nevertheless, Lady Gregory deserves great credit for establishing the idiom and making it widely known by her resourceful and sustained use of it in her translations of heroic legend and folk-tales, and by indicating its possibilities for drama in *Cathleen ni Houlihan* and in *The Pot of Broth*, both written by her and Yeats in collaboration. As Lady Gregory was the first to exploit fully in prose the rich vein opened up by Hyde, so Synge, taking her hint, was the first to exploit it fully in drama. A comparison between a passage from *Cuchulain of Muirthemne*[71] and one from Synge's *Deirdre of the Sorrows* may give some notion of what Synge made of his source. Here is Lady Gregory's Deirdre lamenting the death of her lover Naisi and his two brothers, Ainnle and Ardan, the sons of Usnach:

I am Deirdre without gladness, and I at the end of my life, since it is grief to be without them, I myself will not be long after them.

The sons of Usnach fell in the fight like three branches that were growing straight and nice, and they destroyed in a heavy storm that left neither bud nor twig of them.

Naisi, my gentle, well-learned comrade, make no delay in crying him with me; cry for Ardan that killed the wild boars, cry for Ainnle whose strength was great.

It was Naisi that would kiss my lips, my first man and my first sweetheart; it was Ainnle would pour out my drink, and it was Ardan would lay my pillow. Their birth was beautiful and their blossoming, as they grew to the strength of manhood; sad is the end today, the sons of Usnach to be cut down.

Dear their grey eyes that were loved by women, many looked on them as they went; when they went freely searching through the woods, their steps were pleasant on the dark mountain.

I do not sleep through the night; my senses are scattered away from me, I do not care for food or drink. I have no welcome today for the pleasant drink of nobles, or ease, or comfort, or delight, or a great house, or the palace of a king.

What is country to me, or land, or lordship? What are swift
horses? What are jewels? Och, It is I will be lying tonight on the
strand like the beautiful sons of Usnach.

Here is Synge's Deirdre in a similar position:

> It is I who am desolate; I, Deirdre, that will not live till I am
> old. It's you three will not see age or death coming – you that
> were my company when the fires on the hill-tops were put out
> and the stars were our friends only. I'll turn my thoughts back
> from this night, that's pitiful for want of pity, to the time it was
> your rods and cloaks made a little tent for me where there'd
> be a birch tree making shelter and a dry-stone; though from this
> day my own fingers will be making a tent for me spreading out
> my hairs and they knotted with the rain.
>
> Let us throw down clay on my three comrades. Let us cover
> up Naisi along with Ainnle and Ardan, they that were the
> pride of Emain. It was a clean death was your share, Naisi, and
> it is not I will quit your head, when its many a dark night
> among the snipe and plover that you and I were whispering
> together, when we saw the stars among the clear trees, or the
> moon pausing to rest her on the edges of the hills.
>
> I have put away sorrow like a shoe that is worn out and
> muddy, for it is I have had a life that will be envied by great
> companies. . . . It was not a low thing to be chosen by Con-
> chubor, who was wise, and Naisi had no match for bravery. It
> is not a small thing to be rid of grey hairs, and the loosening of
> the teeth. It was the choice of lives we had in the clear woods,
> and in the grave we're safe surely (336–44).

Remembering that Lady Gregory was not trying to write a play
and that the speech of her Deirdre is effective in its context, we
may, without censuring her, remark how much more vivid and
intense Synge's writing is. He adds a more personal and human
note without losing the universal quality of ritual; he assimilates
the Biblical element so that it is not at all obtrusive; he is more
concrete and evocative in his use of words, images and allusions;
and he matches the word-order to speech rhythms, varying his
movement, his pauses and stresses, as feeling dictates.

Lady Gregory's use of the Anglo-Irish idiom, or Kiltartan, as
she called it from the part of Ireland where she studied it and had

her home, has been variously praised and censured. Yeats, Boyd
and Malone see considerable value in it, but Moore, Ervine and
Reid find it a 'curiously monotonous, facile and charmless dialect, which has neither the pictorial vividness of the Synge idiom,
nor the beauty of Mr Yeats's own manner'.[72] There seems little
doubt that she provides a 'faithful transcript of actual peasant
speech . . . having a natural savour which makes its use in comedy
highly effective', but that she does not shape it with sufficient
imagination, and having little of Synge's high poetic quality she
does not secure his intensely memorable and beautiful effects.[73]
Synge's use of the Anglo-Irish idiom has been much more widely
and unreservedly acclaimed. Even Corkery allows[74] that Synge
surpasses all other Anglo-Irish writers, his speech being 'more
unified than theirs, more thoroughly kneaded by a more strongly
creative spirit', and that Synge has 'created from the living
speech about him an idiom which has won universal praise'.
Corkery quotes approvingly the high praise of Téry and Mair,
and this of Boyd: 'It is evident that Anglo-Irish is to Synge a
medium in which he has obtained absolute freedom, he uses it
with the same effect as the Elizabethans used English.' Corkery's
criticism is that at times the rich colour and sound are laid on too
thick and slab, the idiom becomes too 'shiny' or luscious and
gaudy, and awkward for the actor to speak, and that a too facile
use is made of the cadence, 'the hour of death', 'the fogs of dawn',
'the stars of night', to end a sentence. Something of this seems to
have been glimpsed by Bourgeois, for while praising the powerful
literary quality of Synge's idiom he observes that it is too elevated
or fantastic to typify real speech. A similar view, expressed more
boisterously, comes from Lynd who sees Synge's style as 'gauded
and overwrought, with bagfuls of wild phrases' and from Ervine
who sees it as 'contrived literary stuff, entirely unrepresentative of
peasant speech'. Now Synge did not write as he did merely because he knew no better. If he had wished to reproduce the actual
speech of Irish peasants he could have done so (with much less
effort than the writing of his poetic dialogue took); his prose
works prove how accurately he was able to report speech when
necessary.[75] Moreover, he knew the people well, among them he
mastered both Anglo-Irish and Gaelic, after having studied
Gaelic at Trinity, Dublin, and attended special advanced courses
in Breton and Old Irish at the Sorbonne, Paris; so that, as Greene

says,[76] he had 'a linguistic equipment which his colleagues could
only envy and an insight sharpened by his knowledge of Continental Celticism'. Hence the speech of his plays was the result of
conscious artistic choice. The strictures upon this speech of
Ervine and others add up to the view that dramatic dialogue
should approximate very closely to the dialogue of everyday life.
This view, as Ervine himself recognizes elsewhere, would lead
to the rejection of all poetic drama and of most prose drama that
does more than sketch the surface of things. As Eliot says:[77]

> is not every dramatic representation artificial? And are we not
> merely deceiving ourselves when we aim at greater and greater
> realism? Are we not contenting ourselves with appearances, in-
> stead of insisting upon fundamentals? . . . I say that prose
> drama is merely a slight by-product of verse drama. The human
> soul, in intense emotion, strives to express itself in verse. It is
> not for me, but for the neurologists, to discover why this is so,
> and why and how feeling and rhythm are related. The tendency,
> at any rate, of prose drama is to emphasise the ephemeral and
> superficial; if we want to get at the permanent and universal
> we tend to express ourselves in verse.

Or, as Yeats said in the very useful leaflet the Abbey used to send
out to budding playwrights, 'A work of art, though it must have
the effect of nature, is art because it is not nature, as Goethe said:
and it must possess a unity unlike the accidental profusion of
nature.' All this Synge understood. He knew that dramatic
speech has to be more precise, beautiful and meaningful than
ordinary speech, if it is to make any significant impact upon an
audience in an hour or two. Accordingly, like that of all considerable dramatists, his dialogue is a selection from living language,
not a copy of it. George Moore declared[78] that Synge 'discovered
great literature in barbarous idiom as gold is discovered in quartz,
and to do such a thing is a great literary achievement', but to
create dialogue which is 'a vivid reflection of racial temperament
and yet subtly adapted to individual character moods' [79] Synge
had to mine and refine the material, and it is in this process that
genius is most necessary. Strong recognizes this:[80]

> Synge's idiom (like Shakespeare's) is a *selection* from the idiom
> of his day. The language of Synge's plays is *not* the language of

the peasants, insomuch that no peasant talks consistently as Synge's characters talk: it *is* the language of the peasants, in that it contains no word or phrase a peasant did not actually use.

Boyd sums up well:[81]

> But where Hyde was a too cautious experimenter, and Lady Gregory a perceptible literary reporter, Synge showed himself a master. . . . Synge does not mechanically reproduce what he has heard in the cottages; he moulds the raw material, as it were, of peasant speech until it corresponds exactly to the impulse of his own imagination. Hence the delicate harmony of thought and phrase. He had so completely identified himself with the life of the people, and so thoroughly coloured his vision with the Gaelic spirit of its original conception, that he could create where others reported.

And if, to make assurance doubly sure, yet more evidence is required of the authenticity of Synge's idiom, it comes from the unimpeachable Colum:[82]

> The speech of the Irish country-people is fine material for the dramatist, and the Irish dramatists have made good use of it. Synge's dialogue reproduces the energy and extravagance of the people's speech. . . . It is true that Synge's dialogue is a splendid convention; all the characters speak to the same rhythm and their speech is made up of words and phrases from different parts of the country with Gaelic idioms, authorized and unauthorized. Nevertheless, I feel as much reality in Synge's as in the speech of that acknowledged master of Irish life and manners – William Carleton.

A careful and scholarly examination of the construction of this Anglo-Irish idiom has been made by the Celtic philologist, A. G. van Hamel. He declares that Synge has 'learned and loved that passionate mixture of Irish and English well' and that Synge's characters speak 'a very realistic and vigorous Western Anglo-Irish'. Consequently, in his article 'On Anglo-Irish Syntax', van Hamel draws his examples from Synge's plays and from one or two of Yeats. Nearly all the constructions peculiar to Anglo-Irish arise from the influence of Gaelic. Prominent among these is the extensive use of the verb 'to be'. In English stress is important, and the meaning of the sentence 'Do you fear the police?'

can be varied according to the stress laid on particular words. But in Gaelic, and therefore in Anglo-Irish, the sentence construction emphasizes the meaning, and the most important word comes immediately after the verb 'to be': 'Is it yourself is fearing the polis?' and 'It was my own son hit me.' The object may be made prominent: 'it's great luck and company I've won me in the end of time' or an adverbial adjunct: 'It's soon he'll be falling asleep.' The verb 'to be' is widely used to form tenses, to form moods such as the imperative: 'Let you be making yourself easy and saying a prayer', with 'after' to express the perfect: 'you're the one I'm after lacing in my heart-strings half an hour gone by', and to suggest habit or frequency: 'would anyone believe the things they do be saying in the glen?' A general preference for the interrogative form, particularly to make an affirmative stronger, is noticeable: 'And it's that you'd call sport is it, to be abroad in the darkness with yourself alone?' and: 'Amn't I after saying it is himself has me destroyed, and he a lier on walls, a talker of folly?'

As there is a comparative shortage of common verbs in Gaelic very much use is made of prepositions, and this is carried over to Anglo-Irish. The Gaelic preposition *ar* (= on) is always used of an emotion; hence: 'My leg's bit on me' and: 'Her husband was after dying on her'; 'for' is sometimes used to suggest something creditable: 'isn't it true for Father Reilly, that all drink's a curse' (i.e. 'how wise Father Reilly is to say that all drink is a curse'); and 'with' is used to denote the agent or cause with passive verbs: 'It's with bare starving people the water should be used'. Likewise, since in Gaelic the word for 'and', *agus*, is used very frequently in place of most conjunctions and to introduce subordinate clauses, 'and' is so used in Anglo-Irish, e.g.:

Time clause: 'What way would I live, and I an old woman' (i.e. 'when I am an old woman').

Adjective clause: 'the Lord God sent him this road to make a second husband to the widow Quin, and she with a great yearning to be wedded'.

Concessive clause: 'And to think it's me is talking sweetly, and I the fright of seven townlands for my biting tongue'.

Finally, the translating of common Gaelic expressions into Anglo-Irish produces 'the way' meaning 'so that': 'not a decent house within four miles, the way every living Christian is a bona fide'; 'in it' meaning 'in existence': 'It's a hard thing they'll be saying below if the body is washed up and there's no man in it to make the coffin'; and 'self' not used reflexively but to denote 'so': 'Yet, if it is itself, who can help it at all?' or to denote 'even': 'If it was a hundred horses you had itself'.

The effect of these and other related constructions, as used by Synge, is to produce a sequence of assorted cadences unified in a full sure rhythm which gives unobtrusively a basic pattern, as in some kinds of Jacobean blank verse, yet provides for ejaculations of single syllables or phrases and for numerous variations wherever appropriate. It is this felicitous and seemingly irresistible flow that gives to Synge's dialogue something of that sense of ritual which all art must have while being linked to recognizable everyday actualities, and it exemplifies the great creative principle of similarity in dissimilarity. Synge's rhythms are similar enough to ordinary English speech for us to accept and understand them without undue effort, yet they are also dissimilar enough to give us a sense of novelty and freshness, to refurbish our words and to make us grasp them more fully and as if for the first time.

> Oh, I'm raving with a madness that would fright the world. There was one time I seen ten scarlet divils letting on they'd cork my spirit in a gallon can; and one time I seen rats as big as badgers sucking the lifeblood from the butt of my lug; but I never till this day confused that dribbling idiot with a likely man. I'm destroyed surely (247).

> Draw a little back with the squabbling of fools when I am broken up with misery. I see the flames of Emain starting upward in the dark night; and because of me there will be weasels and wild cats crying on a lonely wall where there were queens and armies and red gold, the way there will be a story told of a ruined city and a raving king and a woman will be young for ever (343).

Clearly, Synge's use of Anglo-Irish cadences is most distinctive and masterly. But no less outstanding is his use of imagery within these cadences:

> I'm telling you there isn't a wisp on any grey mare on the ridge of the world isn't finer than the dirty twist on your head. There

isn't two eyes in any starving sow isn't finer than the eyes you were calling blue like the sea (124).

As Grattan Freyer observes[83] 'similes or richly descriptive comparisons occur with almost rhythmic frequency in the plays', though, one adds, they are much more abundant in the comedies than in the tragedies, and there can be few writers who surpass Synge in the use of imagery for comic purposes. There is a kinship between Falstaff's:

Have I lived to be carried in a basket, like a barrow of butcher's offal, and to be thrown in the Thames? . . . The rogues slighted me into the river with as little remorse as they would have drown'd a bitch's blind puppies,

and Christy's:

following after me like an old weasel tracing a rat, and coming in here laying desolation between my own self and the fine women of Ireland, and he a kind of carcase that you'd fling upon the sea,

or Michael Flaherty's:

aren't you a louty schemer to go burying your poor father unbeknownst when you'd a right to throw him on the crupper of a Kerry mule and drive him westwards, like holy Joseph in the days gone by, the way we could have given him a decent burial, and not have him rotting beyond, and not a Christian drinking a smart drop to the glory of his soul?

Added point is given to this last speech by the fact that Flaherty has just described 'a decent burial': 'flows of drink, the way when we sunk her bones at noonday in her narrow grave, there were five men, aye, and six men, stretched out retching speechless on the holy stones.' Here 'flows' suggests unceasing motion from glasses through throats and so on: 'sunk' continues the notion of immersion (in liquid) – how inappropriate would 'laid', say, have been – 'noonday' makes it more comically extravagant since night is the usual time for drinking but these men have been drinking all through the night right up to the height of day; the amendment about the number of men shows a characteristic desire to report exactly this vital ritual; and 'retching speechless' gains sound

value from surrounding words ('stretched'), carries on the notion
of 'flow' and makes a startling and ironic contrast with 'holy
stones'. Synge is also a master of the direct poetic statement for
a variety of effects: humorous fantasy:

> Doesn't the world know you reared a black ram at your own
> breast, so that the Lord Bishop of Connaught felt the elements
> of a Christian, and he eating it after in a kidney stew? Doesn't
> the world know you've been seen shaving the foxy skipper from
> France for a threepenny-bit and a sop of grass tobacco would
> wring the liver from a mountain goat you'd meet leaping the
> hills? (204).

and an unadorned sublimity which Matthew Arnold might very
well have taken as a 'touchstone' of 'high seriousness': 'It's a
great wonder she wouldn't think of the nails, and all the coffins
she's seen made already'.[54] Synge is sparing of metaphor and
verbal symbolism, and he favours the simple simile derived
usually from the everyday world of man and nature: 'he went
down at my feet like an empty sack'; 'naked as an ash-tree in the
moon of May'; 'joy and sorrow do burn out like straw blazing
in an east wind'; 'a head as bald as an old turnip you'd see rolling
round in the muck'; 'Did you never hear tell of the skulls they
have in the city of Dublin, ranged out like blue jugs in a cabin of
Connaught?'; 'and they find her stretched like a dead sheep with
the frost on her, or the big spiders maybe, and they putting their
webs on her, in the butt of a ditch'. There is a homely verbal
texture and a grasp of the single animating detail here which
recall the best early seventeenth-century poetry, just as there is
something of a metaphysical hyperbole in: 'his chin the way it
would take the bark from the edge of an oak board you'd have
building a door'; 'you with a stack of pint bottles above reaching
the sky'; 'If the mitred bishops seen you that time, they'd be the
like of the holy prophets, I'm thinking, do be straining the bars of
Paradise to lay eyes on the Lady Helen of Troy, and she abroad,
pacing back and forward, with a nosegay in her golden shawl.'
Synge can group similes effectively: 'crossing the hills when the
fog is on them, the time a little stick would seem as big as your
arm, and a rabbit as big as a bay horse, and a stack of turf as big
as a towering church in the city of Dublin'. He can make a social
comment: 'she after going by with her head turned the way

you'd see a priest going where there'd be a drunken man in the side ditch talking with a girl'. He can particularize a conventional image and make it fresh: 'that whitish yellowy hair she has does be soon turning the like of a handful of thin grass you'd see rotting, where the wet lies, at the north end of a sty'. And typically he draws upon religion: 'I went on wandering like Esau or Cain and Abel', and also upon a pagan delight in vigour for its own sake: 'the great queens of Ireland, with white necks on them the like of Sarah Casey, and fine arms would hit you a slap the way Sarah Casey would hit you'. Probably the salient feature of these comparisons is the degree to which they are made specific; the associations are palpable, the pregnant detail is unerringly placed, and so the effect is apt, tangible and immediate.

The foregoing cadences and images, then, are characteristic of the idiom which Synge used to create plays of power and beauty, and, aided by Lady Gregory, he established the Anglo-Irish idiom as the distinctive medium of the revived Irish drama in the first and most important phase of its development. The idiom attracted a number of imitators of little ability, and in time it became debased in their hands. It was parodied, amusingly, in *The Mist That Does Be On The Bog* by Gerald MacNamara, and, from 1910 onwards, avoided by the more intelligent dramatists. A phase of naturalism, in theme and treatment, followed, and despite the efforts of Sean O'Casey to bring poetry back, this still prevails. It might seem that Edward Martyn, rather than Yeats, has triumphed. Martyn, both by his financial support and also by his two best plays, *The Heather Field* and *Maeve*, produced in 1899 and 1900, did much to set the dramatic movement on its feet. He venerated Ibsen and wished to see the naturalistic play dealing with serious contemporary ideas dominant in the Irish drama. Yeats, however, wanted the poetic play based on heroic and folk material. In 1901, about the time that the Fay brothers joined with Yeats, Martyn withdrew from the company, and George Moore followed him. The Fays, Yeats, and Lady Gregory, reinforced by 'A.E.' and a bit later by Synge, and aided by Miss Horniman's generosity, carried on, and the poetic plays of the Abbey Theatre became famous. From the beginning one or two naturalistic plays were put on, and when the poetic drama declined rapidly after the death of Synge in 1909, these soon became predominant. At first sight, then, there might seem to be truth in Moore's remark:

'Yeats founded a realistic theatre'. But T. S. Eliot, taking a longer view and with unequalled insight,[84] shows that Yeats was right:

> Yeats started writing plays at a time when the prose-play of contemporary life seemed triumphant, with an indefinite future stretching before it; when the comedy of light farce dealt only with certain privileged strata of metropolitan life; and when the serious play tended to be an ephemeral tract on some transient social problem. We begin to see now that even the imperfect early plays he made are probably more permanent literature than the plays of Shaw; and that his dramatic work as a whole may prove a stronger defence against the successful urban Shaftesbury Avenue vulgarity which he opposed as stoutly as they. . . . He cared, I think, more for the theatre as an organ for the expression of the consciousness of a people, than as a means to his own fame or achievement.

And Malone concludes[85] that Synge and Yeats in expressing the Irish spirit in English were right:

> In Ireland the English language has so firmly established itself that all effort to eradicate it in the future must prove vain, and it is in the English language that the spiritual difference between the people in Ireland and the people in all other geographical entities will of necessity be best expressed.

This view expressed by Malone – and others – has been strenuously resisted by all official Irish spokesmen since the country became independent in 1921. Each political party has constantly proclaimed that one of its chief and most sacred aims is the relegation of English and the making Ireland a Gaelic-speaking nation. Much money and energy have been devoted to this policy, and hardly anyone publicly has dared to question the wisdom of it or whether all that is being done to realize it is having any effect. Privately, however, there has been much doubt as to whether the end, if desirable, is attainable; after forty years of independence and intense propaganda for Gaelic, English is more widely used than ever and the number of Gaelic speakers has barely increased. This fact has become so obvious that even the political parties cannot much longer refuse to acknowledge it, and two of them, Fine Gael and Labour, independently, in the autumn of 1959,

declared that the efforts to replace English by Gaelic were
vain and were harming the country and that a re-appraisal,
however agonizing to traditional Gaelic nationalists, must be
made.

It is clear then that the Anglo-Irish idiom has as good an expectation of life as any other European tongue, and that the finest use
of it, in Synge's writings, should be studied more and more.

Yeats and Synge

Probably the most satisfying utterances about Synge are those by
Yeats, and some account of them must now be given, though it
cannot do more than merely hint at their wisdom and inspiration.
They provide an invaluable insight into the writings of Yeats and
Synge, the Irish literary renaissance and the principles of naturalistic and poetic drama, and they affirm memorably the status of the
artist and the imagination and of literature as 'the great teaching
power of the world, the ultimate creator of all values'.[86] Yeats was
in that line of geniuses which runs from Blake, Wordsworth and
Coleridge through, strangely enough, John Stuart Mill and
Matthew Arnold, to D. H. Lawrence, a line which while recognizing the immense material benefits that the systematic applica-
tion of scientific method has brought to mankind believes that the
dominance of unimpassioned reason, of habits of analysis and
logic (essential for the solution of many problems) enfeebles
human personality, the instinctive or spiritual life, stifling feeling
and the sense of wonder and fixing abstractions or stereotypes between an individual and reality. It is the belief symbolized in
Blake's 'Sick Rose' and in Coleridge's 'Ode in Dejection'; the
belief that makes Wordsworth's *Prelude* a vital document for education today and Coleridge's *Biographia Literaria* central in literary
criticism; it was constantly proclaimed by Mill after poetry had
cured him of the almost mortal illness brought on by an exclusively rationalistic education; it sustained Arnold's long struggle
against the Philistines and the worship of 'machinery'; it means
that Lawrence's presentation of human passion (whatever its
extravagancies) cannot be ignored; and it caused Synge to wish to
settle on Inishmaan, to wonder on a cliff in Kerry why anyone
lived in the cities and to show in *The Playboy* the supreme power

of the imagination. It pervades the writings of Yeats and can be
seen in such poems as 'The Realists', in the Blake-like

> *Locke sank into a swoon;*
> *The Garden died;*
> *God took the spinning-jenny*
> *Out of his side,*

and in the prayer to be guarded

> *from those thoughts men think*
> *In the mind alone;*
> *He that sings a lasting song*
> *Thinks in a marrow-bone.*

It can be seen dramatically in *The Hour Glass* exposing the hollow-
ness of the Wise Man's rationalism, and in *The King's Threshold*
which proclaims the absolute value of poetry, admitting no compromise, however seemingly reasonable, with rulers or friends or
anyone, and bringing to mankind, if the poet is willing to suffer
for his art (as Seanchan was in the play, and as Yeats and Synge
were in life) priceless fruits of joy and heroism:

> *Cry out that the King's money would not buy,*
> *Nor the high circle consecrate his head,*
> *If poets had never christened gold . . .*
> *. . . cry out that not a man alive*
> *Would ride among the arrows with high heart*
> *Or scatter with an open hand, had not*
> *Our heady craft commended wasteful virtues.*

Poets are the source of spiritual power more enduring than the
material world:

> *Cry aloud*
> *That when we are driven out we come again*
> *Like a great wind that runs out of the waste*
> *To blow the tables flat.*

The betrayal of their function would mean the impoverishment
of mankind; if the poet had compromised:

> *The kiss of multitudes in times to come*
> *Had been the poorer.*

or, as Yeats said, referring, probably, to Synge as a man of a 'passionate serving kind' who had given people 'loftier thought, Sweeter emotion working in their veins', but who had

> *been driven from the place,*
> *And insult heaped upon him for his pains,*
> *And for his open-handedness, disgrace.*

This principle was at the heart of the conflict about Synge's plays, and in sustaining it he and Yeats were taking a crucial part in the never-ceasing struggle for the supremacy of the poet. The disregard of imagination and the consequent bias towards what could be materially assessed and systematized led to a commercialized utilitarianism coupled with philistine nationalism which, crudely propagated by the popular press, was producing a population which could hardly think consistently or feel deeply but which could be roused to fanatical hatred or adulation of abstractions or stereotypes. Repeatedly Yeats makes this point:[87]

> newspaper government and the scientific movement are bringing upon us all these phrases and generalizations made by minds that would grasp what they have never seen . . . in the machine shop of the realists . . . churlish logicians . . . like some noisy and powerful machine of thought that has no part of wisdom but the apologetic of a moment are filling people with abstractions and images created not for their own sake but for the sake of party. . . . Certain generalizations are everywhere substituted for life. Instead of individual men and women and living virtues differing as one star differeth from another in glory, the public imagination is full of personified averages, partisan fictions, rules of life that would drill everybody into the one posture, habits that are like the pinafores of charity-school children.

Briefly, Yeats was opposing the subordination of art to propaganda, even when it was for a worthy cause. With all his admiration for Douglas Hyde, Yeats felt that in ceasing to create Gaelic poetry and plays and fine versions of legend and folk-lore with their important translations into the Anglo-Irish idiom, and in immersing himself in ephemeral writing and propaganda, Hyde was forsaking his true vocation. Unhappily Hyde

> *had beaten into prose*
> *That noble blade the Muses buckled on,*

and Yeats mourned[88] for 'the greatest folklorist who ever lived, for the great poet who died in his youth . . . and took for model the newspaper upon his breakfast table and became beloved by multitudes, the cajoler of crowds' (Moore describes[89] Hyde at a public meeting 'a torrent of verbiage, threats, denunciations pouring through his drooping black moustache like porter'). Hyde acted out of a deep sense of duty and patriotism, but he was mistaken, for the dissemination of gross simplifications of bits of truth hardened into dogmas, and the stirring-up of hatred, although perhaps helpful in ridding a nation of foreign rule, harm the nation's mind and imagination: 'A community that is opinion-ridden, even when those opinions are in themselves noble, is likely to put its creative minds into some sort of prison.' [90] How fundamental this was to Yeats may be seen further in his 'A Prayer for My Daughter', with its censure of the woman he loved for degrading her matchless gifts:

> *An intellectual hatred is the worst,*
> *So let her think opinions are accursed.*
> *Have I not seen the loveliest woman born*
> *Out of the mouth of Plenty's horn,*
> *Because of her opinionated mind*
> *Barter that horn and every good*
> *By quiet natures understood*
> *For an old bellows full of angry wind?*

The writer best serves his country, and mankind generally, by refusing to write with a palpable design or to accept[91]

the rough-and-ready conscience of the newspaper and the pulpit in a matter so delicate as literature. . . . We have to make the theatre a place of intellectual excitement, a place where the mind goes to be liberated as it was liberated by the theatres of Greece and England and France at certain great moments of their history, and as it is liberated in Scandinavia today. If we are to do this we must learn that beauty and truth are always justified of themselves, and that their creation is a greater service to our country than writing that compromises either in the seeming service of a cause. . . . The dramatist produces a moment of intense and abundant life, an activity of the souls of the characters, an energy, an eddy of life purified from every-

thing but itself and the imaginative delight it gives enlarges the
energy of a people by the spectacle of energy, adding to their
being if not to their knowledge, and nourishing that charity
that is the forgiveness of sins will make us understand men no
matter how little they conform to our expectations.

In this there is nothing soft; literature is not vague or mawkish, no
poet has ever been, in his writings, a sentimentalist, Yeats affirms,
and expresses[92] his horror at a treatment of heroic legend 'full of
sedentary refinement and the spirituality of cities, every emotion
made as dainty-footed and dainty-fingered as might be', just as,
at the end of his life, he was, with great honesty, to mock himself
in the remarkable poem 'The Circus Animals' Desertion' for the
dreamy artificiality of his early plays. In fact, and here Yeats
enunciates[93] a truth confirmed later by such varied writers as
D. H. Lawrence, Grahame Greene, E. M. Forster, F. R. Leavis
and Richard Hoggart,

> The sentimentalists are practical men who believe in money, in
> position, in a marriage bell, and whose understanding of hap-
> piness is to be so busy whether at work or play, that all is for-
> gotten but the momentary aim.

The true peasant is not sentimental, Yeats knew, describing the
disdain of a village shoemaker, a great reader, for novelists who
sentimentalized the people and the man's wish for a literature
which would show the people 'in their naked hideousness'. Yeats
concluded:[94] 'That is the peasant mind as I know it, a mind that
delights in strong sensations whether of beauty or of ugliness, in
bare facts, and it is quite without sentimentality.' Not seeking,
then, to hide ugliness with false beauty, the writer must try to see
life clearly and see it whole, the horror, the boredom and the
glory, an appalling task, costing not less than everything, for 'he
only can create the greatest imaginable beauty who has endured
all imaginable pangs',[95] but when accomplished giving to us all,
both writers and readers

> in the creative joy an acceptance of what life brings, because
> we have understood the beauty of what it brings, or a hatred
> of death for what it takes away, which arouses within us,
> through some sympathy perhaps with all other men, an energy
> so noble, so powerful, that we laugh aloud and mock, in

the terror or the sweetness of our exaltation, at death and oblivion.[96]

Thus Synge created. But since 'all minds that have a wisdom come of tragic reality seem morbid to those that are accustomed to writers who have not faced reality at all',[97] and since Synge, instead of writing 'plays that get an easy cheer because they make no discoveries in human nature but repeat the opinions of the audience or the satire of its favourite newspapers',[98] wrote plays that with their astringent vitality assaulted the popular ikons, he was savagely denounced. Again Yeats understood thoroughly:[99]

> The root of it all is that the political class in Ireland have suffered through the cultivation of hatred as the one energy of their movement, a deprivation which is the intellectual equivalent to a certain surgical operation. Hence the shrillness of their voices. They contemplate all creative power as the eunuchs contemplate Don Juan as he passes through Hell on the white horse;

or, as he said in a poem 'On Those That Hated *The Playboy of the Western World*, 1907'

> *Once, when midnight smote the air*
> *Eunuchs ran through Hell and met*
> *On every crowded street to stare*
> *Upon great Juan riding by:*
> *Even like these to rail and sweat*
> *Staring upon his sinewy thigh.*

Yeats concluded:

> Hatred as a basis of imagination helps to dry up the nature and make the sexual abstinence, so common among young men and women in Ireland, possible. This abstinence reacts in its turn on the imagination, so that we get at last that strange eunuch-like tone and temper. For the last ten or twenty years there has been a perpetual drying of the Irish mind with the resultant dust-cloud.

Yeats's analysis of the psychology of popular movements, of misconceptions about science and the irrational adulation of

abstractions, and of the effect of these on the writer is both profound and topical. It anticipates, for example, George Orwell's
demonstration in *1984* of the links between sexual deprivation and
fanaticism and of how deterioration in language is bound up with
coarsening human life. After Matthew Arnold with his warnings
about the 'wave of more than American vulgarity' about to engulf
us, Yeats was one of the first to point to the degrading effects of
commercialized mass media:[100]

> All exploitation of the life of the wealthy, for the eye and the ear
> of the poor and half poor, in plays, in popular novels, in musical
> comedy, in fashion papers, at the cinema impoverishes and
> vulgarizes the imagination, seeming to hold up for envy and to
> commend a life where all is display and hurry, passion without
> emotion, emotion without intellect, and where there is nothing
> stern and solitary.

The commercial theatre is demoralizing[101]

> not because it delights in the husband, the wife, and the lover,
> a subject which has inspired great literature in most ages of the
> world, but because the illogical thinking and insincere feeling
> we call bad writing make the mind timid and the heart effemin-
> ate.

It had developed out of 'that brooding over scientific opinion that
so often extinguished the central flame in Tennyson', it was a
product of naturalism, the notion that plays must reflect the
surface of life;[102]

> the author of *Caste* made a reputation by putting what seemed
> to be average common life and average common speech for the
> first time upon the stage in England, and by substituting real
> loaves of bread and real cups of tea for imaginary ones. He was
> not a very clever nor a very well-educated man, and he made his
> revolution superficially; but in other countries men of intellect
> and knowledge created that intellectual drama of real life, of
> which Ibsen's later plays are the ripened fruit. This change
> coincided with the substitution of science for religion in the
> conduct of life, and is, I believe, as temporary, for the practice
> of twenty centuries will surely take the sway in the end.

To show the inadequacies of ephemeral prose drama by creating something better,[103] 'to ascend out of the common interests, the thoughts of the newspapers, of the market-place, of men of science, but only so far as we can carry the normal passionate reasoning self, the personality as a whole', was the chief task of the theatre of Yeats and Synge.

Not that Yeats denied a place for naturalism or that historically it was necessary to end crude melodrama or farce and to bring adult themes on the stage; part of his complaint against commercialism was that despite its pretensions it was not realistic enough:[104] 'Let us press the popular arts on to a more complete realism – that would be their honesty – for the commercial arts demoralize by their compromise, their incompleteness, their idealism without sincerity or elegance.' Within limits he admired Ibsen. He hated *A Doll's House*: 'what was it but Huxley and Tyndall all over again', and, repeating Goethe's dictum that art is art because it is not nature, he resented 'being invited to admire dialogue so close to modern educated speech that music and style were impossible'.[105] Yet, 'Ibsen was the one great master of the modern stage';[106] neither Yeats nor his generation could escape Ibsen because though they and he had not the same friends they had the same enemies. Yeats's feelings about Shaw too were divided. He risked all that he had built up in the Abbey Theatre in order to stage *The Shewing-up of Blanco Posnet* in defiance of the authorities. He listened to *Arms and the Man* with admiration and hatred, it seemed to him 'inorganic, logical straightness and not the crooked road of life' yet he stood 'aghast before its energy';[107]

> Presently I had a nightmare that I was haunted by a sewing-machine, that clicked and shone, but the incredible thing was that the machine smiled, smiled perpetually. Yet I delighted in Shaw, the formidable man. He could hit my enemies and the enemies of all I loved, as I could never hit, as no living author that was dear to me could ever hit.

Yeats encouraged Martyn and Lennox Robinson and the 'Cork Realists', and he hoped that some dramatist would create plays about the life of Irish drawing-rooms 'and means to play them as truthful as a play of Ibsen's upon the Scandinavian stage'.[108] But he was not himself interested in that kind of work, he did not believe that it was as important as contemporary critics thought it

was and he hoped that their imagination would not turn 'too long
to the quarter of the Scandinavian winds'.[108] In short, the trouble
was that the naturalistic dramatists, with all their intellect, wit,
moral purpose and craftsmanship, lacked poetry:[109] 'Ibsen has sincerity and logic beyond any writer of our time, and we are all
seeking to learn them at his hands; but is he not a good deal less
than the greatest of all times, because he lacks beautiful and vivid
language?' Probably Yeats did not take sufficient account of the
inevitable loss of power in translation, and of *Peer Gynt* and Ibsen's
last great symbolic plays. But about the mass of naturalistic plays
he was right, and his discernment of their limitations, at a time
when naturalism was engrossing both the serious and the commercial theatres, was astounding and prophetic:[110]

> Of all artistic forms that have had a large share of the world's
> attention, the worst is the play about modern educated people
> . . . with its meagre language and its action crushed into the
> narrow limits of possibility. . . . Except where it is superficial or
> deliberately argumentative it fills one's soul with a sense of
> commonness as with dust.

Then, making a notable comparison with the novel which is 'a
permanent form because having the power of psychological
description it can follow the thought of a man who is looking into
the grate',[110] Yeats goes to the heart of the matter; the naturalistic
play

> has one mortal ailment. It cannot become impassioned, that is
> to say, vital, without making somebody gushing and senti-
> mental. Educated and well-bred people do not wear their hearts
> upon their sleeves, and they have no artistic and charming
> language except light persiflage and no powerful language at all,
> and when they are deeply moved they look silently into the
> fireplace . . . modern drama while expressing life directly has
> been driven to make indirect its expression of the mind, which
> it leaves to be inferred from some .commonplace sentence or
> gesture . . . by a stage picture, a man holding a woman's hand
> or sitting with his head in his hands in dim light by the red glow
> of a fire.[110]

With naturalism comes a decline in dramatic energy: 'after all, is
not the greatest play not the play that gives the sensation of an

external reality but the play in which there is the greatest abundance of life itself, of the reality that is in our minds';[111]

> *actors lacking music*
> *Do most excite my spleen,*
> *They say it is more human*
> *To shuffle, grunt and groan,*
> *Not knowing what unearthly stuff*
> *Rounds a mighty scene.*[112]

It was by an infusion of the 'unearthly stuff' that drama was to be revived, not from the meretricious pleasures of musical comedy or from going back to 'the worn-out conventions of English poetic drama' but from a return to the roots of life to

> *where all the ladders start*
> *In the foul rag-and-bone shop of the heart.*

There must be a proper sense of values. In contrast to the contemporary theatre with its stress on personalities, on the mechanics of production, on elaborate settings and spectacle, there was to be in Yeats's theatre a classical economy, and, while all worked together, fundamentally the poet was more important than the actor and the actor more important than the scenery. Always language was at the root of the matter:[113]

> Literature decays when it no longer makes more beautiful, or more vivid, the language which unites it to all life, and when one finds the criticism of the student, and the purpose of the reformer, and the logic of the man of science, where there should have been the reveries of the common heart, ennobled into some raving Lear or unabashed Don Quixote.

The remedy was to do as the Russians had done in the eighteen-seventies, to go back to people whose imagination and language were still vital, who lived rather as they did in the great ages of literature and delighted in the heroic and the homely in legend and in ordinary life: 'a community bound together by imaginative possessions, by stories and poems which have grown out of its own life and by a past of great passions which can still awaken the imagination'.[114] Language was the great mediator:

> the English idiom of the Irish-thinking people of the west is the only good English spoken by any large number of Irish people

today, and we must found good literature on a living speech.
. . . May it not be that the only realistic play that will live as
Shakespeare has lived will arise out of the common life, where
language is as much alive as if it were new come out of Eden?[115]

There was to be then a certain distancing of theme and language to
give distinction and universality. Again like Arnold, Yeats sought
the great themes, actions transcending common life and speech
yet illuminating reality far more profoundly than any adherence
to surface appearances could.[116]

> The play that is to give people a quite natural pleasure should
> tell them either of their own life, or of that life of poetry where
> every man can see his own image, because there alone does
> human nature escape from arbitrary conditions. . . . Have we
> not been in error in demanding from our playwrights person-
> ages who do not transcend our common actions any more than
> our common speech? If we are in the right, all antiquity has been
> in error. . . . The arts are at their greatest when they seek for a
> life growing always more scornful of everything that is not
> itself and passing into its own fullness, as it were, ever more
> completely as all that is created out of the passing mode of
> society slips from it. . . . It is only by extravagance, by an
> emphasis far greater than that of life as we observe it, that we
> can crowd into a few minutes the knowledge of years. Shake-
> speare or Sophocles can so quicken, as it were, the circles of the
> clock, so heighten the expression of life, that many years can
> unfold themselves in a few minutes, and it is always Shake-
> speare or Sophocles, and not Ibsen, that makes us say, 'How
> true, how often I have felt as that man feels'; or 'How intimately
> I have come to know those people on the stage.' . . . The
> greatest art symbolizes not those things that we have observed
> so much as those things that we have experienced.

This conception of Yeats of a theatre with a base of realism and an
apex of beauty, the expression, in language drawn from country
speech, of folk-life and lore and traditional romance and legend,
is wonderfully summed up in his 'The Municipal Gallery Revisited':

> (*An image out of Spenser and the common tongue*).
> *John Synge, I and Augusta Gregory, thought*
> *All that we did, all that we said or sang*

Must come from contact with the soil, from that
Contact everything Antaeus-like grew strong.
We three alone in modern times had brought
Everything down to that sole test again,
Dream of the noble and the beggar-man.

It is a main part of Synge's greatness that he alone fully realized
this dream in drama. This Yeats recognized.

Lady Gregory made an invaluable contribution with her knowledge of peasants, country townsfolk and landowners, her resource
and flair for collaboration and her astounding energy that led her
when advanced in middle age to write plays that were the staple
diet of the Abbey Theatre and to undertake successfully public
lecturing and theatre management, as during the hectic tour of the
U.S.A. in 1911. Yeats appreciated all this, and particularly her
ability swiftly to grasp and to supply what was needed in both
business and dramatic matters and to hold together various
temperaments and forces. He expressed his deep gratitude on
several occasions; most movingly in 'Coole Park, 1929':

I meditate upon a swallow's flight,
Upon an aged woman and her house,
A sycamore and lime-tree lost in night
Although that western cloud is luminous,
Great works constructed there in nature's spite
For scholars and for poets after us,
Thoughts long knitted into a single thought,
A dance-like glory that those walls begot.

There Hyde before he had beaten into prose
That noble blade the Muses buckled on,
There one that ruffled in a manly pose
For all his timid heart, there that slow man,
That meditative man, John Synge, and those
Impetuous men, Shawe-Taylor and Hugh Lane
Found pride established in humility,
A scene well set and excellent company.

They came like swallows and like swallows went,
And yet a woman's powerful character
Could keep a swallow to its first intent;

And half-a-dozen in formation there,
That seemed to whirl upon a compass-point,
Found certainty upon the dreaming air,
The intellectual sweetness of those lines
That cut through time or cross it withershins.

Here, traveller, scholar, poet, take your stand
When all those rooms and passages are gone,
When nettles wave upon a shapeless mound
And saplings root among the broken stone,
And dedicate – eyes bent upon the ground,
Back turned upon the brightness of the sun
And all the sensuality of the shade –
A moment's memory to that laurelled head.

Some of her plays continue to have intrinsic as well as historical value, Una Ellis-Fermor affirms, but Lady Gregory's chief part was in sensitively evaluating and harmonizing disparate elements, in creating conditions in which genius could flower, rather than in creating masterpieces. And she would probably have been the first to acknowledge Synge's superiority.

Yeats at first had little to learn from Synge who 'wished to become a writer. He had, however, nothing to show but one or two poems and impressionistic essays . . . which come, not out of life, but out of literature, images reflected from mirror to mirror'.[117] And it was Yeats, with his rare instinct for quality, who initially gave most fully – advice to go to Aran, where Synge realized himself. But after seeing Synge's subsequent work Yeats understood that he was doing what Yeats knew should be done but had not been able to do himself. Yeats took note of the advice given him by Arthur Symons after seeing *The Shadow of the Glen* 'to write no more peasant plays', and from the time of his friendship with Synge dates Yeats's dissatisfaction with the dreamy languors, the rather precious romanticism of his early work, the 'pale brows, passion-dimmed eyes and long heavy hair', his consequent abandoning of 'a coat | Covered with embroideries | Out of old mythologies', his awareness that 'there's more enterprise | In walking naked' and that 'Romantic Ireland's dead and gone | It's with O'Leary in the grave', and his development beyond Pre-Raphaelitism towards the use of tougher idioms, of irony, satire and invective and the production of lasting poetry, profound, astringent and lovely; a process summed up most notably in 'The Circus Animals' Desertion'. He consistently acknowledged that he had learned from Synge both that an idealization remote from ordinary actuality was inadequate: 'I did not see, until Synge began to write, that we must renounce the deliberate creation of a kind of Holy City in the imagination, and express the individual',[118] and also that the habit of theorizing and immersion in controversy, political or artistic, producing 'intellectual hatred', was debilitating for the artist.

Synge embodied in his plays, better than Yeats or anyone could, Yeats's vision of drama; he blended dream and actuality, yet such was the relationship between the two (resembling that between Wordsworth and Coleridge), the cross-fertilization of mind and mind, of belief and practice, that Synge's plays both fulfilled and at the same time transcended and developed Yeats's vision. Synge did not use heroic and legendary material (apart from *Deirdre of the Sorrows*), instead he did something more valuable and rare. He created a mythology of his own. His characters are clearly drawn from the soil, they are instinct with life, recognizably human and authentic, yet they are also big enough to be types or symbols of humanity, they carry something of that weight of enduring universal significance that only figures in epic or legend or great poetic drama carry – as Yeats perceived when he likened them to Falstaff. When Synge did deal with heroic legend he gave credible human qualities, individuality, 'a local habitation and a name' to the traditional figures without detracting from their grandeur or diminishing their typical power. He produced palpable peasants having legendary qualities and fabulous nobles having earthy realism. Yeats understood this, modifying his dramatic theory and practice, and instead of the aloof grace, the conscious beauty of his early plays,

> *Building a sorrowful loveliness*
> *Out of the battles of old times,*

he moulded national issues such as the Easter 1916 Rising with legend and earlier history in *The Dreaming of the Bones* and *The Death of Cuchulain*, and in these and in one or two later plays (notably *Purgatory*) laid future poetic dramatists under obligation to him.

It is no wonder, then, that Synge was among that very small number of people to whom Yeats sometimes deferred on literary matters, that he discussed Synge more than any other writer, and that at the height of his international acclaim as he received the Nobel Prize he praised Synge warmly. Synge was a genius, one of those unaccountable manifestations of spiritual energy at the right time and place. Into an Ireland where there 'was no longer an impartial imagination delighting in what is naturally exciting' Synge came, 'the rushing up of the buried fire, an explosion of all that had been denied or refused, a furious impartiality, an indifferent turbulent sorrow'.[119] Synge gave his country what it really needed, though not what it fancied it wanted:

> He was a solitary, undemonstrative man, never asking pity, nor complaining . . . all folded up in brooding intellect, knowing nothing of new books and newspapers, reading the great masters alone; and he was but the more hated because he gave his country what it needed, an unmoved mind where there is a perpetual last day, a trumpeting, and coming up to judgement.[120]

Synge was truly a National writer, one who could create only in Ireland, whose *Playboy* 'is the strangest, the most beautiful expression in drama of that Irish fantasy which is the unbroken character of Irish genius' [121] and whose *Deirdre* is the noblest and most human embodiment of the finest of Irish legends. Yet at the same time he is universal, 'one of those who define races and create everlasting loyalties':[122] 'Synge alone has written of the peasant as he is to all the ages; of the folk-imagination as it has been shaped by centuries of life among fields or on fishing-grounds.' [123] He, with Yeats, 'led the drama of the English-speaking people back to the paths of poetry and power, making way, in both countries, for the first body of plays which can seriously compare with the Elizabethans',[124] and with Synge 'the reference back is to Molière, to Cervantes, to Jonson':[125]

> Synge belongs to those who, like Wordsworth, like Coleridge, like Goldsmith, like Keats, have little personality, so far as the casual eye can see, but fiery and brooding imagination. . . . Synge has in common with the great theatre of the world, with that of Greece and that of India, with the creator of Falstaff, with Racine, a delight in language, a preoccupation with

individual life . . . his speech has the flavour of Homer, of the Bible, of Villon.[126]

Synge was the living model of the dedicated artist, seeking to unite stoicism, asceticism and ecstasy:

> He had that egotism of the man of genius which Nietzsche compares to the egotism of a woman with child. Neither I nor Lady Gregory had ever a compliment from him. . . . He had under charming and modest manners, in almost all things of life, a complete absorption in his own dream. . . . For him nothing existed but his thought. He claimed nothing for it aloud. He never said any of those self-confident things I am enraged into saying, but one knew that he valued nothing else. He was too confident for self-assertion. . . . One did not think of him as an egotist. He was too sympathetic in the ordinary affairs of life and too simple. In the arts he knew no language but his own. I have often envied him his absorption as I have envied Verlaine his vice.[127]

Synge was a whole person; his joy in the natural world, in what is good, true or beautiful in thought, action or feeling, in the uncalculating life of people and creatures, went together with his irony, his brooding awareness of decay and death, his relish for the grotesque and naturally savage:

> He could not have loved had he not hated, nor honoured had he not scorned; though his hatred and his scorn moved him but seldom, as I think, for his whole nature was lifted up into a vision of the world, where hatred played with the grotesque and love became an ecstatic contemplation of noble life . . . in his plays the core is always as in all great art, an overpowering vision of certain virtues.[128]

'Synge was a sick man picturing energy, a doomed man picturing gaiety',[129] his view of life was the tragic view, but he wrung from it that wholesome ecstasy which is at the heart of tragedy, as Yeats proclaims in 'Lapis Lazuli'. Synge's death was then, as Yeats put it in a most fitting epitaph,

> a misfortune for the living that must work on, perhaps in vain, to magnify the minds and hearts of our young men, and not for the dead that, having cast off the ailing body, is now, as I believe,

all passionate and fiery, an heroical thing. Our Daimon is as dumb as was that of Socrates, when they brought in the hemlock; and if we speak among ourselves, it is of thoughts that have no savour because we cannot hear his laughter, of the work more difficult because of the strength he has taken with him, of the astringent joy and hardness that was in all he did, and of his fame in the world.[130]

Yeats's evaluation of Synge exemplifies again the fact that the great poets are also the best critics. It is unique and just, a worthy tribute to Synge (and to Yeats himself) and it should become increasingly regarded as a main avenue of approach to Synge and as one of the foremost examples of Yeats's discrimination and vision. Occasionally, of course, he is too generous, but he is never wrong on fundamentals, and these are not set forth in general terms alone but arise from reality, from a penetrating study of the words on the page or the play in the theatre. They reveal the relative qualities of poetic and naturalistic drama, and they establish the primacy of language, restoring to words their ancient sovereignty in the drama. But they were too prophetic to be understood at first. After its first decade the Abbey Theatre moved in directions which Yeats did not care for, though he continued to work for its welfare. He said to Craoibhin Aoibhin (Douglas Hyde),

> *When we are high and airy hundreds say*
> *That if we hold that flight they'll leave the place,*
> *While those same hundreds mock another day*
> *Because we have made our art of common things,*

and to Lady Gregory,[131]

Oh yes, I am listened to – am I not a founder of the theatre? – and here and there scattered solitaries delight in what I have made and return to it again; but some young Corkman, all eyes and ears, whose first rambling play we have just pulled together or half together, can do more than that. He will be played by players who have spoken dialogue like his every night for years, and sentences that it had been a bore to read will so delight the whole house that to keep my hands from clapping I shall have to remind myself that I gave my voice for the play's production and must not applaud my own judgement.

He did not set out to create this sort of theatre and its success was a discouragement and a defeat. Hence George Moore was able to exclaim with glee that Martyn had triumphed and that Yeats had founded a naturalistic theatre. But this was not the end, we now see, and the realization is growing that it is to Yeats that we should return for help in reviving poetic drama:

> although the Abbey Theatre would seem to have lost its distinctive literary purpose, and the Irish dramatic movement to have yielded its birthright to the romance of regional naturalism, the example of a theatre called into being by a literary need is yet so rare, and the practical discoveries of Yeats of such continuing importance, that they seem to claim our primary attention. Yeats's magnificent creative impetus formed the general achievement.[132]

And T. S. Eliot, who stands with Yeats well above all English poets of this century and who in turning to write for the theatre has had to deal with similar problems to Yeats's and who has been indebted to Yeats for help in solving them and in writing his own remarkable plays, sums up Yeats's achievement well:

> I do not know where our debt to him as a dramatist ends – and in time, it will not end until that drama itself ends. In his occasional writings on dramatic topics he has asserted certain principles to which we must hold fast: such as the primacy of the poet over the actor, and of the actor over the scene-painter; and the principle that the theatre, while it need not be concerned only with 'the people' in the narrow Russian sense, must be for the people; that to be permanent it must concern itself with fundamental situations. Born into a world in which the doctrine of 'Art for Art's sake' was generally accepted, and living on into one in which art has been asked to be instrumental to social purposes, he held firmly to the right view which is between these, though not in any way a compromise between them, and showed that an artist, by serving his art with entire integrity, is at the same time rendering the greatest service he can to his own nation and to the whole world. . . . Yeats was one of those few whose history is the history of their own time, who are part of the consciousness of an age which cannot be understood without them. This is a very high position to assign to him: but I believe that it is one which is secure.[133]

Synge's Notions about Literature

Nearly all the foregoing beliefs about literature were held by Synge as well as by Yeats, and were mainly a product, hardly analysable into individual components, of their minds in communion. Nevertheless, some note should be taken of the views Synge expressed about drama and poetry, of his individual emphases or variations on the fundamental attitudes shared by him and Yeats, because of the intrinsic value of these views and variations, of the light they throw on Synge's writings, and also because they too embody the theme of dream and actuality.

Synge was well aware of the dangers of abstraction:

All theorizing is bad for the artist, because it makes him live in the intelligence instead of in the half-subconscious faculties by which all real creation is performed. This is one reason why hostile criticism is harmful to an artist, because it forces him to construct systems and defend and explain his own work. Young and therefore living truths, views, what you will, have a certain diffidence or tenderness that makes it impossible to state them without the accompanying emotional or imaginative life in which they naturally arise. That is, they are stated in the arts when they are dead, only the flesh is cleared away and the naked skeletons are shown by essayists and metaphysicians.[134]

There is much truth in this notable passage, for in art, as Keats knew, axioms do not exist 'until they are proved upon our pulses', yet the artist, without constructing systems or trying to justify or rationalize his work, may, very properly, record his notions and experiences concerning the creative process to assist himself and others; the work of many of our better writers reveals a healthy interaction between theory and practice. Fortunately Synge saw this too:

No one is less fond of theories and divisions in the arts than I am, and yet they cannot altogether be gone without. In these matters we need not expect to say anything very new, but in applying for ourselves, to our own life, what is thought in different ways by many, we are likely to hit on matters of some value.[135]

And he has left us an essence of valuable criticism, consisting of three brief prefaces, a few reviews and some jottings in his note-books.

After his unsuccessful attempts in Paris to become a cos-mopolitan writer Synge realized the importance of having a national mood to interpret, of living contacts with his own country, its people and traditions. A profound work of art, he declared, was always distinct and inimitable, 'possible to only one man at one period and in one place'.[136] His own work and the best of that of his Irish contemporaries fulfilled these requirements, and he strenuously, and mainly successfully, opposed the suggestion by Miss Horniman and Yeats that the Abbey should build up a repertoire of foreign masterpieces produced in a grand style along the lines of the continental municipal theatres. The performance of new plays by native authors, though generally inferior to inter-national classics, was what alone justified the existence of the Abbey and gave it special worth.[137] The national spirit, in legend and in country life, could be best expressed in Anglo-Irish. Gaelic was a living speech in merely a few remote areas, and no matter how well the revival went Gaelic would hardly ever become used widely and fluently enough to provide material for literature com-prehensive of the varieties and complexities of existence.

> English is likely to remain the language of Ireland; and no one, I think, need regret the likelihood. If Gaelic came back strongly from the west, the feeling for English which the present generation has attained would be lost again, and in the best circumstances it is probable that Leinster and Ulster would take several centuries to assimilate Irish perfectly enough to make it a fit mode of expression for the finer emotions which now occupy literature. In the meantime, the opening culture of Ireland would be thrown back indefinitely and there would perhaps be little gain to make up for this certain loss.[138]

Synge therefore viewed the activities of the Gaelic League with some distrust; he felt that it might mar the rareness and beauty of what peasant Gaelic remained and that it should not try to do more than 'keep the cruder powers of the Irish mind occupied'. The Gaelic promoted by the League was tainted by modern commercialism and journalese and was far removed from the real Gaelic tradition, Synge argued, and he warmly denied the asser-tions of the Gaelic League that Irish traditions and life could be understood only through Gaelic. MacKenna says that Synge loathed the Gaelic League for urging the youth of Ireland to learn modern Irish 'because it would give them access to the grand old Saga literature', and he never forgot the bale in Synge's eyes when he read this and cried: 'That's a bloody lie; long after they know modern Irish, which they'll never know, they'll still be miles and years from any power over the Saga.' [139] And in a letter which he did not send to a Dublin newspaper Synge declared: [140]

> Much of the writing that has appeared recently in the papers takes it for granted that Irish is gaining the day in Ireland and that this country will soon speak Gaelic. No supposition is more false. The Gaelic League is founded on a doctrine that is made up of ignorance, fraud and hypocrisy. . . . I believe in Ireland. I believe in the nation that has made a place in history by seventeen centuries of manhood, a nation that has begotten Grattan and Emmet and Parnell will not be brought to complete insanity in these last days by what is senile and slobbering in the doctrine of the Gaelic League. . . . This delirium will not last always. It will not be long till some young man with blood in his veins, logic in his wits and courage in his heart, will sweep over the backside of the world to the uttermost limbo this credo of mouthing gibberish. (I speak here not of the old and magnificent language of our manuscripts, or of the two or three dialects still spoken, though with many barbarisms, in the west and south, but of the incoherent twaddle that is passed off as Irish in the Gaelic League.) This young man will teach Ireland again that she is part of Europe, and teach Irishmen that they have wits to think, imaginations to work miracles, and souls to possess with sanity.

Synge's foresight was remarkably accurate; after intensive propaganda for Gaelic it is still no stronger in relation to English than it was sixty or thirty years ago. These colourful denunciations were inspired by Synge's regard for Gaelic, in which few people were as well equipped as he was with his academic training at Dublin and Paris universities and his contacts with the Gaeltacht peasants. He feared that the Irish tradition would suffer by misrepresentation; from the Gaelic League, and also from translators who diffused a rosy sentimental glow over the past. Historical fiction, making remote figures speak in idioms which have had no life for generations, could hardly be sincere, and 'the drama of swords' was out: 'Few of us except soldiers have seen swords in use; to drag them out on the stage is babyish. They are so rusted for us with the associations of pseudo-antique fiction and drama.' [141] The only possible beauty then was in peasant drama; but it could come only through the imaginative presentation of the whole of reality, not just the admirable parts of it; 'the romantic note and the Rabelaisian note' (the dream and the actuality) must work together. Replying to MacKenna's friendly suggestions that he should restrict the reality of his plays, for which the Irish were 'blessedly unripe', and write innocent, graceful and archaic entertainments, Synge said:

> Heaven forbid that we should have morbid sex-obsessed drama in Ireland, not because we have any peculiar sanctity, which I utterly deny – blessed unripeness is sometimes akin to damned rottenness, see percentage of lunatics in Ireland and causes thereof – but because it is bad as drama and is played out. On the French stage you get sex without its balancing elements. On the Irish stage you get the other elements without sex. I restored sex and the people were so surprised they saw the sex only . . . no drama can grow out of anything other than the fundamental realities of life which are never fantastic, are neither modern nor unmodern and, as I see them, rarely spring-dayish, or breezy or Cuchulainoid. . . . When I deny Ireland's peculiar sanctity, I do so as compared with other potato-fed, thinly populated lands of same latitude. I have as you know perambulated a good deal of Ireland in my thirty years and if I were to tell, which Heaven forbid, all the sex horrors I have seen I could a tale unfold that would wither up your blood. I think of course that single plays may and should be spring-dayish etc. But while life is what it is and men are what they are, I do not think any group of writers will write such work chiefly unless they do so with a wilful insincerity of joy that would make their work useless, and destroy the power of their souls. I think squeamishness is a disease, and that Ireland will gain if Irish writers deal manfully, directly and decently with the entire reality of life. I think the lawmaker and the law-breaker are both needful in society . . . and I think the law-maker is tending to reduce parts of Ireland to a dismal, morbid hypocrisy that is not a blessed unripeness.

On the other hand I feel of course the infinitely sweet and healthy piety of a great deal of Irish life. I will use it gladly in my work, and meanwhile it is perfectly safe from any fear of contamination from my evil words.[142]

This is noteworthy and well put, and it shows how conscious and intelligent an artist Synge was. And well and consistently did Synge apply these principles in his writings. Consequently he was not favourably inclined towards most of the trends in the drama and poetry of his day. His objection to the naturalistic problem play derived from Ibsen and Strindberg, which Martyn advocated, was that it was obtrusively didactic. Like Keats, Synge hated art that has a palpable design upon one, and he found the 'playhouse too often stocked with the drugs of many seedy problems'. These problems, handled in a rather theoretical and unimpassioned way, were sometimes based on peculiar social circumstances which were bound to change and so deprive the plays of much of their meaning:

> The drama, like the symphony, does not teach or prove anything. Analysts with their problems, and teachers with their systems, are soon as old-fashioned as the pharmacopoeia of Galen – look at Ibsen and the Germans – but the best plays of Ben Jonson and Molière can no more go out of fashion than the blackberries on the hedges.[143]

Where the naturalistic play dealt with real human issues it did so in a drab manner, presenting a chunk of life insufficiently distanced and shaped, and tending to produce depression and bewilderment rather than exhilaration and insight. Furthermore, in striving for greater approximation to surface appearances it was inclined to emphasize the ephemeral and to lose touch with the realities of joy and poetry:

> We should not go to the theatre as we go to the chemist's, but as we go to a dinner where the food we need is taken with pleasure and excitement.[144] On the stage one must have reality, and one must have joy; and that is why the intellectual modern drama has failed. . . . Ibsen and Zola deal with the reality of life in joyless and pallid words.[145]

On the other hand a richness remote from the 'profound and

common interests of life' was no better than a prosaic adherence
to external reality, and in this respect 'A.E.' and the Art for Art's
sake group failed, and Yeats was occasionally in danger. An
esoteric hot-house richness, the preserve of a private clique, was
incapable of giving 'the reality which is the root of all poetry, in a
comprehensive and natural form'.

Both sides, then, were partly right and partly wrong. The
supporters of the intellectual naturalistic drama, seeing that art
should embody a criticism of life and deal with serious issues,
were right in their conception of 'ends', but in their 'means' they
were wrong, being propagandists rather than artists; they gave
'instruction' but little 'delight'. The Art for Art's sake group
realizing that art should be richer, more exact and shapely, than
ordinary life were right in their 'means', but their view about
'ends' was inadequate; they gave 'delight' of a kind but no 'instruction'. Great art, whether the approach was classical or
romantic, blended delight and instruction, reality and richness:

> For a long time I have felt that poetry roughly is of two kinds,
> the poetry of real life – the poetry of Burns and Shakespeare
> and Villon, and the poetry of a land of fancy – the poetry of
> Spenser and Keats and Ronsard. That is obvious enough, but
> what is highest in poetry is always reached when the dreamer
> is leaning out to reality, or when the man of real life is lifted out
> of it, and in all the poets the greatest have both these elements,
> that is they are supremely engrossed with life, and yet with the
> wildness of their fancy they are always passing out of what is
> simple and plain.[146]

This perceptive statement, and Synge's analysis of the shortcomings of the writing of his day, are valid, except that he is too
severe upon Ibsen. He is, perhaps, thinking of the plays of Ibsen's
middle period and not of the more valuable early poetic plays and
the later symbolical drama, though these plays of the middle
period have more merit than Synge allows. They did, however,
arouse much curiosity and contention, and became, through no
fault of Ibsen's, an unhealthy influence on drama, forcing it into a
naturalistic mould. It is of this influence, and of the undistin-
guished plays that were being produced in imitation of Ibsen, that
Synge was probably thinking; and it speaks highly of his insight
that he was able to indicate the limitations of the naturalistic play

at a time when most writers and critics were much taken with it, and that he did this without falling into the opposite error, which Yeats did not always avoid, of cultivating an aloof, dream-like fancy.

In his criticism Synge did not expect to say anything moment-ously new; nor did he. Yet he is almost unique among his con-temporaries in hitting on ideas set forth by the great Romantic critics and subsequently largely neglected. Synge's notion that art should be rooted in the serious and enduring concerns of mankind, yet should present these concerns in a form that would give joy, refreshment and illumination, recalls the insistence of Keats (and Hazlitt) that the artist must know 'the agonies, the strife | Of human hearts' but must create art of an 'intensity capable of making all disagreeables evaporate from their being in close relationship with Beauty and Truth'. Synge believed, with Keats, that the artist should 'not dispute or assert, but whisper results to his neighbour', and that the values and relationships of art were felt and implied, not argued: 'The drama is made serious not by the degree in which it is taken up with problems that are serious in themselves, but by the degree in which it gives the nourishment, not very easy to define, on which our imaginations live'.[147] This brief statement of the way in which art is a powerful moral agent reminds one of Shelley's wise words:

> The great instrument of moral good is the imagination; and poetry administers to the effect by acting upon the cause. Poetry enlarges the circumference of the imagination by re-plenishing it with thoughts of ever new delight. . . . Poetry strengthens the faculty which is the organ of the moral nature of man, in the same manner as exercise strengthens a limb.[148]

In addition, Synge's assertion that in art one must have richness and reality, that the artist must be 'supremely engrossed with life' yet must shape it into something rich and strange and joyous is a reiteration of the celebrated account by Wordsworth and Coler-idge of 'the two cardinal points of poetry, the power of exciting the sympathy of the reader by a faithful adherence to the truth of nature, and the power of giving the interest of novelty by the modifying colours of imagination'.[149] Just as Wordsworth turned away from what he felt were the artificial elegancies and insin-cerity of eighteenth-century town life and poetry to rustic life, so

Synge turned away from the sterility, the squalor and the false
joy which he found in modern towns, to the life of the Irish
country folk. Believing that 'All art is a collaboration' he felt that
only among the peasants, whose imagination was virile and healthy,
could he get the stimulus and material for the kind of drama he
wanted to write:

> In my plays I have used one or two words only that I have not
> heard among the country people of Ireland, or spoken in my
> nursery before I could read the newspapers. A certain number of
> the phrases I employ I have heard also from herds and fisher-
> men, or from beggar-women and ballad-singers . . . and I am
> glad to acknowledge how much I owe to the folk-imagination
> of these fine people. . . . All art is a collaboration; and there is
> little doubt that in the happy ages of literature, striking and
> beautiful phrases were as ready to the story-teller's or the
> playwright's hand, as the rich cloaks and dresses of his time. It is
> probable that when the Elizabethan dramatist took his ink-horn
> and sat down to his work he used many phrases that he had just
> heard. . . . In Ireland, those of us who know the people have
> the same privilege. . . . In countries where the imagination of
> the people, and the language they use, is rich and living, it is
> possible for a writer to be rich and copious in his words, and at
> the same time to give the reality, which is the root of all poetry,
> in a comprehensive and natural form. . . . In a good play every
> speech should be as fully flavoured as a nut or apple, and such
> speeches cannot be written by anyone who works among
> people who have shut their lips on poetry. In Ireland, for a few
> years more, we have a popular imagination that is fiery and
> magnificent and tender; so that those of us who wish to write
> start with a chance that is not given to writers in places where
> the springtime of the local life has been forgotten, and the
> harvest is a memory only, and the straw has been turned into
> bricks.[150]

Synge rarely missed an opportunity of praising the peasants and
of acknowledging his debt to them, and here his generosity has
caused him to overstate his case and to be unduly modest about
his own achievement. It is true that the way of life and the
imagination of these people did give him an initial advantage
over many twentieth-century dramatists, but, as *Juno and the*

Paycock, *Venus Observed* and *The Cocktail Party* show, it is possible to write plays about modern urban life, which have both reality and a kind of poetic richness and depth. Furthermore Synge glosses over the immense labour he put into his writing; although the idiom of the peasants was unusually vivid it still had to be shaped into apt, significant and sounding dramatic diction. He did not just collect words and images and string them together; like all good dramatic speech, the speech in Synge's plays is not a mere copy of everyday speech however vivacious. Synge made a selection from the idiom of the peasants and created language authentic and credible and more exact, compact and beautiful than the actual utterance of anyone.

He did something similar with regard to character and plot. He found in tramp and peasant life a singular colour and wildness that gave it 'romance and a peculiar value for those who look at life in Ireland with an eye that is aware of the arts also', and in creating characters in his plays he drew upon his experiences of the remarkable individuals he had met during the course of his wanderings about Ireland; yet he had, inevitably, to develop and heighten and intensify what was already more animated than the average. His plots too were based upon incidents and stories he had come across, but these, concise and lively as they were, had still to be made more splendid, taut and economical for the life of the theatre. Thus although Synge's raw materials were one stage nearer the finished product of drama than those of nearly all twentieth-century dramatists, they had to go through the imaginative process before they became art. Like most good writers he took language, character and situation from actual life, embellishing and improving them, and bringing out their essence.

As the foregoing paragraphs indicate, there runs through all Synge's critical notions the tension between dream (richness) and actuality (reality). He appears to have wished to resolve this tension in art. In life he was aware of a basic incompatibility between dream and actuality, and he probably believed that it was one of the prime functions of art to fuse these disparate elements into a new whole, a finer reality. How far he succeeded in this, and how far he carried out his theories in his work, we shall see as we examine it.

CHAPTER THREE

Prose Works

The Aran Islands

One of the remarkable features of Yeats is his biographical power, his ability to suggest in poetry something of the essence of the individuals he knew; among the finest was Synge:

> *And that enquiring man John Synge comes next,*
> *That dying chose the living world for text*
> *And never could have rested in the tomb*
> *But that, long travelling, he had come*
> *Towards nightfall upon certain set apart*
> *In a most desolate stony place,*
> *Towards nightfall upon a race*
> *Passionate and simple like his heart.*[151]

In the summer of 1896 Yeats had been on that 'desolate stony place', the Aran Islands, and had seen the 'passionate and simple' people there. His imagination was still 'full of those grey islands where men must reap with knives because of the stones' when he first met Synge on 21 December 1896 in Paris, and he soon advised Synge:[152]

> Give up Paris; you will never create anything by reading Racine, and Arthur Symons will always be a better critic of French literature. Go to the Aran Islands. Live there as if you were one of the people themselves; express a life that has never found expression.

In May 1898 Synge went; and from this time until the end of 1902 he spent part of each summer or autumn on the Aran Islands, and most of the rest of each year in Paris recollecting, and recording what he had experienced.

Although the material conditions of life must often have been

trying for him Synge did live, so far as he could, as one of the
islanders themselves. In a state of wise passiveness he slowly
absorbed the spirit of the life around him; spending hours lying
in the sun gossiping with the older men, or walking on the calm,
star-lit nights with Michael, the young man who was helping to
improve his Gaelic. He had his own corner in the homes of the
people where he would sit, alert and patient 'talking of the sorrows of the people till it was late in the night' (210); he shared the
leisure of the islanders: 'For the greater part of the afternoon we
sat on the tops of empty barrels in the public-house, talking of
the destiny of Gaelic' (93). He knew where to find the various
kinds of conversation: 'This afternoon – it was Sunday, when
there is usually some interesting talk among the islanders – it
rained, so I went into the schoolmaster's kitchen, which is a good
deal frequented by the more advanced among the people' (149).
He never once complains of personal hardship, but it is clear that
he was willing to undergo considerable discomfort to hear something that might be interesting. Moreover – and this probably
helped to gain him the confidence of the islanders – he was ready
to accept their judgements; on two occasions at great risk to his
own life. Once he boarded a curragh with a hole in it 'plugged
with a piece of sacking, and we set off with nothing but a piece of
torn canvas between us and the Atlantic' (64); and another time,
when the priest and the schoolmaster had advised him not to make
a sea-passage because of the bad weather, he says simply: 'but my
crew had gone towards the sea, and I thought it better to go after
them' (127). Without being diffident yet without obtruding, he
was eager to join in the work and recreation of the islanders
when they asked him. Being conscious of his obligations to them
he never expected the natives to perform for his diversion; in
fact he was ready to amuse them, playing his fiddle, performing
conjuring tricks and simple feats of gymnastics, and telling them
news of the outside world. By these and similar means Synge
devoted himself to understanding the spirit of the place.

He gained this understanding; and it is clear that the nature-
mysticism, which is an important feature of Synge's plays, is
derived to a considerable extent from his contact with these
people who lived in communion with the natural world. He says:

In Inishmaan one is forced to believe in a sympathy between

man and nature . . . (51). I am only beginning to understand the nights . . . and the influence they have had in giving distinction to these men who do most of their work after night-fall . . . (152).
their mood accorded itself with wonderful fineness to the suggestions of the day . . . (177).

   A week of sweeping fogs has passed over and given me a strange sense of exile and desolation. I walk round the island nearly every day, yet I can see nothing anywhere but a mass of wet rock, a strip of surf, and then a tumult of waves. The slaty limestone has grown black with the water that is dripping on it, and wherever I turn there is the same grey obsession twining and wreathing itself among the narrow fields, and the same wail from the wind that shrieks and whistles in the loose rubble of the walls. At first the people do not give much attention to the wilderness that is round them, but after a few days their voices sink in the kitchen, and their endless talk of pigs and cattle falls to the whisper of men who are telling stories in a haunted house (46–7).

Synge too felt this power. He describes his walk in a storm, and ends: 'After a few hours the mind grows bewildered with the endless change and struggle of the sea, and an utter despondency replaces the first moment of exhilaration' (112). But after a hurricane he remarks: 'The suggestion from this world of inarticulate power was immense, and now at midnight, when the wind is abating, I am still trembling and flushed with exultation' (113). Like Keats he is able, imaginatively, to take part in the existence of birds: 'As I lie here hour after hour, I seem to enter into the wild pastimes of the cliff, and to become a companion of the cormorants and crows' (48). And again at night: 'The sense of solitude was immense. I could not see or realize my own body, and I seemed to exist merely in my perception of the waves and of the crying birds, and of the smell of seaweed' (153). The sea affected him deeply:

   The black curragh working slowly through this world of grey, and the soft hissing of the rain, gave me one of the moods in which we realize with immense distress the short moment we have left us to experience all the wonder and beauty of the world (171).

In a curragh in heavy seas he experienced 'a far more intimate feeling of the glory and power of the waves than [he] had ever known in a steamer'. So that he thought if he were 'dropped into the blue chasm of the waves, this death, with the fresh sea saltness in one's teeth would be better than most deaths one is likely to meet' (93). The accuracy, restraint and sensitiveness of his writing give a singular potency to the transitory incident and set up reverberations which seem to go beyond it. The whole book is like this. Synge avoids abstractions and mere information, and is wary of making generalizations based only upon his own experience. With the artist's feeling for the significant, he selects, and sets forth, the vivid, concrete particular in such a way that it suggests something universal. He ends a description of a girl in her teens with this:

> At one moment she is a simple peasant, at another she seems to be looking out at the world with a sense of prehistoric disillusion and to sum up in the expression of her grey-blue eyes the whole external despondency of the clouds and sea (121).

For Synge an important characteristic of Aran life was its primitiveness. He did not stay long on Aranmor, the largest of the three islands, because he felt that it was becoming tainted with modern commercialism. So he left it for Inishmaan, where 'the life is perhaps the most primitive that is left in Europe' (10), and most of his book refers to this island. He speaks of his 'exquisite satisfaction' in moving away from civilization in the 'rude canvas canoe of a model that has served primitive races since man first went to sea' (15). Yet this primitiveness was to some degree refined and wholesome, and as far removed from the ignorance and crudity of some savage tribes as it was from the corrupt sophistication of much town life:

> the general simplicity of their lives has given them many points of physical perfection. Their way of life has never been acted on by anything much more artificial than the nests and burrows of the creatures that live round them, and they seem, in a certain sense, to approach more nearly to the finer types of our aristocracies – who are bred artificially to a natural ideal – than to the labourer or citizen, as the wild horse resembles the thoroughbred rather than the hack or cart-horse (33).

It was a world something like that which William Morris dreamed of, in which utility and beauty, work and play, life and art – and, Synge would say, using his own terms, reality and richness – were one:

> I have never heard talk so simple and attractive as the talk of these people (181).
>
> The kitchen itself where I will spend most of my time is full of beauty and distinction. The red dresses of the women who cluster round the fire on their stools give a glow of almost Eastern richness, and the walls have been toned by the turf-smoke to a soft brown that blends with the grey earth-colour of the floor. . . .
>
> Every article on these islands has an almost personal character, which gives this simple life, where all art is unknown, something of the artistic beauty of mediaeval life . . . all articles are full of individuality, and being made from materials that are common here, yet to some extent peculiar to the island, seem to exist as a natural link between the people and the world that is about them (17–18).

There were no class distinctions; sociability was marked, and all work done in common, such as kelp-burning and thatching, was regarded as a sort of festival. Life was integrated:

> It is likely that much of the intelligence and charm of these people is due to the absence of any division of labour, and to the correspondingly wide development of each individual, whose varied knowledge and skill necessitates a considerable activity of mind. Each man can speak two languages. He is a skilled fisherman, and can manage a curragh with extraordinary nerve and dexterity. He can farm simply, burn kelp, cut out pampooties, mend nets, build and thatch a house, and make a cradle or a coffin. His work changes with the seasons in a way that keeps him free from the dullness that comes to people who have always the same occupation. The danger of his life on the sea gives him the alertness of a primitive hunter, and the long nights he spends fishing in his curragh bring him some of the emotions that are thought peculiar to men who have lived with the arts (156–7).

But there was a grim side too. Aran, with all its attractions, was no Utopia; nor, Synge felt, does the nature of things permit one anywhere, for nothing can prevent decay, desolation and death from bringing 'the eternal note of sadness in'. Synge was very conscious of this, and *The Aran Islands*, in common with all his writings, is built around the theme of dream against actuality. I remark here three aspects of this theme.

The first aspect is the one we are now touching on: the fact that those conditions which give so much distinctive grace and wholesomeness to island life, are, at the same time, responsible for making the islanders unusually susceptible to the harsher realities of life. What adds richness to the dream makes actuality more bitter. The austere loveliness of the scenery, the 'intense insular clearness' of the atmosphere 'that makes the whole island glisten with the splendour of a gem, and fills the sea and sky with a radiance of blue light' (47), are dependent on weather conditions which bring frequent storms, and days of mist and rain making all 'indescribably desolate', and preventing crops from ever being more than scanty. The remoteness and simplicity which keep them an integrated community unpolluted by the world also cut them off from the benefits of modern science, and accentuate their feeling of dread and isolation in the face of vast, uncontrollable forces. And the sea, which offers a livelihood, and helps to develop admirable qualities, brings also suffering and death. Moreover it is more difficult for the islanders to ignore actuality than it is for most of us to do so: they – as *Riders to the Sea* shows – cannot rest in the dream – as, say, the villagers of *The Well of the Saints* can. These characteristics, implicit throughout, are focused, with arresting starkness and economy, in the accounts of two funerals.

Synge found the funeral keen particularly impressive and symbolic of the pain both of the islanders and of humanity confronted with actuality:

The grief of the keen is no personal complaint for the death of one woman, but seems to contain the whole passionate rage that lurks somewhere in every native of the island. In this cry of pain the inner consciousness of the people seems to lay itself bare for an instant, and to reveal the mood of beings who feel their isolation in the face of a universe that wars on them with winds and seas. They are usually silent, but in the presence of death all outward show of indifference or patience is forgotten, and they shriek with pitiable despair before the horror of the fate to which they all are doomed.

Before they covered the coffin an old man kneeled down by the grave and repeated a simple prayer for the dead.

There was irony in these words of atonement and Catholic belief spoken by voices that were still hoarse with the cries of pagan desperation (52).

Such scenes undoubtedly brought home to Synge the horror of death with singular intensity; and his writing, in turn, communicates this intensity to the reader, yet mingled with that pleasure with which art invests even the most sombre subject. The second funeral has this climax: an old woman, the mother of the dead man, took up a skull – it was her own mother's – out of the grave

and came back to the coffin, and began to beat on it, holding the skull in her left hand. This last moment of grief was the most terrible of all. The young women were nearly lying among the stones, worn out with their passion of grief, yet raising themselves every few moments to beat with magnificent gestures on the boards of the coffin. The young men were worn out also, and their voices cracked continually in the wail of the keen (215).

How well these passages exemplify Synge's prevailing attitude as the sympathetic observer; involved enough to be deeply moved by the experience yet able to understand the wider significance of it, and to appreciate the irony of the prayer and the magnificence of the girls' gestures. After the funeral Synge felt that he had to be alone, and he wandered along the shore for some time thinking. Characteristically, he does not describe his thoughts, but he speaks of meeting some fishermen, and ends:

As they talked to me and gave me a little poteen and a little bread when they thought I was hungry, I could not help feeling that I was talking with men who were under a judgement of death. I knew that every one of them would be drowned in the sea in a few years and battered naked on the rocks, or would die in his own cottage and be buried with another fearful scene in the graveyard I had come from (216).

The islanders knew this too, though they never spoke of it directly, and they tried to conceal the actuality. Synge noticed shortly after the first funeral some old women 'still sobbing and shaken with grief, yet beginning to talk again of the daily trifles that veil from them the terrors of the world' (52-3). On another occasion, when a woman after examining the clothes taken off a drowned man had declared that it was her brother:

> For a while the people sat silent, and one could hear nothing but the lips of the infant, the rain hissing in the yard, and the breathing of four pigs that lay sleeping in one corner. Then one of the men began to talk about the new boats that have been sent to the south island, and the conversation went back to its usual round of topics (165-6).

Existence, then, is a dream which will be dissolved by the ultimate actuality, death, and the finer the dream the harsher the actuality – this aspect of the tension between dream and actuality is endemic to island life, as it is, in a less palpable and concentrated form, to all life. The second aspect, however, was one beginning to be felt when Synge was there, and one which has since ended in the triumph of actuality.

Synge was conscious throughout that the developments of modern commercial life (the actuality) were beginning to encroach upon the traditional way of life (the dream). The corruption was noticeable already upon the largest island, Aranmor, though it had not touched Inishmaan:

> I am in the north island (Aranmor) again, looking out with a singular sensation to the cliffs across the sound. It is hard to believe that those hovels I can see on Inishmaan are filled with people whose lives have the strange quality that is found in the oldest poetry and legend. Compared with them the falling-off that has come with the increased prosperity of this island is full of discouragement. The charm which the people over there share with the birds and flowers has been replaced here by the anxiety of men who are eager for gain (125).

The pain is made deeper by the realization that there seems to be a basic incompatibility between material security and an integrated way of life allowing scope for emotional and imaginative fulfilment; as the physical conditions of the people are improved so they tend to lose the richness and distinction of their way of life. This can be seen in the description of the eviction by sheriffs and police from the mainland of islanders who had failed to pay rent:

> When the anchor had been thrown it gave me a strange throb of pain to see the boats being lowered, and the sunshine gleaming on the rifles and helmets of the constabulary who crowded into them . . . (76).

> After my weeks spent among primitive men this glimpse of the newer types of humanity was not reassuring. Yet these mechanical police, with the commonplace agents and sheriffs, and the rabble they had hired, represented aptly enough the civilization for which the homes of the island were to be desecrated . . . (77).

This disclosure of deep feeling, and this censure of the eviction party and all they represent, coming from the normally reticent Synge, are worth noting. Taken with the following passage they lead to the third aspect of the tension between dream and actuality.

This aspect is centred in Synge himself. In Galway, returning from his first visit to the islands, he writes:

> I have come out of an hotel full of tourists and commercial travellers, to stroll along the edge of Galway Bay, and look out in the direction of the islands. The sort of yearning I feel towards those lonely rocks is indescribably acute. This town, that is usually so full of wild human interest, seems in my present mood a tawdry medley of all that is crudest in modern life. The nullity of the rich and the squalor of the poor give me the same pang of wondering disgust; yet the islands are fading already and I can hardly realize that the smell of seaweed and the drone of the Atlantic are still moving round them (101).

These passages, built on the tension between two modes of being, reveal something of the quality of island life; they are part of a book which sets forth, memorably, the essence of that life. In doing so, the book also sets forth the essence of the character of Synge; it is probably the most self-revealing of anything he wrote. All books, both by what they describe and by what they leave out, imply something about their authors; and Synge's plays and prose-works, and his poems to a lesser extent, by his choice of subjects and his treatment of them, give us a fairly sound idea of his nature. But in *The Aran Islands* these hints and guesses are supplemented by important direct evidence consisting of certain phrases which occur at important junctures in the book and which seem, as it were, to have been wrenched out of the normally reticent Synge. We have had some examples of them already: he speaks of his 'exquisite satisfaction' in approaching Inishmaan; his 'indescribably acute yearning' towards the islands; the 'singular sensation' he has looking towards them; and the 'strange throb of pain' he feels when the eviction party lands. He speaks of an old woman who

> recited the verses with exquisite musical intonation putting a wistfulness and passion into her voice that seemed to give it all the cadences that are sought in the profoundest poetry.
>
> The lamp had burned low, and another terrible gale was howling and shrieking over the island. It seemed like a dream that I should be sitting here among these men and women listening to this rude and beautiful poetry that is filled with the oldest passions of the world (118).

'It seemed like a dream' – this is a key-phrase; life on Inishmaan was, for Synge, the dream; the rest of the world, by contrast, harsh actuality. He found on the island a depth of joy and peace which he had never thought existed anywhere; the life satisfied some hunger in his heart, and he longed to partake of it for ever. In a curragh with some islanders he is filled with well-being, 'a dreamy voluptuous gaiety', and he goes on:

> Their mood accorded itself with wonderful fineness to the suggestions of the day, and their ancient Gaelic seemed so full of divine simplicity that I would have liked to turn the prow to the west and row with them for ever. I told them I was going back to Paris in a few days to sell my books and my bed, and that then I was coming back to grow as strong and simple as they were among the islands of the west (177–8).

Leaving the islands he 'saw the three low rocks sink down into the sea with a moment of inconceivable distress', and 'the lamentation of the cold sea' against the sides of the ship 'became almost unendurable' (134). His joy on returning is presented with the same moving power:

> It gave me a thrill of delight to hear their Gaelic blessings and to see the steamer moving away, leaving me quite alone among them. . . . In the cottage everything was as usual. . . . As I

sat down on my stool and lit my pipe with the corner of a sod, I could have cried out with the feeling of festivity that this return procured me (146-7).

But (and the pang for Synge was not much less severe than it was for his Deirdre) 'There's no safe place, on the ridge of the world.' Actuality would break in. Synge knew no matter how much he admired the islanders and sympathized with them, he was unsuited to share their life fully; and there is pathos – unintentional, for Synge was stating the facts as he saw them, not angling for sympathy – in his realization that he could never set up his everlasting rest on Inishmaan:

> On some days I feel this island as a perfect home and resting place and on other days I feel that I am a waif among the people (120).
>
> I sat for nearly an hour beside the fire . . . and as I waited, with just light enough from the chimney to let me see the rafters and the greyness of the walls, I became indescribably mournful, for I felt that this little corner on the face of the world, and the people who live in it, have a peace and dignity from which we are shut out for ever (217).

Some cause has been shown for saying that *The Aran Islands* is a piece of writing of distinctive merit, not only because it embodies so admirably the main theme of Synge's writings: the tension between dream and actuality, between two inimical ways of life; the interaction between Man and the natural world; the awareness of mutability. It could also be said, truthfully, that the experiences on which this book is based were, for Synge, essentially similar to those derived from a work of art. He received from his life on the Aran Islands that exaltation and poise, that serious and intense understanding of the nature of human existence, which art can give. Aran was a microcosm of all that Synge considered to be important in the world; and it offered the essence of life, not stale, diffuse and incoherent, but fresh, compact and comprehensible. This is implicit throughout, and is stated on several occasions: 'the simple life has something of the artistic beauty of mediaeval life', and the islanders are 'people whose lives have the strange quality that is found in the oldest poetry and legend'. He finds links between the artist and the islanders whose daily work brings them 'some of the emotions that are thought peculiar to men who have lived with the arts'. And on a glorious day after a storm he says: 'The continual passing in this island between the misery of last night and the splendour of today seems to create an affinity between the moods of these people and the moods of varying rapture and dismay that are frequent in artists' (49). Thus, on the Aran Islands, the tang of existence, with all its tensions, loveliness and desolation, could be felt more purely and exactly than it could anywhere else. In short, the Aran Islands fused both richness and reality, and brought the whole soul of Synge into activity. By the excellence of his writing he, in turn, is able to do something similar to us.

It is generally recognized that the Aran Islands gave Synge tales and incidents for his plays and helped him considerably towards his unique understanding of the peasant and towards the creation of his distinctive dramatic speech. It is probable that they also gave him his attitudes to life and the main theme of all his writings. Acting on Synge as a work of art acts on us, they showed him life clearly and whole. From this vision he took his attitudes and main theme; these are fully developed in *The Aran Islands*, and remain unchanged in all his subsequent work. Clearly Yeats's instinct in sending Synge to the Aran Islands was extraordinarily fine and right: there Synge found himself both as man and artist.

In Wicklow, West Kerry and Connemara

In May 1908, about ten months before his death, Synge in the course of a letter to Yeats regarding those writings of his which had not been published in book form, said: 'I have a lot of Kerry and Wicklow articles that would go together in a book.' These were published in November 1910 in Volume Four of the first Collected Edition of Synge's works. Along with them in this volume appeared a collection of articles about the 'Congested Districts' of Connemara and Mayo, which Synge had contributed to a newspaper. Thus *In Wicklow, West Kerry and Connemara* is a collection of reprints: two of the Wicklow essays were first published in *The Shanachie*, the others in *The Manchester Guardian*; all the West Kerry section appeared first in *The Shanachie* in three instalments; and all the Connemara articles in *The Manchester Guardian*. The Wicklow and West Kerry sections were revised and partly re-written before publication in book form. The

Connemara section was untouched. Hence *In Wicklow, West Kerry and Connemara* is, as a whole, less compact and finely organized than the rest of Synge's books; nevertheless it is of considerable merit and interest, and has a bearing on the main theme of all Synge's writings. The character of Synge links the three sections of the book, yet each section has its individual traits, and each may be examined separately.

Synge came from a large and well-known County Wicklow family, and was born in Rathfarnham, near Dublin. He spent most of his youth in County Wicklow, and it was here that he began his study of Irish life and scenery. He returned to this district many times during his life, and his deep understanding of the people and their surroundings is apparent in every essay in the Wicklow section of his book. Here, as in all his writings, Synge's approach is akin to that of the artist seeking to express a kind of truth more vivid and universal than that within the province of the historian or the natural or social scientist. With a habit of careful observation and a firm grasp of facts he is not concerned so much with externals and abstractions as with comprehending and setting forth the essential character of the place and its inhabitants. In method too he resembles the poet, building each essay, as if it were a lyric, around some central mood or incident. He says:

> In these hills the summer passes in a few weeks from a late spring, full of odour and colour, to an autumn that is premature and filled with the desolate splendour of decay; and it often happens that, in moments when one is most aware of this ceaseless fading of beauty, some incident of tramp life gives a local human intensity to the shadow of one's mood (6).

This sentence is important for the proper understanding of these essays, and indicates something of their main quality: a fine apprehension of nuances, illuminating and admirable, among pervasive decay. The last line has a connexion with this passage from *A Midsummer Night's Dream*:

> *And, as imagination bodies forth*
> *The forms of things unknown, the poet's pen*
> *Turns them to shapes, and gives to airy nothing*
> *A local habitation and a name.*

Like Shakespeare, Synge objectifies, gives shape ('local habitation' or 'human intensity') to his private states of mind ('airy nothings', 'shadows of a mood'). Furthermore, the words 'local human' suggest that the essays are representative of the locality and that there is in this place an interaction between Man and the natural world. The word 'intensity' indicates that Synge shapes his material so that the essays have both economy of wording and range of suggestion and provide heightened excitement and insight.

Synge usually starts an essay with a brief general statement, and then presents some pregnant incident illustrating this, and expressing the feelings and attitudes both of himself and of the people of the district. He liked to make use of stories he had heard from the people, and he constructed these as carefully as he did the speeches in his plays. It was not his habit to take notes while people were speaking to him – they would hardly have been so friendly had he done so – instead, he heard all that they had to say, then wrote out a version as soon as possible, and went on improving it and shedding all that was clumsy and redundant, until the story or experience emerged purely and completely expressed. He skilfully retained the native rhythms and turns of phrase, and his essays combine a precision and shapeliness of utterance, never found in extempore speech, with an undeniable authenticity. The following story is a good example of this blending of richness and reality:

It was the law at that time that if there was sickness on any person in the town of Sligo you should notice it to the Governors, or you'd be put up in the gaol. Well, a man's wife took sick, and he went and noticed it. They came down with bands of men they had, and took her away to the sick-house, and he heard nothing more till he heard she was dead, and was to be buried in the morning. At that time there was such fear and hurry and dread on every person, they were burying people they had no hope of, and they with life within them. My man was uneasy a while thinking on that, and then what did he do, but slip down in the darkness of the night and into the dead-house, where they were after putting his wife. There were beyond twoscore bodies, and he went feeling from one to the other. Then I suppose his wife heard him coming – she wasn't dead at all – and 'Is that Michael?' says she. 'It is then,' says he; 'and,

oh, my poor woman, have you your last gasps in you still?' 'I
have, Michael,' says she; 'and they're after setting me out here
with fifty bodies the way they'll put me down into my grave at
the dawn of day.' 'Oh, my poor woman,' says he; 'have you the
strength left in you to hold on my back?' 'Oh, Micky,' says she,
'I have surely.' He took her up then on his back, and he carried
her out by lanes and tracks till he got to his house. Then he
never let on a word about it, and at the end of three days she
began to pick up, and in a month's time she came out and began
walking about like yourself or me. And there were many people
were afeard to speak to her, for they thought she was after
coming back from the grave (22–3).

In the Wicklow essays the tension between dream and actuality
is mingled with the contrast between two ways of life; between
the desolation of the people of the glens and the vigorous enterprise of the roaming tramps and tinkers. The people of the glens
are oppressed by their surroundings, and find existence more of a
nightmare than a dream. Against the harshness of actuality they
are able to place only the dream of emigrating to America, the
one haven among the 'three shadowy countries that are never
forgotten in Wicklow – America (their Eldorado), the Union and
the Madhouse'. They are people who have been abandoned, and
who are lingering in the ruins of the way of life based on the
Anglo-Irish Protestant Ascendancy. Synge came at the right time
and was particularly suited for the task of depicting these circumstances, for he was Ascendancy by birth (though Nationalist
by conviction) and as his life and writings show he was always
drawn to subjects which offered scope for evoking something of
the 'desolate splendour of decay'. So, with a poetic exactness and
delicacy which make the essays of enduring worth, he embodies
in them the spirit of the time and place, the feeling of pervasive
blight and frustration twined with regret at the passing of something unique and valuable. Although he sympathized mainly with
the peasants, Synge realized that the Ascendancy landlords had
made a remarkable contribution to Irish life, particularly with
regard to the arts, and that their downfall had produced a dreary
lacuna in which the people of the glens scratched for a livelihood:

Everyone is used in Ireland to the tragedy that is bound up with
the lives of farmers and fishing people; but in this garden one

seemed to feel the tragedy of the landlord class also, and of the innumerable old families that are quickly dwindling away. These owners of the land are not much pitied at the present day, or much deserving of pity; and yet one cannot quite forget that they are the descendants of what was at one time, in the eighteenth century, a high-spirited and highly-cultivated aristocracy. The broken greenhouses and mouse-eaten libraries, that were designed and collected by men who voted with Grattan, are perhaps as mournful in the end as the four mud walls that are so often left in Wicklow as the only remnants of a farmhouse (52-3).

With the landlords gone, the whole countryside, which depended on them, crumbled. The active peasants emigrated, and nearly all the people left were in the position of the old man who said to Synge: 'That's the profession I have now – to be thinking of all the people, and of the times that's gone.' In contrast to *The Aran Islands*, which gives a picture of life still wholesome and vigorous, caught in its fullness before it became tainted with commercialism, the Wicklow essays give a sense of being at the end of a phase. One is constantly aware of the 'ceaseless fading of beauty' and of an atmosphere of weariness and anxiety. 'The Oppression of the Hills' shows this perhaps more directly than most of the other essays.

It opens with a plain general statement: 'Among the cottages that are scattered through the hills of County Wicklow I have met with many people who show in a singular way the influence of a particular locality' (13). A description of the natural world follows, and, because there is a close link between environment and inhabitant, the description also enables us to comprehend something of the mental condition of the people:

At every season heavy rains fall for often a week at a time, till the thatch drips with water stained to a dull chestnut. . . . Then the clouds break, and there is a night of terrific storm from the south-west . . . when the winds come down through the narrow glens with the congested whirl and roar of a torrent, breaking at times for sudden moments of silence that keep up the tension of the mind. At such times the people crouch all night over a few sods of turf and the dogs howl in the lanes (13-14).

The tension between dream and actuality is reflected in the

natural world which is normally dreary and harsh, like actuality, but which is occasionally irradiated with beauty, like a dream. This essay shows how the nightmare and horror may be relieved by a few hours of extraordinary loveliness and exhilaration: 'When the sun rises there is a morning of almost supernatural radiance, and even the oldest men and women come out into the air with the joy of children who have recovered from a fever' (14). But, like all beauty, this interlude quickly passes: 'in the evening it is raining again', and the cycle of dull despair goes on. The essay continues with a human incident exemplifying the opening statement; an old man tells of a herd who went mad during a storm and died on the hills. The old man ends: 'I remember when you'd see forty boys and girls below there on a Sunday evening, playing ball and diverting themselves; but now all this country is gone lonesome and bewildered, and there's no man knows what ails it' (15). All are 'lonesome and bewildered', intense nervousness is common even with young people, and Synge himself begins to feel the pervading influence:

> The rushes were shining in the moonlight, and one flake of mist was lying on the river. We looked into one bog-hole, and then into another, where a snipe rose and terrified us. We listened; a cow was chewing heavily in the shadow of a bush, two dogs were barking on the side of a hill, and there was a cart far away upon the road. . . . Among these emotions of the night one cannot wonder that the madhouse is so often named in Wicklow (18).

Among these glens, the weather and the natural world are easily the most powerful forces determining the character and the occupations of the people. This characteristic, implicit, in varying ways, in all the essays, reaches its most notable expression in 'Glencree', an essay which typifies very aptly the salient features both of the district and of the essays. At first sight this essay may seem to be nothing more than a piece of competent descriptive writing, but closer examination reveals that by means of this description Synge is presenting in terms of sensation the quality of the lives of the people and their surroundings. A clear morning entices Synge into the glens, and he walks

> between sheets of sickly moss and bog-cotton that is unable to

thrive. The road is caked with moss that breaks like pie-crust under my feet, and in corners where there is shelter there are sheep loitering, or a few straggling grouse . . . (58).

Then the fog comes down, distorting everything:

The little turfy ridges on each side of the road have the look of glens to me, and every block of stone has the size of a house . . . the sense of loneliness has no equal . . . even weasels run squealing past me on the side of the road. . . . Then the fog lifts and shows the white empty roads winding everywhere, with the added sense of desolation one gets passing an empty house on the side of the road. . . . In most places I can see the straight ending of the cloud, but above the lake grey fingers are coming up and down, like a hand that is clasping and opening again. . . .

There is a dense white fog around the cottage, and we seem to be shut away from any habitation. All round behind the hills there is a moan and rumble of thunder coming nearer, at times with a fierce and sudden crash. The bracken has a nearly painful green in the strangeness of the light. Enormous sheep are passing in and out of the sky line (58–60).

How well the restraint and accuracy of this writing convey the recurrent motifs of desolation, nightmare fancies and anxiety.

There is a strange depression about the cottage tonight. The woman of the house is taken ill and has got into bed beside her mother-in-law, who is over ninety and is wandering in her mind. The man of the house has gone away ten miles for medicine, and I am left with the two children, who are playing silently about the door. The larches in the haggard are dripping heavily with damp, and the hens and geese, bewildered with the noise and gloom, are cackling with uneasy dread. All one's senses are disturbed. As I walk backwards and forwards, a few yards above and below the door, the little stream I do not see seems to roar out of the cloud.

Every leaf and twig is heavy with drops, and a dog that has passed with a sad-eyed herd looked wet and draggled and afraid (61).

But an effect of unrelieved drabness is not good artistically –

some note of fresh colour and life is necessary if only to highlight the predominant sombre mood. Synge, therefore, once more blended richness with reality; in this case by making good use of the fact that the drabness was not unrelieved, for there were tramps and tinkers who moved through the glens from time to time, and who were immune from the blight. Just as the predominant dreariness of the natural world was underlined by brief gleams of beauty, so the desolation of the dwellers in the glens was underlined by the vigour of the tramps. Accordingly the last quarter of 'Glencree' depicts a scene quite different from that of the rest of the essay. It is the same place, but on one of those rare days when the natural world is benign and lovely: 'The sky was covered with white radiant clouds, with soft out-lines, broken in a few places by lines of blue sky of wonderful delicacy and clearness' (62). And the human being in the picture is a tramp, resourceful and carefree, who saunters in, washes his shirt in the spring, puts it on, and wanders towards the village, 'picking blackberries from the hedge'. Thus in the essays, the tramps, along with the tinkers – 'gallous lads for walking round through the world' – represent a comparatively wholesome way of life, and this is contrasted with the decaying way of life, the nightmare, of the people of the glens, whose dream is of escape to America.

In both *The Aran Islands* and *In Wicklow, West Kerry and Connemara* Synge understands and sympathizes with the people but in the latter he does not become involved emotionally with them as he does in the former. This may be exemplified by a comparison of his account of the Blasket Islands with his account of the Aran Islands. The Blaskets are six small islands off the extreme southwest coast of Ireland, in Synge's day inhabited by people with a simple, traditional way of life, who obtained a living by fishing and farming. Synge gained a good deal from his contact with these people, and he had a considerable admiration for them, but he was not moved profoundly, and his experiences there were nothing like so momentous as they were on Aran. His description of his first journey to the Blaskets is reminiscent of one to the Arans: 'The day was admirably clear, with a blue sea and sky, and the voyage in the long canoe – I had not been in one for two or three years – gave me indescribable enjoyment' (83). He found there a way of life much more colourful and wholesome than that in any part of Ireland, except Aran, which he had visited, and he was shown courtesy and kindness. On one occasion he speaks of the people of the Blaskets in terms that recall key-passages in *The Aran Islands*:

> The women, as usual, were in their naked feet, and whenever there was a figure for women only there was a curious hush and patter of bare feet, till the heavy pounding and shuffling of the men's boots broke in again. The whirl of music and dancing in this little kitchen stirred me with an extraordinary effect. The kindliness and merry-making of these islanders, who, one knows, are full of riot and severity and daring, has a quality and attractiveness that is absent altogether from the life of towns, and makes one think of the life that is shown in the ballads of Scotland (104–5).

But further than this his feelings were not engaged, and he never had any desire to share their life. There he did not experience the quality of beauty and tragedy, the intensified awareness – rich and real as in a work of art – of all that is fundamental to life, which he experienced on Aran. Consequently, the third aspect, centred on Synge himself, of the tension between dream and actuality does not occur in *In Wicklow, West Kerry and Connemara*. Nor, in this book, is the first aspect of this tension present – the conflict between the community and the sea – for, unlike the people of Aran, the people of the Blaskets did not risk their lives constantly. 'There has been no one drowned on this island for forty years' an old man told Synge.

Taking the West Kerry section as a whole it is the second aspect of the tension between dream and actuality which we notice: the tension between beauty and material security, which arises from the fact that loveliness is somehow bound up with sorrow and desolation and that as physical conditions of life are improved so qualities of imagination tend to be lost:

> The little group of blue-coated men lying on the grass, and the group of girls further off, had a singular effect in this solitude of rocks and sea; and in spite of their high spirits it gave me a sort of grief to feel the utter loneliness and desolation of the place that has given these people their finest qualities (98).

Again, in a fine descriptive passage which reminds one of Edgar's speech at Dover in *King Lear*, he says:

> It is a place of indescribable grandeur, where one can see Carrantuohill and the Skelligs and Loop Head and the full sweep of the Atlantic, and, over all, the wonderfully tender and searching light that is seen only in Kerry. Looking down the drop of five or six hundred feet, the height is so great that the gannets flying close over the sea look like white butterflies, and the choughs like flies fluttering behind them. One wonders in these places why anyone is left in Dublin, or London, or Paris, when it would be better, one would think, to live in a tent or hut with this magnificent sea and sky, and to breathe this wonderful air, which is like wine in one's teeth (81).

But here actuality comes in: 'there are little villages of ten or twenty houses, closely packed together without any order or roadway . . . they are often infested with typhus'. Synge, as usual, makes no direct comment; he places the two facts together and leaves them to make their effect. Occasionally, however, he sums up his feelings in a moving sentence. He has been describing the people going to chapel, and ends:

> This procession along the olive bogs, between the mountains and the sea, on this grey day of autumn, seemed to wring me with the pang of emotion one meets everywhere in Ireland – an emotion that is partly local and patriotic, and partly a share of the desolation that is mixed everywhere with the supreme beauty of the world (71).

Synge was a solitary, a wanderer who had no home and no roots except in the power and tradition of art and the imagination, and although he hardly ever mentions his own solitariness, he was quick to sense the loneliness of other people and places. In one spot where 'the weather was gloomy and wild, there was something nearly appalling in the loneliness of the place'. And he noticed at Puck Fair many people 'who had come in for amusement only, and were walking up and down, looking at each other – a crowd is as exciting as champagne to these lonely people, who live in long glens among the mountains' (122). Puck Fair, held each August, was the 'greatest event in West Kerry', and eagerly looked forward to by all; but after the three days of

excitement, companionship and bargaining, actuality asserts its
hold. As they started homewards:

> rain was coming up over the hills of Glen Car, so that there
> was a strained hush in the air, and a rich, aromatic smell com-
> ing from the bog myrtle, or boggy shrub that grows thickly in
> this place. The strings of horses and jennets scattered over the
> road did not keep away a strange feeling of loneliness that
> seems to hang over this brown plain of bog (127).

Against this dreariness the people tried to maintain barriers,
important among which was the still fairly vigorous tradition of
folk-literature and music. Synge gives his own version of some
folk-tales, and the best of these, based on a long English doggerel
sung to him, is a further example of his mastery of English prose:

> A poor scholar went to Maynooth and had great success in his
> studies, so that he was praised by the bishop. Then he went
> home for his holiday, and a young woman who had great riches
> asked him into her parlour and told him it was no fit life for a
> fine young man to be a priest, always saying Mass for poor
> people, and that he would have a right to give up his Latin
> and get married to herself. He refused her offers and went back
> to his college. When he was gone she went to the justice in great
> anger, and swore an oath against him that he had seduced her
> and left her with child. He was brought back for his trial, and
> he was in risk to be degraded and hanged, when a man rode
> up on a horse and said it was himself was the lover of the lady,
> and the father of her child (105).

Nevertheless, commercial entertainment was beginning to have
a coarsening effect on the small towns, which were already
wretched enough. Synge's regret at the expense of spirit and
energy in something approaching a waste of brutality and
squalor in these places, and his distaste for crude entertainment
are perceptible in his description of the circus in Dingle. The
night was foul, the place filthy, the tent, with its naked flares and
billowing structure, dangerous, and the performance over an hour
late in starting:

> It was begun by the usual dirty white horse, that was set to
> gallop round, with a gaudy horse-woman on his back who did

the ordinary feats, the horse's hoofs splashing and possing all the time in the green slush of the ring. . . . A little later the clown came out, to the great delight of the people. He was followed by some gymnasts, and then the horse-people came out again in different dress and make-up, and went through their old turns once more. After that there was prolonged fooling between the clown and the chief horse-man, who made many mediaeval jokes (77).

In contrast to the people of Aran, who, although often passionate and vehement in speech and gesture, were rarely drunk and hardly ever brutal, the people of West Kerry were easily led into drunkenness and violence. Synge never heard 'the men talk for half an hour of anything without some allusion to drink'; one night he was awakened by 'a furious drunken uproar coming from a canoe that was somewhere out in the bay. It sounded as if the men were strangling or murdering each other'; and after the sports there was, as one man said, 'great sport':

> They were all beating and cutting each other on the shore of the sea. Four men fought together in one place till the tide came up on them, and was like to drown them; but the priest waded out up to his middle and drove them asunder. Another man was left for dead . . . and the postman was destroyed for ever (138).

Synge records this, and makes no comment, but in his next paragraph he says: 'I have been out to Bolus Head, one of the finest places I have met with.' One gets the impression that Synge sometimes moved in this way from Man to the natural world, perhaps more frequently in this section than in any other part of his prose works. He seems to have been more deeply affected by the natural world than by anything else in Kerry, and the most noteworthy parts of this section are moulded round some description of natural scenery. Corkery says:[153] 'We often come on a picture that Jack Yeats or Paul Henry might have painted: it is easy to know that he had lived much among painters and pictures.' There is truth in this, as the following passage indicates:

> In the evening as I was coming home, I got a glimpse that seemed to have the whole character of Corkaguiney – a little line of low cottages with yellow roofs, and an elder tree without

leaves beside them, standing out against a high mountain that seemed far away, yet was near enough to be dense and rich and wonderful in its colour. . . . The blueness of the sea and the hills, the singular loneliness of the hillside I was on, with a few choughs and gulls in sight only, had a splendour that was almost a grief to the mind (150).

In the last line the main theme is heard once more: sadness because beauty and desolation are mingled. Synge appears to have 'spent much of [his] time looking at the richness of the Atlantic on one side and the sad or shining greys of Dingle Bay on the other', and he is drawn, as one would expect, to what is 'grey, wild and magnificent. . . . The cold sea and surf, and the feeling of winter in the clouds, and the blackness of the rocks, and the red fern everywhere, were a continual surprise and excitement.' In these last phrases, and in the following sentence concluding a description, the epithets reveal the qualities that attracted him: 'The whole sight of wild islands and sea was as clear and cold and brilliant as what one sees in a dream, and alive with the singularly severe glory that is in the character of this place' (86–7). These pictures, more than anything else, seem to give 'local intensity' to the sombreness of his mood. It is not that he distorts the scene to suit his own obsessions – for each object is perceived and presented with remarkable accuracy – but that these scenes call up certain emotions in him which he transmits to us by means of objective description.

Of the Connemara section of *In Wicklow, West Kerry and Connemara* the publishers rightly say: 'although only the hastily written records of a journey through the West of Ireland, they contain characteristic passages which it is felt those interested in Synge's work will wish to have in this permanent form'. It is said that Cromwell offered the defeated Irish the alternative of Hell or Connacht. Some feel that he gave no real choice: torment lay in either direction. Malone says:

Connacht is the wildest and the poorest of the Irish provinces, awesome . . . but also pathetic in the squalid poverty of its inhabitants. It is a veritable paradise to the artist, but it is as veritably a hell to the social reformer and the statesman. The painter delights in its scenery, the poet revels in the wild and

vividly-coloured phraseology of the people . . . but to the
statesman and the sociologist Connacht is simply a 'Congested
District', that is, not a densely populated district as might be
supposed, but simply a place where the land is not fertile
enough to provide sustenance and livelihood for the people
who try to live upon it. Its scenic splendour and its poverty-
ridden inhabitants are both primitive.[154]

Synge's assignment meant that he had to try to look at the
Congested Districts of Connemara and Mayo in Connacht with
the eyes of the social investigator. He seems to have done this
successfully, and, what is more, done it without inhibiting the
artist in him. Yet the acute perception and the imaginative sympathy of the artist were, in this case, used as means to the end of
social improvement; not used for delight and, probably through
delight, for instruction; but used for direct instruction, and, only
incidentally, for delight. Most of the time he is more concerned
with living conditions than with scenery, and he asks people about
their work and their crops and pay, and not about folk-literature.
He says that they once 'spent the rest of the evening talking and
drinking and telling stories in Irish', but he records no stories.
Nor is he interested mainly in individuals but in groups – of
fishermen, labourers, unemployed – though he cannot resist giving expression in a moving style to the deep pathos of a ferry-
man's position. This man seemed to typify the simple courage of
the people in the face of desolation and misfortune:

'I have a young family growing up, for I was snug for a while;
and then bad times came, and I lost my wife, and the potatoes
went bad, and three cows I had were taken in the night with
some disease of the brain, and they swam out and were drowned
in the sea. . . . So here I am now with no pigs, and no cows, and
a young family with no mother to mind them . . . If it wasn't
for them I'd be off this evening, and I'd earn my living easy
on the sea, for I'm only fifty-seven years of age, and I have good
health; but how can I leave my young children? And I don't
know what way I'm to go on living in this place that the Lord
created last, I'm thinking, in the end of time . . . where even
the judges and quality do come out and lower our rents when
they see the wild Atlantic driving in across the cursed stones'
(185–6).

In some of the less remote districts there was not so much poverty, and Synge notices three distinct social groups among the people dressed in their best coming from Mass: the police and coastguards in their smartest uniforms, and the shopkeepers dressed like the people of Dublin; the more well-to-do country people in local clothes of good quality; the destitute in threadbare or ragged local clothes, 'the women mostly barefooted, and both sexes pinched with hunger and the fear of it'. Synge, characteristically, wishes that the last group may be levelled up to the second group, and that this group, which retains the local customs, may thrive, but he adds, with a touch of sadness, 'except in a few districts this group is not numerous, and it is always aspiring after the dress of the shop-people or tending to sink down again among the paupers'. Here once more we have the main theme of all Synge's writing – the tension between a full imaginative, emotional life and material progress, between the dream and the actuality. This comes out in the first article, and is the prime consideration underlying them all:

> One's first feeling as one comes back among these people and takes a place, so to speak, in this noisy procession of fishermen, farmers and women, where nearly everyone is interesting and attractive, is a dread of any reform that would tend to lessen their individuality rather than any very real hope of improving their well-being. One feels that it is part of the misfortune of Ireland that nearly all the characteristics which give colour and attractiveness to Irish life are bound up with a social condition that is near to penury (158).

Synge's writings show that he was aware of this misfortune, and it determines the main lines of his approach to the social problems of the Congested Districts. He is always anxious lest unimaginative, though well-intentioned, official action should destroy the distinctive character of a district, and he suggests that the peasants 'should be left as free as possible to arrange their houses and way of life as it pleases them':

> Traditions are destroyed for ever when too sweeping improvements are made in a district, and the loss is a real one . . . the rearrangement and sale of holdings to the tenants must be carried out on a large scale, but in doing so care should be taken

to disorganize as little as possible the life and methods of the people. . . . For instance, there is no pressing need to substitute iron roofs – in many ways open to objection – for the thatch that has been used for centuries, and is part of the constructive tradition of the people. . . . In the same way the improvements in the houses built by the Board are perhaps a little sudden. It is far better, wherever possible, to improve the ordinary prosperity of the people till they begin to improve their houses themselves on their own lines, than to do too much in the way of building houses that have no interest for the people and disfigure the country (201–2).

Synge is anxious to preserve what grace and beauty there are in the lives and surroundings of the people, and one of his rare disclosures of personal emotion comes during a dreary journey in a slow cart when he sees people sunk hopelessly in squalor; he is as much moved by the ugliness and the deadening of the imagination that poverty can bring, as he is by the physical suffering it brings also:

In Mayo the people cutting turf in the bogs, and their draggled colourless clothes – so unlike the homespuns of Connemara – added indescribably to the feeling of wretchedness one gets from the sight of these miserable cottages, many of them with an old hamper or the end of a barrel stuck through the roof for a chimney, and the desolation of the bogs (205).

He contrasts the well-being of those people who are fully engaged upon the traditional work of kelp-making with the degradation of the unemployed who are compelled to take up relief work for a shilling a day; he remarks that no one begs, even in a round-about way; and he shows how eager the people are to help themselves and adopt improved methods that are of value, instancing the old woman, who, unable to afford the contrivance for spraying potatoes against the blight, got a bucketful of the solution and spattered her potatoes with an old broom.

In the face of these articles alone it is difficult to see how anyone can truthfully accuse Synge of being antagonistic to the Irish peasantry, particularly when we observe running through these articles, as indeed through much of his work, a tension between the peasants on the one hand and the officials and the shopkeeper

class on the other. Without sentimentalizing them, Synge was
usually on the side of the peasants, and critical of the arrogance
of some officials and of the greed of those shopkeepers who
exploited their position as sole employers, and sole buyers and
sellers of produce, in a district.

But Synge is aware of the complicated nature of the problem,
and he propounds no quick and easy solution. He points out that
acts which seem thoroughly laudable such as the suppression of
poteen-making can cause distress, and he gives an amusing account of the reminiscences of a man about the good old times
when the laws against illicit distillation were not enforced and
'you'd see the police itself down on their knees blowing the fire
with their own breath to make a drink for themselves'. This
patient, watchful sympathy is present throughout; Synge makes
allowance for human failings and is always fair; he never over-
states a case, nor does he draw general conclusions merely from
a few selected or fortuitous instances. The literary merits of these
articles are not considerable, but they show at least that Synge
had the ability to approach and comprehend a serious practical
social problem, to observe acutely, to fix on all relevant details,
to present his material logically and attractively, and to draw conclusions, tentative but noteworthy.

Synge's two prose works are valuable in at least four ways:
they provide the sources for most of Synge's plays and poems,
and so throw an exceptionally revealing light upon the aims,
methods and principles not only of Synge but, perhaps, of other
artists, and they fit in completely with all Synge's other works,
and in reiterating in different ways the main themes of Synge's
life and writings, they help to stress how fundamental these
themes are; they give a unique and profound insight into the
nature of Synge himself; they embody a fund of folk-lore and
folk-literature, expressed in a style which retains the essential
features of peasant speech, endowing it with heightened concise-
ness and beauty, and they are the first, and the still unequalled,
accounts of primitive and traditional ways of life which have since
passed away: books by natives of these places are valuable too, but
Synge brought to his task in addition to an acute intelligence and
sensitivity and a deep sympathy for the people, the cultured mind
and imagination of a remarkable artist, and an experience of

peasant life in other lands and of life in great cities; they have a kind of vitality and significance independent of any particular relation, and are not means but ends, created things with a life of their own offering that extension and refinement of sensibility peculiar to works of art. Although the interest of Synge's prose works is partly dependent on the fact that Synge was an important dramatist, they are also valuable in themselves, and would be noteworthy even if Synge had written nothing else.

CHAPTER FOUR

Poems and Translations

Synge was a fastidious critic of his own work, and he wrote
much more than he published. Drafts of plays, essays, poems
and a novel, previously hardly known about, have recently
been mentioned and quoted in the biography by Greene and
Stephens. From an early age Synge wrote verse, much of it
rather naïve reflections of his feelings or commonplace nature
stuff imitative of his favourite poet, Wordsworth, yet showing
traces of individual worth. He let MacKenna read an immense
wad of verse, but eventually only twenty-two poems and seventeen translations were published. The translations were mainly
exercises made at a time when he was experimenting with the
peasant idiom to see if it was adaptable to other purposes. Most
of the published poems were written during the last three years of
his life and were mainly influenced by his feelings for Molly Allgood (Maire O'Neill) and his apprehensions of death. It cannot
be maintained that Synge's poems and translations are of high
merit, yet they, together with his observations on poetry, have
a certain historical importance, and some of his poems remain
intrinsically valuable. Synge's verse is also interesting as a supplement to his other work, and to our impression of the man.

Synge believed that no good writer can ever be translated, and
some of his translations were put into the Cuala Press edition of
his *Poems* only 'To make it a little less thin.' Nevertheless the
translations, as a whole, have charm; Bourgeois says of them:

They are felicitous attempts at rendering fragments of European literature into dialect. . . .' Some of them are almost
literal, like the translation of Walther von der Vogelweide.
Others, almost more original than Synge's original poems, are
independent paraphrases, or rather re-creations, like the Villon
pieces.[155]

Laying aside any reference to the originals one remarks about these translations their closeness, both in matter and style, to the plays. Each piece could be assigned with propriety to a character in the plays; and nearly all of them display that feeling for the simple everyday object and situation, and that awareness of a link between Man and the natural world, which are prominent in the plays. Consider 'An Old Woman's Lamentations', probably the best of the translations:

> The man I had a love for – a great rascal would kick me in the gutter – is dead thirty years and over it, and it is I am left behind, grey and aged. When I do be minding the good days I had, minding what I was one time, and what it is I'm come to, and when I do look on my own self, poor and dry, and pinched together, it wouldn't be much would set me raging in the streets.
>
> Where is the round forehead I had, and the fine hair, and the two eyebrows, and the eyes with a big gay look out of them would bring folly from a great scholar? Where is my straight shapely nose, and two ears, and my chin with a valley in it, and my lips were red and open?
>
> Where are the pointed shoulders were on me, and the long arms and nice hands to them? Where is my bosom was as white as any, or my straight rounded sides?
>
> It's the way I am this day – my forehead is gone away into furrows, the hair of my head is grey and whitish, my eyebrows are tumbled from me, and my two eyes have died out within my head – those eyes that would be laughing to the men – my nose has a hook on it, my ears are hanging down, and my lips are sharp and skinny.
>
> That's what's left over from the beauty of a right woman – a bag of bones, and legs the like of two shrivelled sausages going beneath it.
>
> It's of the like of that we old hags do be thinking, of the good times are gone away from us, and we crouching on our hunkers by a little fire of twigs, soon kindled and soon spent, we that were the pick of many.

A good deal of Synge is here: the tension between the dream of the past (in paragraphs two and three) and the actuality of the present (in paragraphs four and five); the sharp consciousness of the transience of youth and beauty, and the notion that once love has gone life is misery; the liking for 'a great rascal'; and a somewhat opulent redundancy of style. As in the plays Synge gains his effects by means of repetition – 'sameness with difference' in idea and expression – by rhetorical question, by colloquial turns of phrase and homely images, and by a distinctive rhythm.

Yet although the piece has a richness seldom found in Synge's verse it is, from one point of view, lacking in reality. To people who speak the idiom upon which this and all Synge's translations are based, the translations can be both rich and real; but to the rest of us they can be little more than singular and charming, because they are too remote from our everyday speech. We find the subject matter engaging and we admire the craftsmanship, but we cannot make the translations part of us, we cannot feel them on our pulses, as we can poetry based upon the rhythms of our speech. This fact does not mar the plays. In them the speech is in character, and we enjoy it, because, although its rhythms are not our own, we know that they are the rhythms used by the people represented on the stage. The Playboy's emotions are expressed accurately in his speech; but our emotions find neither satisfactory expression nor extension in the rhythms of Synge's translations. In a way we are reading a foreign language, and the English of Skelton, of *Paradise Lost* and of Gray, is nearer to us than is the language of passages like this:

And she has left me after her dejected and lonesome, turning back all times to the place I do be making much of for her sake only, and I seeing the night on the little hills where she took her last flight up into the heavens, and where one time her eyes would make sunshine and it night itself.

Turning to Synge's poems one soon notices that death is easily the predominant subject. There are two main attitudes to death, similar to those in the plays and translations: that the dream of love alone can make life worthwhile, but that once this dream is shattered, death is the only resort, and that for those who have not experienced deep love, nor been awakened to actuality, any sort of life is better than death. One of the better poems, 'Queens', embodies a tension between two attitudes to death: the 'romantic' and the 'realistic'. Using a method similar to the method of

contrast used in his plays, Synge places the dream of the splendour
of queens against the actuality:

> *Seven dog-days we let pass*
> *Naming Queens in Glenmacnass*
> *All the rare and royal names*
> *Wormy sheepskin yet retains. . . .*
> *Queens whose finger once did stir men,*
> *Queens were eaten of fleas and vermin,*
> *Queens men drew like Monna Lisa,*
> *Or slew with drugs in Rome and Pisa. . . .*

The jaunty, doggerel-like manner continues to hint mockingly
that queens were by no means uniformly exquisite. The queens
are drawn from many sources – Classical, Biblical, Medieval, Irish
– and Synge shows skill in linking them together; but, however
different or magnificent they were in life, they are now all the
same – eaten by vermin; and even the records of them are worm-
eaten:

> *We named Lucrezia Crivelli,*
> *And Titian's lady with amber belly,*
> *Queens acquainted in learned sin,*
> *Jane of Jewry's slender shin:*

The next couplet foreshadows T. S. Eliot's method of placing
two apparently unrelated elements together ('Whether on the
shores of Asia, or in the Edgware Road') to bring out hidden
resemblances, and to imply an evaluation of them both:

> *Queens who wasted the East by proxy,*
> *Or drove the ass-cart, a tinker's doxy. . . .*

Cleopatra too was a doxy; and she was partly responsible for
bringing ruin to many people, whereas a tinker's doxy, who
drives the cart and does some poaching, is comparatively harm-
less. The inescapable facts of decay and dissolution, implicit
throughout, are stressed in the last lines:

> *Yet these are rotten – I ask their pardon –*
> *And we've the sun on rock and garden;*
> *These are rotten, so you're the Queen*
> *Of all are living, or have been.*

The main theme of the poem is that the present is the only tangible actuality, and that the poet's beloved – apart from the qualities which make her 'Queen of all are living' – is infinitely more lovely than any queen of history merely because she is alive. One gets the impression of a sensitive mind so harrowed by the notion of the havoc caused by time that it has to adopt this mildly sardonic tone, and to turn to personal affections and to the natural world for comfort.

The poem 'In Kerry' resembles 'Queens'. It shows how the solace of the natural world is spoiled by evidences of death, then hints that love creates 'a new wild paradise', a dream, that transfigures harsh actuality; but only temporarily. Here too an ironic levity is assumed towards death, to make the contemplation of it less painful. This sudden transition from enjoyment of the natural world to a grim smile at awareness of the omnipotence of death is seen again in 'To the Oaks of Glencree', where, as he leans against the tree, Synge realizes that the whirligig of time will bring in his revenges, and the tree (it too changed into coffin boards) will embrace him; but – the last twist of the knife – it will not keep out worms. Again, his horror at the thought that death will reduce him, and those he loves, to clods over which mediocrities will trample, is apparent in 'I've Thirty Months', and in the savage intensity of 'A Question':

> *I asked if I got sick and died, would you*
> *With my black funeral go walking too,*
> *If you'd stand close to hear them talk or pray*
> *While I'm let down in that steep bank of clay.*

> *And, No, you said, for if you saw a crew*
> *Of living idiots pressing round that new*
> *Oak coffin – they alive, I dead beneath*
> *That board – you'd rave and rend them with your teeth.*

Synge could, however, use his preoccupation with death to more purely comic effect as is shown by his 'Epitaph' on a priest:

> *If fruits are fed on any beast*
> *Let vine-roots suck this parish priest,*
> *For while he lived, no summer sun*
> *Went up but he'd a bottle done,*

And in the starlight beer and stout
Kept his waistcoat bulging out.

Then Death that changes happy things
Damned his soul to water springs.

The merit of the foregoing poems may be seen if we place against
them one of Synge's feebler compositions:

A silent sinner, nights and days,
No human heart to him drew nigh,
Alone he wound his wonted ways,
Alone and little loved did die.

And autumn Death for him did choose,
A season dank with mists and rain,
And took him, while the evening dews
Were settling o'er the fields again.

This diffuse and commonplace piece is plainly derivative (one
catches echoes of Gray's 'Elegy', *In Memoriam, A Shropshire Lad*)
and it lacks the glint of irony or humour which often gives individuality to Synge's verse.

A characteristic piece in his debunking vein is 'The Passing of
the Shee', written after looking at one of 'A.E.' 's pictures:

Adieu, sweet Angus, Maeve and Fand,
Ye plumed yet skinny Shee,
That poets played with hand in hand
To learn their ecstasy.

We'll stretch in Red Dan Sally's ditch,
And drink in Tubber fair,
Or poach with Red Dan Philly's bitch
The badger and the hare.

This is akin to 'Queens' and proclaims Synge's dislike for the
insubstantial splendour of Celtic Romance as depicted by 'A.E.'
and his followers, and his preference for the 'life of sensations'
of people who are neither heroic nor graceful. In the first stanza
Synge mocks an outworn style and uses 'poetic' words to show

the incongruity of the Shee. They wear 'plumes' – the trappings of majesty – yet are empty, fictitious queens; 'skinny Shee', lacking in life and voluptuousness. The poet with the outlook expressed in 'A.E.' 's picture has to adopt some conventional posture and 'To learn [his] ecstasy' instead of creating it from his senses and imagination. Nor can he come into any kind of intimate contact with his subject; he must behave like a courtier to his Shee, and 'play with' them 'hand in hand' in some unreal ritual. Synge rejects this dream of a legendary past, and advocates an immersion in the actuality of contemporary life, and a cessation of the vain attempt to gain vitality from attitudes and conventions which have served their purpose and passed away.

Synge was disturbed because poetry had become removed from the interests and activities of the majority of people; and he tried to close the breach. On several occasions he discussed the problem with John Masefield, and the two writers seem to have felt that the re-creation of ballad poetry was both desirable and possible. Synge's approach to the ballad resembled his approach to drama; he turned to communities which had a resource in the use of language, and a way of life still, in some respects, similar to those which obtained when the ballad was most in favour. Furthermore, as is shown by the tales, ballads and songs which Synge heard and recorded in his prose works, the tradition of folk-literature was by no means dead in rural Ireland. Synge got the notion for the ballad, 'The 'Mergency man' from an incident he heard about in West Kerry. Synge's prose version of this is unexceptionable, but comparison between it and the verse shows that the ballad is more noteworthy. Using no more words and not omitting anything of relevance Synge incorporates in the ballad a number of features not found in the source. The ballad indicates how unwelcome the 'Mergency Man was: he could get no lodgings and had to share 'the half of the bailiff's room'. It evokes the storm vividly, with the hyperbole of:

> *Till a black night came in Coomasaharn,*
> *A night of rains you'd swamp a star in.*

and with the picture of a night so inclement that 'The hares itself will quit the heather'; a line which economically reveals also that the tenants have been hiding in the heather. The triplet contrasts the blackness of the night with the white fury of the flood, and shows the admiration of the people for the bravery of the 'Mergency Man, even though he is their enemy:

The night was black at the fording place,
And the flood was up in a whitened race,
But devil a bit he'd turn his face.

The 'peelers', with their knowledge of the locality, warn him of the great danger, and then give expression to the usual human desire to avoid responsibility: 'We'll wash our hands of your bloody job.' The 'Mergency Man, however, accustomed – because he is enforcing the hated foreign laws – to having all people against him, defiantly goes on – to his death:

He made two leps with a run and dash,
Then the peelers heard a yell and splash;

And the 'mergency man in two days and a bit
Was found in the ebb tide stuck in a net.

This piece, with its realism, and its austere presentation of the facts, unadorned with any direct moral reflections, has much of the real ballad flavour. So too has 'Danny', perhaps the best of Synge's poems. Its theme is one favoured by Synge: about a man of some distinction opposing mediocre men who are tolerable as individuals but who become inhuman when swayed by mob passions. The 'Erris men' are aware of their own virtue and respectability, and – perhaps because they find these qualities unsatisfying – they feel outraged when Danny breaks their social codes and refuses to conform to their patterns of behaviour. Accordingly they band together into a sort of Vigilantes or Ku Klux Klan, and judge him worthy of death. Danny's vitality is shown throughout, and his marked enjoyment of life – which always arouses the envy of the mediocrities – continues right to his end:

It wasn't long till Danny came,
From Bangor making way,
And he was damning moon and stars
And whistling grand and gay.

Till in a gap of hazel glen –
And not a hare in sight –
Out lepped the nine-and-twenty lads
Along his left and right.

How well the line, 'And not a hare in sight' expresses the sinister nature of the place of ambush: not even animals who can escape quickly dare linger there. Synge makes clever use of magic numbers: Danny has the strength of seven, and it takes three groups of seven men to overthrow him:

> *But seven tripped him up behind,*
> *And seven kicked before,*
> *And seven squeezed around his throat*
> *Till Danny kicked no more.*

> *Then some destroyed him with their heels,*
> *Some tramped him in the mud,*
> *Some stole his purse and timber pipe,*
> *And some washed off his blood.*

With all their sanctimoniousness the 'Erris men' are most brutal, and not above looting. Further irony and pathos occur at the end:

> *And when you're walking out the way*
> *From Bangor to Belmullet,*
> *You'll see a flat cross on a stone,*
> *Where men choked Danny's gullet.*

Society crushes the free vigour and resource of Danny, and re-places a vital 'gullet' with a cold, stone cross – symbol of mercy and love.

Probably the salient characteristic of Synge's verse is that it is different from nearly all the verse written between 1890 and 1908. At this period many poets still trusted the main current of nine-teenth-century verse, broadly Romantic, to sustain and inspire them, although this, as we today can see, was becoming stagnant. Other poets tried to cut new channels, but mostly ended in neglected backwaters, or in the sand. Synge was one of the first in this century who went back to early seventeenth-century springs, and also one of the small number who indicated the new directions which the more vital poetry of our day has taken. Synge's poems are few, and his observations on poetry not ex-tensive, but taken together they constitute a considerable achieve-ment, and show a remarkable insight into the condition and needs of the poetry of the time.

Synge found little to inspire and aid him in the poetry of the nineteenth century. Just as the nineteenth century felt that much of the diction of eighteenth-century verse was 'poetic' – gaudy and insincere – so Synge felt that a good deal of nineteenth-century verse was 'poetic' in a similar undesirable sense. It laid too much stress on the visionary elements of poetry, and in its straining after exaltation it tended to lose touch with the everyday concerns of mankind. In trying to put poetry on a pedestal many poets were succeeding only in putting it on the shelf. Hence all aspects of poetry suffered:

> The poetry of exaltation will always be the highest; but when men lose their poetic feeling for ordinary life, and cannot write poetry of ordinary things, their exalted poetry is likely to lose its strength of exaltation, in the way men cease to build beautiful churches when they have lost happiness in building shops.[156]

For the contemporary practitioner the remedy was, first of all, to look for guidance to a time when the 'poetry of ordinary things' flourished. The eighteenth century, with all its merits, was considered to be too restricted in scope and manner, and too remote in spirit, to offer the right kind of impetus. But Synge found an exciting congeniality of spirit in the literature of the early seventeenth century which gave him constant delight and inspiration. So, without imitating them, he tried to do what Jonson and Herrick had done; he tried to write occasional verse. And in this his instinct was right, for it is doubtful whether he had the ability to write elevated lyrics in the English idiom. He avoided anything that was rarefied or merely pretty, and produced verse which is well suited, as he intended, to be 'read by strong men, and thieves, and deacons, not by little cliques only'. His poetry is tough, seemingly casual, yet precise; marked by conversational rhythms, colloquial wording, and a feeling for the concrete in word and object. He recalls, what had been forgotten for many years, that irony, invective and humour can be used for serious ends in poetry; and in one or two of his technical devices – the use of juxtaposition and implication, doggerel, assonance – he adumbrates some of the methods popular among poets of our day.

His ideas about poetry too, new and startling in his day, are now generally accepted as valid. Nevertheless it should be remembered that at a time when Yeats had hardly begun to loosen

his allegiance to the Pre-Raphaelites, Synge had insight enough
to make statements such as this:

> In these days poetry is usually a flower of evil or good; but it
> is the timber of poetry that wears most surely, and there is no
> timber that has not strong roots among the clay and worms.
> . . . It may also be said that before verse can be human again
> it must learn to be brutal.[157]

Yeats was obviously a far greater poet than Synge, yet Synge was
the first of the two to insist on the necessity for anchoring poetry
– no matter how ecstatic it may be – in the common concerns of
mankind: a view which Yeats accepted later. In addition, Synge's
remark that the poets of the seventeenth century 'used the whole
of their personal life as their material', and his notion that some
unusually significant change took place in poetry in the seventeenth century presage two of T. S. Eliot's observations (on wit
and metaphysical poets and on 'a dissociation of sensibility')
which have achieved prominence. Synge may be no more than
a minor poet, but he is one of those minors who have played a
part in the major changes of poetry.

CHAPTER FIVE

Early Shorter Plays

The Shadow of the Glen

Synge's work is remarkably homogeneous, and some of the main features of his writings may be discerned through a comparison of his first play, *The Shadow of the Glen*, with its source, a tale told by Pat, an old Gaelic story-teller, and succinctly translated into English, in *The Aran Islands*, by Synge. The story-teller relates how, while travelling one night, he was driven by bad weather to seek shelter at a cottage. A woman admitted him and he saw a body on the table. She said it was her husband who had died suddenly. The wife gave the story-teller food, and went out. Then the 'dead man' got up and said he was only pretending to be dead in order to catch his wife with her lover. He laid himself out again, and soon the wife returned with a young man who went into the bedroom to rest. Later, the wife, making some excuse, followed him there. After a while the husband got up, took a big stick, went into the bedroom, and battered his wife and her lover to death.

This version of an ageless story that has been found in various forms in several continents is in a sound tradition; it is an eye-witness account, clear, robust and free from introspection. Sanity and a sense of proportion prevail throughout; as in the opening, where the human need for food and shelter, and the reflection 'he that's dead can do no hurt', overcome the fear of a dead body; and again in the appreciation of essentials and simple comforts: the clean house; the cup, 'with a saucer under it'; the 'fine sugar and bread'; 'the fine clean shirt' and 'the fine flannel drawers' (of the man). The style has something of the vigour of the better kind of folk-tale or fable: adjectives are used very sparingly, verbs are nearly always active, and there is accurate observation of significant detail: 'The dead man hit him a blow with the stick so that the blood out of him leapt up and hit the gallery.' The story-teller shows little emotion; he is not interested in people's feelings, least of all in his own; he is solely concerned to give an exact and lively account of what he has seen. He does not consider motives or values or try to examine the forces at work behind the facts; and there is no trace of individuality in the figures, they are timeless – a Husband, a Wife, a Lover, seen by a Story-teller. Pat's story, then, presents at a fairly primitive level a situation common to every generation; could Synge distil from it dramatic richness and reality?

He begins by making a decisive change of emphasis. Instead of a stark account of a cuckold's swift vengeance he offers a play concerning figures who have recognizable human characteristics and who represent, to some extent, differing attitudes. Synge, in spite of what his detractors say, was not interested in violent action for its own sake. The adultery and slaughter of the tale do not occur in the play, and Corkery's description of a woman 'wearing her lusts upon her sleeve, a being all appetite and no faculty' [158] fits the wife of the tale much more accurately than it fits Nora. The cunning and ruthlessness of the husband are the salient features of the tale; the predicament of Nora Burke is the central issue of *The Shadow of the Glen*.

Nora embodies the tension between free emotional fulfilment and material security, between imaginative insight and everyday appearances (coupled always with a consciousness of the transience of youth and beauty) which is at the heart of Synge's life and work. In the tale we have the unparticularized figure of the slippery wife; in the play we see the particular and the universal blended in the character of Nora. She is a fine, ardent woman who has found in marriage a few material goods and a dwelling, but no satisfaction of her emotional and imaginative needs. She is caught between two ways of life: the one, with her husband, humdrum, restricted, lonely, but fairly safe; the other represented by the Tramp, more adventurous, offering scope for emotional and imaginative experience, but often hard and insecure. It would be best, Nora knows, to mingle both ways into one, but, as Synge constantly implies, this is hardly ever practicable, and in Nora's case is clearly impossible. Her husband and her environment are inimical, but to leave them is to forfeit such security as she has, and needs. Eventually she is forced to go off with the Tramp and is impressed enough by his account of the life they may enjoy together, to feel that she is taking the more tolerable course, although she shows herself fully aware of its drawbacks. She is 'a hard woman to please' and never 'afeard of beggar or bishop or any man at all'. What she does fear is revealed after she has given her reason for marrying Dan:

> What way would I live if I didn't marry a man with a bit of a farm, and cows on it, and sheep on the back hills?
>
> I do be thinking in the long nights it was a big fool I was that time, Michael Dara; for what good is a bit of a farm with cows on it, and sheep on the back hills, when you do be sitting looking out from a door the like of that door, and seeing nothing but the mists rolling down the bog, and the mists again and they rolling up the bog, and hearing nothing but the wind crying out in the bits of broken trees were left from the great storm, and the streams roaring with the rain (25–6).

This evokes the desolation of the surroundings and, at the same time, describes the desolation of Nora's life with Dan. The anguish at her heart is also felt in the following lines with their graphic images and falling cadences:

> Isn't it a long while I am sitting here in the winter and the summer, and the fine spring, with the young growing behind me and the old passing, saying to myself, to look on Peggy Cavanagh, who had the lightest hand at milking a cow that wouldn't be easy, or turning a cake, and there she is now walking round on the roads, or sitting in a dirty house, with no teeth in her mouth, and no sense, and no more hair than you'd see on a bit of hill and they after burning the furze from it (26).

In the play the husband, Dan, is presented in a more unfavourable light than he is in the tale, probably in order to increase the unhappiness of Nora's position and to give her strong cause for seeking affection elsewhere. Dan is sour and stingy, prone to complain of being 'destroyed with the drouth' and ready to endanger his scheme for a drink. He is insensitive and cannot understand why his wife and the Tramp should be oppressed by the glen. He dislikes the Tramp for his easy manner, his gift of speech, and his appreciation of Nora's feelings, all of which Dan dismisses as 'blathering'. Dan is not above exploiting his age:

'I'm getting old, God help me, though I've an arm to me still', and although he does not strike Nora he torments her effectively when he discovers her dread of loneliness, fading beauty and old age:

> Walk out now, Nora Burke, and it's soon you'll be getting old with that life, I'm telling you; it's soon your teeth'll be falling and your head'll be the like of a bush where sheep do be leaping a gap. . . .
> It's lonesome roads she'll be going and hiding herself away till the end will come, and they find her stretched like a dead sheep with the frost on her, or the big spiders maybe, and they putting their webs on her in the butt of a ditch (29–30).

The incompatibility between husband and wife is finely brought out at this point. Dan's evocation of physical decay arouses Nora to anger, but her outburst is followed by a note of remarkable compassion, as she half turns away, and speaks plaintively: 'Yet, if it is itself, Daniel Burke, who can help it at all, and let you be getting up into your bed, and not taking your death with the wind blowing on you, and the rain with it, and you in your skin' (30). In this context the simple words: 'Yet if it is itself . . . who can help it at all' are moving. It is as if Nora's realization that we shall all grow old apace and die is so intense, and comprehensive of the implications of this fact, that she is able to catch not a little of the charity of Lear's 'None does offend, none, I say, none; I'll able 'em'. She answers Dan's harshness with concern for his well-being, but he cannot understand her forbearance, her need, or her fear, and in a few moments she is preparing to go with the Tramp. Her final speech shows her grasp of realities, and her awareness that the outcome will, probably, be more harmful for Dan than for her, since she was able to look after his physical needs (he seems to have no others) although he was incapable of cherishing her at all fully.

In most ways the Tramp's nature is opposite to that of Dan. The Tramp, although poor, is much more fully alive; he has 'walked a great way through the world . . . and seen great wonders'; and is appreciative of simple comforts. He is sensitive to the moods of people and of the natural world, and susceptible to feelings, language and rhythms. One might regard him as a kind of natural aristocrat – a far more congenial comrade for Nora than Dan is. The opening pages of *In Wicklow, West Kerry and Connemara* show that this rich portrait is based upon reality:

> wherever the labourer of a country has preserved his vitality, and begets an occasional temperament of distinction, a certain number of vagrants are to be looked for. In the middle classes the gifted son of a family is always the poorest – usually a writer or artist with no sense for speculation – and in a family of peasants, where the average comfort is just over penury, the gifted son sinks also, and is soon a tramp on the roadside.
>
> In this life, however, there are many privileges. The tramp in Ireland is little troubled by the laws, and lives in out-of-door conditions that keep him in good-humour and fine bodily health.

Synge, in depicting the Tramp as a superior being to Dan, is clearly building upon his own experience and observation; and his perception of strong links and resemblances between the position of the writer or artist in middle-class society and the position of the vagrant in a peasant community is seminal in the creation of a character who possesses notable imaginative qualities. Moreover, it is significant that Synge identified himself with the vagrant, and in his love-letters to Molly Allgood usually signed himself as 'Your Old Tramp'.

The tale sets forth an 'eternal' situation – the triangle of Husband, Wife, Lover. The situation in the play is different, somewhat more complex, though, probably, no less fundamental – a tension between differing attitudes to life embodied in sharply contrasted characters: Dan, Nora, the Tramp. Michael is not really an independent force, he is akin to Dan; very similar, maybe, to what Dan was thirty years or so earlier. He shares nothing of the Tramp's understanding of natural forces; he has little of Patch Darcy's skill with animals. Like Dan, he dislikes the Tramp and is jealous of Patch. He makes no attempt to appreciate Nora, and while she is disclosing her deepest fears he devotes himself to counting Dan's money and to planning what he will do with Dan's property. Nora realizes his limitations. She warns him that she is a hard woman to please, and when Michael glibly assumes that they will marry and live happily in the glen, she retorts:

> Why should I marry you, Mike Dara? You'll be getting old and I'll be getting old, and in a little while, I'm telling you, you'll be

sitting up in your bed – the way himself was sitting – with a shake in your face, and your teeth falling, and the white hair sticking out round you like an old bush where sheep do be leaping a gap (27).

The emergence of Dan from beneath his sheet at this moment (like a vision of the Michael of the future) reinforces the connexion between these two men. When Michael and Nora are surprised by Dan, Michael panics: 'Get me out of it, Nora, for the love of God,' and his only response to Nora's mute appeal for help is the suggestion: 'there's a fine Union below in Rathdrum'. From this it follows naturally that after Nora and the Tramp have gone, the play ends with Dan and Michael, kindred souls, sitting quietly together and pledging each other's health with 'a taste of the stuff'; an amazing contrast to the end of the tale.

Thus Synge adds individuality to the figures of the tale. He also gives them a setting in the natural world – a local habitation as well as a name. The personality which Synge has so adroitly fused into the tale (without losing the universality of the original) functions in an environment and is conditioned by it. And it might truly be said that in *The Shadow of the Glen*, as the title implies, one of the most active forces is the surrounding country-side. Here again the shaping power of Synge's mind works upon material provided by his experiences in Wicklow:

Among the cottages that are scattered through the hills of County Wicklow I have met with many people who show in a singular way the influence of a particular locality. These people live for the most part beside old roads and pathways where hardly one man passes in the day, and look out all the year on unbroken barriers of heath. At every season heavy rains fall for often a week at a time, till the thatch drips with water stained to a dull chestnut and the floor in the cottages seems to be going back to the condition of the bogs near it. . . . At such times the people crouch all night over a few sods of turf and the dogs howl in the lanes. . . . This peculiar climate, acting on a population that is already lonely and dwindling, has caused or increased a tendency to nervous depression among the people, and every degree of sadness, from that of the man who is merely mournful to that of the man who has spent half his life in the madhouse, is common among these hills.[159]

The effect of this environment is felt throughout the play. People are obsessed by it. They tell the time by the shadow moving up the glen and the sun sinking in the bog and find in their surroundings images of desolation and decay. A kind of blight hangs over them, a malevolent influence, which affects everyone; 'destroying' Michael, unable to control his sheep, and encouraging Dan to brood upon his suspicions, 'it's always upon the hills he was thinking thoughts in the dark mist' Nora says of him. Even Patch Darcy, reared in the district, and skilful at his trade, is at length driven to madness. Upon Nora and the Tramp this influence is intense, but they react in different ways. Nora has never known any landscape except that which oppresses her. Against its power she has tried to build barriers: a home with Dan; later, friendship with Patch, with others, now with Michael. But all in vain: the marriage is barren in every sense; Patch has gone mad and died; Michael fails her; and, lonely and horrified, she gropes against hostile forces in a seemingly endless gloom.

The Tramp provides the way out. He knows Nature in her many different moods and settings, and through patient and ardent intercourse has achieved a certain harmony with her, in which wonder and awe are mingled with understanding and love. Thus, although the mists and shadow of Nora's glen move him so that 'a little stick would seem as big as your arm, and a rabbit as big as a bay horse, and a stack of turf as big as a towering church in the city of Dublin', there is never the slightest danger of his going the way of Patch Darcy. He represents some of the positive values of the play, and his final words, encouraging Nora to follow with him a way of life that is worthwhile, indicate, at the same time, the desirable relation between Man and Nature:

> We'll be going now, I'm telling you, and the time you'll be feeling the cold, and the frost and the great rain, and the sun again, and the south wind blowing in the glens, you'll not be sitting up on a wet ditch, the way you're after sitting in this place, making yourself old with looking on each day and it passing you by . . . you'll be hearing the herons crying out over the black lakes, and you'll be hearing the grouse and the owls with them, and the larks and the big thrushes when the days are warm; and its not from the like of them you'll be hearing a tale of getting old like Peggy Cavanagh, and losing the hair

off you, and the light of your eyes, but it's fine songs you'll
be hearing when the sun goes up, and there'll be no old fellow
wheezing, the like of a sick sheep, close to your ear (31–2).

Synge's play, then, engages a wider and deeper range of experience than does the tale, which never tries to be more than a good
example of the better kind of 'and then, and then' story. Corkery
recognizes[160] that the main interests of the tale are in curiosity
and swift action: 'Beyond the incident itself folk-lore looks neither
before nor after,' but he will not agree that in the play Synge has
embodied pathos, humour and human interests of a serious kind.
He smiles derisively at W. B. Yeats's description of Nora as the
woman 'of the glens, as melancholy as a curlew, driven to dis-
traction by her own sensitiveness, her own fineness', and tries to
refute it by quoting Nora's reasons for marriage, adding, 'Nora
takes to the road as if she had never indulged the Irish peasant's
dream of stability and comfort.' He forbears, however, to mention her next words which reveal that Nora *has* indulged this
dream (marriage with Dan and a farm) but that it has become a
nightmare; nor does he point to the other passages that set forth
her real predicament. He seems to think that because Nora warns
Michael that she is a 'hard woman' it is inaccurate psychology to
make her also a woman of deep feeling: as if a fine sensibility and
strong imaginative qualities are quite inconsistent with physical
and mental maturity and vigour. Regarding humour Corkery
thinks that the best parts of Synge's drama are those 'which make
the audience laugh the loudest', the parts in which the 'happy-go-
lucky comedy in the folk-tale breaks to the surface'. Those of us
who have difficulty in finding any 'happy-go-lucky comedy' in a
stark tale of a ruse which ends in the slaughter of two human
beings, may call to mind Touchstone's remark in *As You Like It*:
'Thus men may grow wiser every day; it is the first time that ever
I heard breaking of ribs was sport for ladies.' There is, perhaps, a
certain grim humour in the folk-tale, and one admires the ingenuity of the husband, but the comedy and excitement of the
play are all Synge's own invention. The mingled surprise and
humour of Dan's arising from his bed with his mocking reiteration of the Tramp's earlier words, 'a man that's dead can do no
hurt'; the humour of Dan's thirst, his difficulties in feigning death,
and the more subdued humour of his second rising (as Nora is

lamenting the inevitability of old age and Michael is promising her a fine life with a young man) – none of these is so much as hinted at in the folk-tale. Yet Corkery is again clearly wrong in saying that in the play 'There is no passage without its titter or laugh': there are hardly any comic passages except the ones just mentioned, and Synge did not intend any more. Nor is it true to say that the play swings incongruously between comedy and tragedy, that it rocks upon its base: actually it is (as we have seen) a firm and clear embodiment of a tension between two modes of being, and the gradations of mood are the inevitable result of the interplay of human and natural forces. In addition, the inweaving of the sombre and the comic in proportions varying according to the main theme is an important device used by many dramatists (Shakespeare, Tchekov and O'Casey are obvious examples) and in *The Shadow of the Glen* the streaks of comedy aptly and naturally relieve and intensify the seriousness of the whole.

It is now possible to see what Synge has made of his source. To it he has added character: Nora, Dan, Michael, the Tramp, are credible individuals with a life of their own; yet, like most notable characters in imaginative writing, they are also representative of certain enduring features of Man's nature and condition. Local human intensity has been gained without the sacrifice of the universality of the tale. Along with this has come the creation of an environment, producing a fresh theme (the interaction between Man and the natural world) which is blended with the main theme. The crude passion and violence of the tale have been replaced by more complex and subtle issues of human relationships. Thus the original theme has been extended in every dimension, and a play of considerable worth created. In it a singular power in the use of words and a mastery of dramatic technique are applied to fuse into a new whole a number of disparate elements: Pat's story; Synge's experiences in Wicklow and Aran; Synge's preoccupation with what he felt was a deep-rooted tension between material security and a free, full imaginative life; and his keen awareness of the transience of youth and beauty. In this distinctive use of material drawn from Irish life and legend, in these methods, in these interests and attitudes, and in this imaginative synthesis, *The Shadow of the Glen* is typical of all Synge's dramatic work: elements similar to these indicated here are central in each of his five other plays.

The Tinker's Wedding

The Tinker's Wedding is usually regarded as the poorest of Synge's plays. It has never been professionally produced in Ireland and amateurs there have put it on only once or twice. Some critics ignore it or give it a derisive dig in passing. A few find patches of merit and promise in it, and one thinks it good. But none of them devotes more than a paragraph or two to the play, and, apart from Denis Donoghue's sensible article on it, there is no piece of criticism which attempts seriously to examine and evaluate the play, and to relate it to the rest of Synge's achievement. It is not as if *The Tinker's Wedding* was a piece of beginner's work, lightly tossed off by the dramatist, and then neglected. There is good evidence to suppose that *The Tinker's Wedding* was the first play Synge wrote, but it is a fact that he returned to the play several times between 1903 and 1906, and that he made some alterations to it after *The Playboy of the Western World* was produced. Nor did he continue to work upon it merely in the hope that he might make some money by polishing it up for public performance. There was never the remotest chance of its being put on the Abbey stage, and the first production of it, in London, did not take place until after Synge's death. Synge was a fastidious writer and a severe critic of his own work, and it is hardly likely that he would have devoted precious time and energy (for he knew that death was not far distant) during the most creative part of his life to work that was clearly below his normal standard. Moreover he allowed the play to be printed in January 1908 during his lifetime, and he left no instructions to keep it out of any complete edition of his works. Since the play has Synge's approval there is at least a case for giving it fuller consideration than it has yet had.

The Tinker's Wedding may be seen as an embodiment of a tension between two ways of life, between a cautious, respectable, more settled way of life and an unrestrained materially insecure way allowing scope for passion and imagination. Normally these two social groups live side by side, and in the play the tension is caused by the desire of the young tinker woman, Sarah Casey, to reject one important custom of her kind and to take on in its place a custom from the alien way of life. The play is, in fact, another variation of the theme of dream versus actuality, and it is a fairly exact complement to *The Shadow of the Glen*.

In both plays a woman is dissatisfied with her condition and tries to change it. In Nora this urge comes from the core of her personality, but in Sarah it is a whim. Nora's dream has become a nightmare, actuality has gone bad on her. She tries to get away, and eventually she goes off with the Tramp, hoping to turn his dream of a fuller life together into a new actuality which will be, at least, better and much more suited to her nature than anything she has known previously. Nora's discontent and longings are very real, arising from her inimical husband and environment; they, together with the vision set forth by the Tramp, are the dreams which may lead to the right actuality for her. Impelled by her deepest instincts, aided by the Tramp, she moves from a condition which has become unbearable to one which will be, at least, tolerable, and which may be happy.

Sarah is a complete contrast to Nora. Sarah's environment is wholesome; the best actuality for her is with Michael and Mary, and her dream of a respectable marriage is a chimera. From the beginning of the play it is made clear that Sarah, along with Michael and Mary, is really thriving and enjoying life on the whole. She has been living contentedly for some years with Michael, and has borne him children. She is in good physical condition and is still an attractive woman. There are other tinkers, such as Jaunting Jimmy, wealthier than Michael, who would like to have Sarah for a mate; and Michael is quickly alarmed when she threatens to leave him. Even her 'mother-in-law', Mary, says she is 'a grand handsome woman, the glory of tinkers, the Beauty of Ballinacree'. Accordingly, Michael and Mary are astonished at Sarah's sudden desire to get married, and even the Priest thinks she is queer. Sarah's haste to get the marriage over before anyone knows of it shows that she is aware that she is doing something that people of her kind would consider strange and unnatural; and she admits it is a whim: 'the spring-time is a queer time, and it's queer thoughts maybe I do think at whiles'. She says she wants to be married so that no one will be able justly to call her 'a dirty name', but she seems to have been more or less happy for years without worrying about such insults, and in any case all the people of her kind are not married, and she clearly despises the respectable people, the ones who might call her the dirty name. Her longings are the caprices of a well-nourished person; Nora's longings arise from the starvation of something vital. Nora, at the end, sets out towards a new and better condition; Sarah, at the end, returns to her rightful condition after a momentary aberration. In accordance with these features the predominant mood of *The Tinker's Wedding* is happy and sunny, sharpened by touches of pathos and melancholy, whereas that of *The Shadow of the Glen* is sombre, relieved by flashes of comedy; and the natural world seems to be in tune with Sarah and the tinkers, but not with Nora.

Some of the most vehement objections to *The Tinker's Wedding* centre on the character of the Priest. These (so far as they attain coherence) would seem to add up to the belief that although in real life a few priests may have characters as unpleasant as, or worse than, that of the Priest, Synge has made a grave moral and artistic error in putting such a figure on the stage. The artistic flaws in *The Tinker's Wedding* are never demonstrated; it seems to be assumed that once moral flaws in Synge's action have been alleged, and proved to the accuser's satisfaction, either artistic flaws must inevitably follow, or else, being condemned on moral grounds, the play deserves no further consideration. Now, it should be possible, without attacking anyone, to try to extend to Synge the same tolerance that he extended to those people with whose views he disagreed. Synge seems to have had little liking for institutional religion, either that of the church his fathers served in, the Church of Ireland, or that of the Church of Rome, but his writings were usually devoid of partisanship. He praises the clergy on several occasions, and he seems to have been on good terms with the curate of the Aran Islands. Synge's attitude to the Church was probably more a Continental one than a modern Irish one, and it is clearly ridiculous to take the Priest in *The Tinker's Wedding* as Synge's considered judgement about the leaders of the majority of his fellow-countrymen. The issue is blurred further by an undue simplification, by seeing the play, as Bourgeois and others do, as a simple representation of the conflict between the Christian and the Pagan elements in the Irish character. Bourgeois, however, is clear-sighted enough to see that this simple antithesis will not do; he finds that it remains incongruous, and he asks two questions: 'Is not the Priest in the play himself a Pagan?' and 'On the other hand, why should the Priest's maledictions frighten the Tinkers if they are really Pagans?' [161] He does not try to answer these questions; but an attempt at answering them must now be made.

The Christian and Pagan elements in the character of any nation or person do not exist in isolated compartments; the one element has influence, more or less, on the other; two ways of life, existing side by side for a long time, are bound to tinge each other a little. Thus, we see, the Priest is not a Christian, but we see also, comparing him to Mary, he is not a Pagan; he is something in between, inferior in important respects to both Christian and Pagan. The Priest is unlikable, not because he is a priest, but because he is not a true priest. He has officially renounced his Pagan instincts but he has not acquired the Christian virtues. He still has the old Pagan craving for the enjoyments of the flesh, but when he tries to satisfy this his pleasure is spoiled by the sense that he is sinning.

On the other hand the Tinkers are essentially Pagan. They have not been influenced in any material way by the Church; they are normally content with their own habits and beliefs, and they try to avoid contact with organized religion, particularly as they find it firmly allied with civil law and power. But they have not been able to avoid acquiring a superficial smattering of religion, as their speech shows, and it is the desire of one of them to adopt an alien religious custom that precipitates the clash. They are occasionally curious about religion, they fear it sometimes, and so, as they are also superstitious, the Priest's maledictions at the end cause them to run, for two good reasons: they naturally fear that his loud curses will bring someone to his aid; this uproar in Latin startles them, they think it may do them harm, and so they run off, just to be on the safe side.

Thus the tension in *The Tinker's Wedding* is between, on one side, a more settled and respectable society which has lost its innocence and sense of enjoyment in life through awareness of sin but which has not attained Grace, a society only nominally Christian; and, on the other side, a Pagan community, thrown off its balance by the transitory delusion of one of its members.

The Priest is fond of pleasure, of passing the night with the doctor, 'playing cards, or drinking a sup, or singing songs, until the dawn of day', but he seems to get no real enjoyment out of these activities. They are spoiled by the feeling that he is doing wrong; and he is constantly beset by fears that he will be tricked by someone, or that his bishop will find out about his habits. Enjoyment has become equated in his mind with sin, and the evident huge delight in life which emanates from Mary seems to him proof that she is 'an old flagrant heathen'; his retort to her sympathetic attempt to cheer him up after his complaints of the hardship of his lot is: 'What is it I want with your songs when it'd be better for the like of you, that'll soon die, to be down on your two knees, saying prayers to the Almighty God' (73). With little understanding of human nature and lacking understanding of the spirit, he tends to lay undue stress on matters of form; he is easily shocked by any breach of orthodox ceremony and is scandalized by Mary's admission that she has never heard a prayer. He seems to think that the mere performance of some ritual is enough, and he agrees to marry Sarah only in order to prevent her from becoming a heathen like Mary. At the end he keeps his word not to inform on the tinkers but breaks the spirit of it: 'I've sworn not to call the hand of man upon your crimes today; but I haven't sworn I wouldn't call the fire of heaven from the hand of Almighty God' (98). The scuffle is really his responsibility since he loses his temper, becomes insulting and provokes Sarah to inveigh against him. Finally, when his unjust accusations and threats have moved the subdued Michael to action, he strikes the first blow, even though he believes that he himself is divinely protected from harm. And it is not until he loses his nerve and runs calling for the police that the tinkers in mere self-defence (since the Priest's word would be believed before theirs) begin to overpower him. Yet unsympathetic as his character is, he is not a monster; he is touched at Sarah's distress when she learns that the marriage-fee is one pound, and he knocks the price down to ten shillings and the tin can; and next morning his caution, if not his generosity, induces him to offer them one shilling in an attempt to persuade them to release him from his promise to perform the marriage ceremony. This portrait of the Priest is the credible one of the man who has taken on a vocation for which he is not suited, who has become ashamed of his natural instincts and senses but has not been able to repress or sublimate them. He senses faintly that his religion should give him solace and insight, but he has not progressed far enough in it to experience that spiritual communion and delight which, presumably, compensate immeasurably for any renunciation of the joys of this world.

In complete contrast and opposition to the Priest is Mary. There is no trace of her in Synge's source; like the Tramp in *The Shadow of the Glen* she is wholly Synge's invention and is the most important character in the play, the one through whom Synge gives his singular and significant twist to the theme and links it firmly with the one theme of all his writings. Mary's first entry immediately marks her as the natural opponent of the Priest; she sings the ballad, 'The Night Before Larry Was Stretched'. Larry seems to be some kind of hero to the tinkers, he has the qualities they admire; passion and courage; a resolve to enjoy life to the last; loyalty to his kind and affection for his doxy; and a refusal to compromise his pagan principles. Larry is a symbol of those pagan forces which are directly opposed to the civil and religious powers which put him to death and which harry the tinkers. There is much of Larry in Mary, and it is significant that she is given these lines from the ballad to sing:

> *And when they asked him what way he'd die,*
> *And he hanging unrepented,*
> *'Begob,' says Larry, 'that's all in my eye,*
> *By the clergy first invented.'*

This is an amusing and ironic expression of the tinker's view on marriage. The tinkers have their own customs and are able to live (as Larry was able to die) without the offices of the Church which (they think) were only created for the benefit of the Church; as is illustrated by the way the Priest bargains to get money for the marriage ceremony. Nevertheless Mary, who knows nothing of the preparations for the marriage, is friendly and respectful towards the Priest. She too has been enjoying herself, but unlike him she is in a happy state of mind. Drink and pleasure only make the Priest sour and more sorry for himself, whereas they increase Mary's natural geniality. She has an immense and unperverted delight in life, and she never doubts that happiness here and now is the natural and desirable condition of humanity. All her senses are fully alert; she has an appreciative eye for the bits of finery with which Sarah is tricking out Michael and herself; and she revels in the natural world:

I having a great sleep in the sun . . . but if sleep's a grand thing, it's a grand thing to be waking up a day the like of this, when there's a warm sun in it, and a kind air, and you'll hear the cuckoos singing and crying out on the top of the hills (81).

Her imagination is vigorous and capable of seeing likenesses between the queens of legend and Sarah: 'I've a grand story of the great queens of Ireland; with white necks on them the like of Sarah Casey, and fine arms would hit you a slap the way Sarah Casey would hit you' (77). And far from being jealous of her 'daughter-in-law's' youth and beauty, she is very appreciative of it:

> you're a grand handsome woman, the glory of tinkers, the pride of Wicklow, the Beauty of Ballinacree . . . let you sit down there by the big bough, and I'll be telling you the finest story you'd hear any place from Dundalk to Ballinacree, with great queens in it, making themselves matches from the start to the end, and they with shiny silks on them the length of the day, and white shifts for the night . . . a story would be fit to tell a woman the like of you in the spring-time of the year (76).

Along with this wholesome opulence goes a fine sensitivity to mood and atmosphere and a keen awareness of the transience of beauty and joy; she knows, if no one else in the play does, that in 'the very temple of delight Veil'd Melancholy has her sovran shrine'. In addition to giving the distinctive life and richness to the play, and contributing much of the abounding fun and comedy, she draws through it that slender thread of sweet sadness which makes the joy more precious:

> What good am I this night, God help me? What good are the grand stories I have when its few would listen to an old woman, few but a girl maybe would be in great fear the time her hour was come, or the little child wouldn't be sleeping with the hunger on a cold night? (*She takes the can from the sacking, and fits three empty bottles and straw in its place, and ties them up.*) Maybe the two of them have a good right to be walking out the little short while they'd be young; but if they have itself, they'll not keep Mary Byrne from her full pint when the night's fine, and there's a dry moon in the sky. (*She takes up the can, and puts the package back in the ditch.*) Jemmy Neill's a decent lad; and he'll give me a good drop for the can; and maybe if I keep near the peelers tomorrow for the first bit of the fair, herself

won't strike me at all; and if she does itself, what's a little
stroke on your head beside sitting lonesome on a fine night,
hearing the dogs barking, and the bats squeaking, and you saying
over, it's a short while only till you die. (*She goes out singing 'The
night before Larry was stretched'*.) (78)

This sombre streak must be used very skilfully, it could easily
wreck a comedy; but here it is exquisite. Mary has just been re-
minded by both the Priest and Sarah that she is 'an old drinking
heathen' who will soon be dead, and she suddenly feels lonely. The
Priest, she assumes, has the comfort of his religion and his private
pleasures; Sarah and Michael are young and have each other; and
so why should she be left out? She too needs some joy and comfort, she is entitled to a drink, and she determines to have what
she can. The passage provides that touch of pathos which high-
lights by contrast the predominant happiness of Mary's character,
making her a fuller and more human dramatic figure; and it
motivates her theft of the can in such a way that we feel she has
some cause for taking it, particularly as she does not envy the
happiness of the others, but merely wants her own share.

Unlike the Priest she is generous and free from hypocrisy. She
welcomes the Priest to their fire, persuades him to share their
porter, listens sympathetically to his recital of the hardships of his
life, and tries to cheer him up. Nor does his rude retort that she
should fall to her prayers upset her. She points out with simple
dignity that it is, apparently, the Priest's job to say prayers; for
the tinkers 'don't have them at all'; then she too, like Sarah, has
her queer wish: to hear the Priest pray, 'a scholar, speaking Latin
to the Saints above'. But he cannot oblige; instead he declares that
he has never met her like for 'hard abominations'. Mary's innocent reply to this: 'Is that the truth?' adroitly emphasizes the gap
between the tinkers and the Priest. What is sin to him is rightful
pleasure to them; yet he judges them by standards which they
neither understand nor acknowledge. Mary, on the other hand, is
slow to condemn, she feels that they must bear with each other:
'Let you not be shy of us, your reverence. Aren't we all sinners,
God help us! Drink a sup now, I'm telling you; and we won't let
on a word about it till the Judgement Day' (71). Her charity is
constant, and she is the only character never to become angry;
even at the end she keeps her good humour, and she is 'sick and

sorry' to tease the Priest. She restrains Sarah and Michael: 'Let you not be rough with him, and he after drinking his sup of porter with us at the fall of night,' and she it is who finds a peaceful solution with the suggestion that the Priest should swear an oath not to inform against them.

Along with a deep knowledge of human nature and a degree of innocent self-awareness – the opposite of brooding and self-pity – she has a comprehensive understanding of the nature and traditions of her kind. As soon as Sarah tells her of the proposed marriage, and Michael says he has agreed to go through with it to prevent Sarah leaving him, Mary goes straight to the heart of the matter: 'And you're thinking it's paying gold to his reverence would make a woman stop when she's a mind to go?' (86). And when Sarah retorts that she has 'as good a right to a decent marriage as any speckled female does be sleeping in the black hovels above, would choke a mule' (86), Mary replies soothingly and perceptively:

> It's as good a right you have, surely, Sarah Casey, but what good will it do? Is it putting a ring on your finger will keep you from getting an aged woman and losing the fine face you have, or be easing your pains; when it's the grand ladies do be married in silk dresses, with rings of gold, that do pass any woman with their share of torment in the hour of birth, and do be paying the doctors in the city of Dublin a great price at that time, the like of what you'd pay for a good ass and a cart? (86).

Mary knows that without the spirit, the letter gives no life; that beneath all ceremony and form there is a basic kinship between all human beings; and that certain actualities must be faced against which sophistication is of no avail. Mary here speaks with a traditional wisdom which is valid, at least for the tinkers, as Sarah, much against her will, has to admit. Mary's insight has been gained by close and sympathetic contact with many people in differing circumstances:

> If you do be drinking a little sup in one town and another town, it's soon you get great knowledge and a great sight into the world. You'll see men there, and women there, sitting up on the ends of barrels in the dark night, and they making great talk would soon have the like of you, Sarah Casey, as wise as a March hare (87).

In contrast to the Priest, who is quick to condemn any action which fails to toe the party line of his orthodoxy, Mary does not assail the Priest's traditions and values, nor does she deny that these may be as precious for the Priest and his followers as their own are for the tinkers. She feels (and here she is expressing one of Synge's deepest convictions) that misunderstanding and tension arise when an attempt is made to impose alien standards and habits upon a living tradition; the main requisite is mutual toleration. This point, the core of the play, is well made by Mary at the end, as she addresses the Priest tied in the sack:

> Be quiet your reverence. What is it ails you, with your wrigglings now? Is it choking maybe? It's only letting on you are, holy father, for your nose is blowing back and forward as easy as an east wind on an April day. There now, holy father, let you stay easy, I'm telling you, and learn a little sense and patience, the way you'll not be so airy again to rob poor sinners of their scraps of gold. That's a good boy now, your reverence, and let you not be uneasy, for we wouldn't hurt you at all. It's sick and sorry we are to tease you; but what did you want meddling with the like of us, when it's a long time we are going our own ways, and it's little need we ever had of going up into a church and swearing – I'm told there's swearing with it – a word no man would believe, or with drawing rings on our fingers would be cutting our skins maybe when we'd be taking the ass from the shafts the time they'd be slippy with going round beneath the heavens in rains falling . . . it's little need we ever had of the like of you to get us our bit to eat, and our bit to drink, and our time of love when we were young men and women, and were fine to look at (95–7).

The wedding-ring is a further example of Synge's genius in investing a simple object with dramatic power. The ring is a symbol, a concrete representation of the undesirability of the Priest's customs for the tinkers. At the beginning of the play Michael is making the ring very unwillingly, and Sarah hopes that she will be married with it; but, as Mary points out, and as Sarah at last understands, the ring, both as an object and as a symbol, is completely unsuitable. Accordingly, Sarah, at the end, puts it on the Priest's finger to remind him of his vow not to inform on them. And how excellent this ending is, in its concise, amusing, and

dramatic summary of all that has gone before. The Priest's characteristic guile which sends the tinkers scampering off; Mary's cry,
as if in admiration of his cunning: 'There's an old villain'; and the
Priest's malediction, typical of authority's habit of casting into
outer darkness what is 'superb and wild in reality'; all these coming
together contrast, for the last time, the shifty self-interest of the
Priest with the ingenuous relish for life of the tinkers.

Synge in his 'A Letter to a Young Man' [162] compliments him
on seeing

> what it seems so impossible to get our Dublin people to see,
> obvious as it is – that the wildness, and if you will, vices of the
> Irish peasantry are due, like their extraordinary good points of
> all kinds, to the *richness* of their nature – a thing that is priceless
> beyond words.

Synge feared that the distinctive qualities and traditions of the
wandering country folk would be lost if they were exposed to
misdirected (though, perhaps, well-meaning) attempts to make
them conform to the standards of the majority of more settled
and respectable people. As always, he asked for humility and
generosity, for, as he says in *The Aran Islands*,[163] after a description of some evictions and an account of the islanders' singular
(and enlightened) attitudes to crime and punishment: 'It seems
absurd to apply the same laws to these people and to the criminal
classes of a city.' *The Tinker's Wedding* is a successful presentation,
in terms of exhilarating comedy, of these considerations, and,
consequently, an integral part of Synge's work.

CHAPTER SIX

Longer Plays

The Well of the Saints

*T*he Well of the Saints, perhaps Synge's most profound and sombre work, is related closely to that kind of play – so far without a name – of which *The Wild Duck* and *The Three Sisters* are examples: the kind that, barely tickled by the comic spirit and mainly unpurged by purely tragic exaltation, deals searchingly with serious issues, and, unblurred by morbidity, reflects, with some compassion, a melancholy vision of the human condition.

Synge's own view of human life appears to have been a melancholy one. He felt that although everyday existence might be, for most people, tolerable, and even happy at times, life in this universe, stripped of all its comforting camouflage, was in essence meaningless: Man's aspirations, his ideas of love, goodness, beauty, vital though they may be for a few years, all find alike the inevitable end; and beyond the grave there is nothing. Consequently, the few people that see life clearly and see it whole are faced with a ghastly spectacle; one which is spared to the vast majority, who, lacking this insight, are accordingly more or less content and find life well worth living. Keats too was aware of this: 'Health and spirits can only belong unalloyed to the selfish Man – the Man who thinks much of his fellows can never be in Spirits . . . lord, a man should have the fine point of his soul taken off to become fit for this world.' One of the great problems for the artist with this outlook is to secure and retain the incentives and attitudes making for a purposeful and not unhappy life, without blunting the fine edge, and without ignoring what he apprehends as actuality, intolerably harsh though he feels that actuality to be. And here, as the life and work of men such as Keats and Synge demonstrates, the imagination is of supreme value.

The Well of the Saints is compounded of materials similar to

those used in all Synge's other plays, and Synge's methods of
synthesis here resemble those he normally adopted. His plot is
again a characteristic variation or transformation of a fable, versions of which have been found in different literatures and centuries. He draws upon his experience of Irish peasant life and upon
his knowledge of folk-lore, without overlooking the experience
and knowledge he has gained in other fields. The intensity of the
local instance is charged with a wider significance, and characters
are projected both as credible individuals and as representative
of certain human traits and attitudes. The theme of the play too is
the theme that is central in all Synge's work – the tension between
dream and actuality; and *The Well of the Saints* in combining four
versions of this theme, each different yet complementary, provides the fullest and most direct treatment of it. The theme is
considered in relation to Mary Doul, to Martin Doul, to the villagers, and to the Saint; for all, whether they know it or not, have
the same problem, and need, in their varying ways, 'to construct
something upon which to rejoice'.

The theme-variation revolving round Mary Doul is the sim-
plest and most easily recognized one. It is in the beginning similar
to that of her husband, Martin, and the opening of the play
demonstrates that life for both of them is, on the whole, interesting and agreeable. Beneath their bickering are fast bonds of
affection, mutual need, and identity of purpose and belief. They
do not complain of their affliction; their other senses are keenly
alert and they enjoy the natural world a good deal; they are
united in the face of the rest of mankind, 'for the seeing is a queer
lot', and yet, because they do a little work and are deserving of
charity, they have a recognized place in the community. They are
known as 'the people is happy and blind', and Timmy the smith
tells the Saint:

> they do be always sitting here at the crossing of the roads, ask-
> ing a bit of copper from them that do pass, or stripping rushes
> for lights, and they not mournful at all, but talking out straight
> with a full voice, and making game with them that likes it
> (116–17).

Their chief joy, however, the main source of their self-respect,
is derived from the belief, fostered by the villagers, that they are
a distinguished couple; that Mary, known as 'the beautiful

woman of Ballinatone' with 'her yellow hair, white skin, and big
eyes is a wonder surely', and that Martin is 'a grand handsome
fellow'. Mary, who never doubts, is the more content; and she
believes the dream so absolutely that Molly Byrne's malicious
hints about the truth are refuted with complacency:

> Molly Byrne was jealous, God forgive her, because Timmy the
> smith was after praising my hair . . . the young and silly do be
> always making game of them that's dark, and they'd think it a
> fine thing if they had us deceived, the way we wouldn't know
> we were so fine-looking at all (103).

Martin, on the other hand, though normally satisfied with the
dream and with his lot, is occasionally harassed by doubt; and to
banish this he desires sight:

> I do be thinking in the long nights it'd be a grand thing if we
> could see ourselves for one hour, or a minute itself, the way
> we'd know surely we were the finest man and the finest woman
> of the seven counties of the east . . . and then the seeing rabble
> below might be destroying their souls telling bad lies, and we'd
> never heed a thing they'd say (103).

In addition, his fancy sometimes plays with a notion of the wonder of human existence, of 'the big women and the young girls,
and all the fine things is walking the world', but this does not
agitate him until the prospect of sight is suddenly offered.

Thus in the first ten minutes of the play Synge, swiftly and
economically, creates a situation in which two people owe their
comparative happiness mainly to their acceptance of a belief
which everyone except themselves knows is not based on the
facts.

Their contentment vanishes instantly when they hear that 'A
fine holy man, a saint of the Almighty God' is coming to cure
their blindness, and they are filled with an overwhelmingly acute
desire for sight. Excitement and hope are increased by the ritual-
like entry of the villagers preparing the approach of the Saint, and
by his appearance. A peak is reached when the blind receive sight
and see the world for the first time since childhood; for a few
fleeting moments they experience the most intense wonder and
delight. Martin is the more demonstrative;

That's Timmy, I know Timmy by the black of his head. . . .
That's Mat Simon, I know Mat by the length of his legs. That
should be Patch Ruadh, with the gamey eyes in him, and the
fiery hair. (*He sees Molly Byrne on Mary Doul's seat, and his voice
changes completely.*) Oh, it was no lie they told me, Mary Doul.
Oh, Glory to God and the seven saints I didn't die and not see
you at all. The blessing of God on the water, and the feet carried it round through the land. The blessing of God on this
day, and them that have brought me the Saint, for its grand
hair you have and soft skin, and eyes would make the saints, if
they were dark awhile, and seeing again, fall down out of the
sky. Hold up your head, Mary, the way I'll see it's richer I am
than the great kings of the east. Hold up your head I'm saying,
for it's soon you'll be seeing me, and I not a bad one at all (121).

What power and irony are here: the culmination of Martin's happiness is at the same time the culmination of his delusion; his
fervent thanksgiving and admiration are soon to turn to bitter
recrimination and curses when the truth becomes known and he
realizes that far from being richer than the great kings of the east
he is poorer than he ever was. The fall from the height of ecstasy
expressed in this speech is shocking, but Synge, with the ruthlessness of the great artist, spares no one: the process of disillusionment is carried through with exactness and speed. There is
pathos in the contrast between Martin's ardent praise and the fact
that he is addressing Molly not Mary, and this pathos increases
as Martin moves around trying to see his dream realized in the
flesh. As each of the three girls in turn scornfully rejects him, fear
and anger grow, until, enraged by the jeers of the villagers, he
bursts out:

Where is it you have hidden her away? Isn't it a black shame for
a drove of pitiful beasts the like of you to be making game of
me, and putting a fool's head on me the grand day of my life?
Ah, you're thinking you're a fine lot, with your giggling, weep-
ing eyes, a fine lot to be making game of myself and the woman
I've heard called the great wonder of the west (123).

Towards the end of this speech 'the great wonder of the west'
herself enters – a hag cured of blindness, asking complacently,
'Which of you is Martin Doul?' Martin wheels round, and for the

first time in their lives the two see each other. This superb
dramatic climax, skilfully prepared for by all that has gone before
– the initial contentment, the sudden excitement, the surging
hope, the passion – is, by contrast, a moment of complete silence
and stillness. Martin and Mary see actuality, and are frozen with
horror. At length the terrible quiet of disillusion is broken by the
taunts of the vindictive Molly, who finds much enjoyment in
driving home the shattering facts:

> MOLLY (*To Martin Doul.*) Go up now and take her under the chin
> and be speaking the way you spoke to myself.
> MARTIN (*In a low voice with intensity.*) If I speak now, I'll speak
> hard to the two of you. . . .
> MOLLY (*To Mary Doul.*) You're not saying a word, Mary. What
> is it you think of himself, with the fat legs on him, and the
> little neck like a ram? (123–4).

At this the blind give vent to their agony in vehement denunciation of each other; Martin's passion finding apt and forceful expression in his rhythms and images which contrast well with the
shorter, reiterated phrases of Mary:

> MARY: If I'm not so fine as some of them said, I have my hair,
> and big eyes, and my white skin.
> MARTIN: Your hair and your big eyes is it? . . . I'm telling you
> there isn't a wisp on any grey mare on the ridge of the world
> isn't finer than the dirty twist on your head. There isn't two
> eyes in any starving sow isn't finer than the eyes you were
> calling blue like the sea.
> MARY: It's the devil cured you this day with your talking of
> sows; it's the devil cured you this day, I'm saying, and drove
> you crazy with lies (124).

Their disillusionment is so strong that it forces them into an
opposite error. It makes them see each other as worse than they
really are, and causes them to charge each other with the creation
of an illusion for which, actually, the villagers have been chiefly
responsible. The peak of their torment follows Martin's unconsciously ironic and prophetic words (which hint that the two will
be blind again, and will welcome blindness):

Go on now to be seeking a lonesome place where the earth can

hide you away; go on now, I'm saying, or you'll be having men
and women with their knees bled, and they screaming to God
for a holy water would darken their sight, for there's no man
but would liefer be blind a hundred years or a thousand itself,
than to be looking on your like (125).

By this time they are speechless, so intense is their anguish and
frustration, and they try to find relief in crude attempts to brain
each other. Already naked actuality is having an unwholesome
effect upon them. The Saint, however, intervenes and they are
parted. He gives the shuddering couple his advice and blessing,
and so brings the act to a quiet close. But it is the quiet of utter
disappointment and exhaustion. For Martin and Mary the blessing
of sight has quickly proved a curse; actuality has destroyed the
comforting fiction which made life much more than bearable, and
it has given them nothing but ugliness and brutality in exchange.
The end of Act One sees them completely disillusioned about each
other. But, for Martin, this, although the most immediate, was not
the only illusion; he still retains one.

Act Two carries the process of disillusion to the limit, and
accordingly Mary plays only a minor part in it. For her disillusion
was complete when she found that she was very far from beautiful, and that Martin was 'a little, old, shabby stump of a man'.
Her life and her dream had been centred solely on herself and her
husband and she had never been concerned with much else.
When blind she had done little in the way of piecing together
notions or dreams about the world or its people, nor when she
has sight does she bother herself about what is going on around
her except where it affects her or Martin with obvious directness.
This is in keeping with her self-sufficient character, and with her
nature as a woman, since apparently the generality of women tend
inevitably to be somewhat more passive and restricted in outlook
than men. Further psychological accuracy can be seen in the way
in which, shortly after one dream has disintegrated, Mary begins
to build up another; so powerful is the natural defence mechanism
fostering beliefs (whether true or false) encouraging a human being
to go on living. Thus, by the end of Act Two, Mary is well on the
way towards inducing a mental condition that will give her comfort and strength; by means of a verbal lashing, which Molly lacks
the resources of language to answer, she gains for herself some

kind of revenge, and a feeling of renewed power and self-satisfaction:

> When the skin shrinks on your chin, Molly Byrne, there won't
> be the like of you for a shrunk hag in the four quarters of
> Ireland. . . . It's them that's fat and flabby do be wrinkled
> young, and that whitish yellowy hair she has does be soon
> turning the like of a handful of thin grass you'd see rotting, at
> the north of a sty. . . . Ah, it's better to have a simple, seemly
> face, the like of my face, for twoscore years, or fifty itself, than
> to be setting fools mad a short while, and then to be turning a
> thing would drive off the little children from your feet (143).

In this ability to ride out a disaster by stifling part of one's sensibility, by ignoring the unpleasant features of the human predicament as much as possible, and by finding or manufacturing something that will make life worth living, Mary is representative of those of us (the majority, I suppose) who are (perhaps unavoidably) limited in our interests and sympathies.

Martin, on the other hand, is different; he has the temperament and the imagination of the artist. This is, properly, not very obvious in Act One where he is linked closely in most ways with Mary. But even here indications of it can be discerned in his marked sensuousness, his delight in words, his sensitivity to moods and surroundings, and his imaginings about the world. The tumult of events and emotions outside the church and the scalding shock of disillusionment rapidly bring the whole soul of Martin into increased activity. His poetic faculties quickly bloom and approach maturity, so that the beggar with all his five senses now fresh and keen is in the position of a poet, with kindling eye in a fine frenzy rolling over all the mighty world of eye and ear. If Act One presents, among other things, an image in terms of peasant life of the awakening of the artist to actuality and the simultaneous shattering of his most familiar and clearly formed dream, Act Two similarly presents the artist anatomizing this actuality, and bringing his other dream, not so completely formed, but wider, mysterious, and quite as precious, to the test of fact.

From the beginning of Act Two it is clear that, in contrast to his position when blind, Martin with sight can find no place in the community. He has little heart or ability to do the odd jobs which

Timmy gives him, and he is continually being charged with laziness and subjected to economic pressure. Traces of bitterness and self-pity are noticeable in his speech and manner. He shows signs of becoming dissatisfied with sight, and the old days of blindness begin to acquire an attractive glow: 'It's more I got a while since, and I sitting blinded in Grianan, than I get in this place, working hard, and destroying myself, the length of the day' (129). He is able to see imperfections with a clarity unattainable by men like Timmy whose perceptions have been dulled by routine; around him there is nothing to wonder at or admire, and the unloveliness of Man and the drabness of the natural world oppress him and disillusion him further:

> For it's a raw beastly day we do have each day, till I do be thinking it's well for the blind don't be seeing them grey clouds driving on the hill, and don't be looking on people with their noses red, the like of your nose, and their eyes weeping and watering, the like of your eyes, God help you, Timmy the smith. . . . It's a hard thing for a man to have his sight, and he living near to the like of you, and if it's a dark day itself it's too well I see every wicked wrinkle round by your eye (130–1).

Timmy's reply to this is interesting:

> It's a queer thing the way yourself and Mary Doul are after setting every person in this place talking of nothing, thinking of nothing, but the way they do be looking in the face. It's the devil's work you're after doing with your talk of fine looks (135).

Devil's work or not, Martin's work in Act Two resembles the work of the artist. Martin with his newly-found sight has the unusual ability to see and feel freshly; his senses and responses have the unique penetration and immediacy of one just awakened to the world. Yeats says: 'The imaginative writer shows us the world . . . not as it seems to eyes habit has made dull, but as we were Adam and this the first morning.' [164] Martin apprehends the world thus; and he acts upon his society in the same way as an artist acts upon our society. Both Martin and the artist have an intensity and comprehensiveness of perception and vision lacking in other men, and both have also the technical skills to give these perceptions and visions coherence and significance. They both

try to remove the veil created by comforting illusions and pre-
judices, which tends to hide some aspects of the truth about human existence, and both try to make Man more adequately aware
of himself, to help him feel the power and the terror, the glory and
the boredom. As Coleridge says,[165] the prime function of the poet
is the

> awakening the mind's attention to the lethargy of custom, and
> directing it to the loveliness and the wonders of the world
> before us; an inexhaustible treasure, but for which, in conse-
> quence of the film of familiarity and selfish solicitude, we have
> eyes, yet see not, ears that hear not, and hearts that neither feel
> nor understand.

So far Martin has seen nothing of the loveliness and wonder of the
world, his surroundings are quite unlike the Garden of Eden, and
he is deeply disappointed with the natural world; consequently he
has been able to give expression only to the hideous aspects of life.
But now an Eve appears; he is alone with Molly, and, he believes,
very close to the essence of all the beauty and delight in the world.
When blind he had been much attracted by the notion of Molly:

> She's a sweet, beautiful voice you'd never tire to be hearing, if
> it was only the pig she'd be calling, or crying out in the long
> grass, maybe, after her hens. It should be a fine, soft, rounded
> woman, I'm thinking, would have a voice the like of that
> (104).

He knew her voice and the sound of her movements exactly, and
from these notions and impressions and from the villagers' gos-
sip he had built up an image of her. The sight of her by the
church had not in any way destroyed this image; nor had her
cruelty, Martin's mind then being oblivious of all else but hatred
of Mary. So now, as Molly lingers there, coolly conscious that she
fascinates, she appears to Martin to symbolize, and to contain
within herself, all that is lovely and desirable in the world. His
mood changes as he speaks to her:

> It's a power of dirty days, and dark mornings, and shabby-
> looking fellows we do have to be looking on when we have
> our sight, God help us, but there's one fine thing we have, to be
> looking on a grand, white, handsome girl, the like of you . . .
> and every time I set my eyes on you I do be blessing the saints,

and the holy water, and the power of the Lord Almighty in the heavens above (136).

Molly's pert rejoinder: 'I've heard the priests say it isn't looking on a young girl would teach many to be saying their prayers,' does not deter him from recalling the great joy and pride he had hearing her voice when he was blind: 'It's of many a fine thing your voice would put a poor dark fellow in mind, and the day I'd hear it it's of little else at all I would be thinking' (136). Then when Molly maliciously puts him in mind of the 'grand day of his life' when he received sight, he replies in graphic images which are an epitome of the whole play:

> A bad black day when I was roused up and found I was the like of the little children do be listening to the stories of an old woman, and do be dreaming after in the dark night that it's in grand houses of gold they are, with speckled horses to ride, and do be waking again, in a short while, and they destroyed with the cold, and the thatch dripping, maybe, and the starved ass braying in the yard (137).

But although Martin has been awakened by disillusionment and is therefore more alert than most people, he still retains one dream, now more precious than all else – that Molly is a world of bliss. In fact by this stage, he is so tired of actuality that he prefers to it his dream of Molly:

> MOLLY: You've great romancing this day, Martin Doul. Was it up at the still you were at the fall of night?
> MARTIN: It was not, Molly Byrne, but lying down in a little rickety shed across a sop of straw, and I thinking I was seeing you walk, and hearing the sound of your step on the dry road, and hearing you again, and you laughing and making great talk in a high room with dry timber lining the roof. For it's a fine sound your voice has that time, and it's better I am, I'm thinking, lying down, the way a blind man does be lying, than to be sitting here in the grey light taking hard words of Timmy the smith (138).

Even the hard Molly is stirred by this, and, looking at him with interest for the first time, she says:

> It's queer talk you have if it's a little, old, shabby stump of a man you are itself.

MARTIN: I'm not so old as you do hear them say.

MOLLY: You're old, I'm thinking, to be talking that talk with a girl.

MARTIN: It's not a lie you're saying, maybe, for it's long years I'm after losing from the world, feeling love and talking love, with the old woman, and I fooled the whole while with the lies of Timmy the smith (138).

There is moving pathos and irony here: Martin, having learned that he has devoted himself to a dream – that he and Mary are a handsome couple – which did not withstand the first touch of actuality, and having been disappointed in men and the natural world, thinks that he has reached the limit of disillusion and that there is nothing left to fear or to be deceived by. He cannot see that just as Timmy and the others have fooled him about Mary, so he is fooling himself about Molly. For now her dallying manner has excited him further and hope suddenly surges in him; perhaps he need not merely dream about her; perhaps he can possess the reality of beauty and love, and know, at last, that life can be truly more ecstatic than any dream:

> I've heard tell there are lands beyond in Cahir Iveraghig and the Reeks of Cork with warm sun in them, and fine light in the sky. And light's a grand thing for a man ever was blind, or a woman, with a fine neck, and a skin on her the like of you, the way we'd have a right to go off this day till we'd have a fine life passing abroad through them towns of the south, and we telling stories, maybe, or singing songs at the fairs (139).

Here Martin makes his last attempt to grasp both actuality and happiness and enjoy them as one. Speaking with a low, furious intensity that startles, then half-mesmerizes, the normally immovable Molly, he pleads that he alone is able truly to appreciate her. Only those who have been blind and then receive sight can see life as it really is. So disturbingly accurate is his vision of the horror, that his wife shuns him and the villagers begin to fear him as one doing the devil's work. Yet only he understands at all fully the fundamental facts of human loveliness and mutability:

> I'm thinking by the mercy of God, it's few sees anything but them is blind for a space. It's few sees the old women rotting for the grave, and it's few sees the like of yourself. Though its

shining you are, like a high lamp would drag in the ships out of the sea (140).

Since he alone can see the horror, he only can adequately comprehend and appreciate a woman's beauty and love. For all other men have had, more or less unconsciously, to deaden part of their sensibilities in order to avoid painful awareness of the harshness of actuality; moreover, their natures have become coarsened by constant immersion in the petty cares of the world. And invariably to shun the unpleasant, and to be concerned exclusively with material success, stunts the imagination, the faculty through which both the horror and the glory are apprehended. Accordingly, blurred with trade, and lacking ideals and vision, other men are far less capable of appreciating beauty and love than is the man, who, preserved through blindness from the world's slow stain, sees actuality clearly when he is given sight, and is able to respond, wholeheartedly and genuinely, to both the horror and the glory:

> And you'd do right not to marry a man is after looking out a long while on the bad days of the world; for what way would the like of him have fit eyes to look on yourself, when you rise up in the morning and come out of the little door you have above in the lane, the time it'd be a fine thing if a man would be seeing, and losing his sight, the way he'd have your two eyes facing him, and he going the roads, and shining above him, and he looking in the sky, and springing up from the earth, the time he'd lower his head, in place of the muck that seeing men do meet all roads spread on the world.

MOLLY: It's the like of that talk you'd hear from a man would be losing his mind.

MARTIN: It'd be little wonder if a man near the like of you would be losing his mind. Put down your can now, and come along with myself, for I'm seeing you this day, seeing you, maybe, the way no man has seen you in the world . . . (140–1).

A parallel between Martin and the artist can be seen here. But Martin is to experience a degree of actual horror, unmitigated by any actual good, that few artists have to endure. For Martin there is no 'balance of good and ill' in actuality; he finds all ill. His ardour has alarmed Molly, and she calls for Timmy, who reaches her side, just as Mary comes in softly and observes all.

This climax to Act Two is quite as masterly as the climax to Act One, which it resembles. As in Act One, disillusionment comes immediately after a passionate speech to Molly, and the impact for Martin is just as shocking and brutal. Molly angrily denounces him and Timmy sternly orders him to march off. Martin realizes that he has failed; he will never have Molly; but he may yet retain his dream. With agony he implores Molly not to shame him by revealing what he has said to her. He knows now that he can never have more than dreams, and he begs Molly to respect them, and to spare him them at least. But all fails: 'The bonds of heaven are slipp'd, dissolved, and loosed,' and chaos comes:

> Let you not put shame on me, Molly, before herself and the smith. Let you not put shame on me and I after saying fine words to you, and dreaming . . . dreams . . . in the night. (*He hesitates, and looks round the sky.*) Is it a storm of thunder is coming, or the last end of the world? (*He staggers towards Mary Doul, tripping slightly over tin can.*) The heavens are closing I'm thinking with darkness and great trouble passing in the sky. (*He reaches Mary Doul, and seizes her left arm with both his hands – with a frantic cry.*) Is it darkness of thunder coming, Mary Doul? Do you see me clearly with your eyes?
>
> MARY (*Snatches her arm away, and hits him with the empty sack across the face.*) I see you a sight too clearly, and let you keep off from me now.
>
> MOLLY (*Clapping her hands.*) That's right, Mary. That's the way to treat the like of him is after standing there at my feet and asking me to go off with him, till I'd grow an old wretched road-woman the like of yourself (142).

It is not easy to praise this passage adequately: one can do little more than point to some of the details that help to create the impression of a soul rendered utterly desolate. There are: the desperation in Martin's words, produced, in part, by his reiterations and questions; the pathetic stumbling over the tin can; the return of blindness, confused with thunder, and symbolic of wrath in the whole universe, and of the death of all light, hope, good; then, the cry of the abandoned soul as darkness submerges it: 'the heavens are closing'; and, finally, like the stroke of death, the swipe across the face, confirming that actuality is brutal and in-human, and, as it were, impressing upon the physical parts the same terrible truth that has just ravaged the mind and imagina-tion. There exist few more searching instances in drama of Man's inhumanity to Man than Mary's swipe and Molly's words; and the effect is reinforced by the use of such simple means, and by the consideration that the agents are two, more or less, normal women.

Mary's defiance of Molly, and her prediction that Molly's prettiness will soon fade and leave her a hag, follow, and break Timmy's slender control of his temper:

> Oh, God protect us from the words of the blind. (*He throws down Martin's coat and stick.*) There's your old rubbish now, Martin Doul, and let you take it up, for it's all you have, and walk off through the world, for if ever I meet you coming again, if it's seeing or blind you are itself, I'll bring out the big hammer and hit you a welt with it will leave you easy till the Judgement Day (144).

Martin, now blind again, makes a great effort to rouse himself. If Timmy has physical strength, Martin has resources of wit and invective, and a new, dearly-bought insight into the nature of things. Urging Molly to see Timmy as he really is, he gives vent to his anger and pain in a trenchant denunciation of his rival. Timmy, however, pushes him aside, and he and Molly, after as-serting their own merits, and reproaching and threatening the blind, go off. Martin, left alone, is now as utterly disillusioned with actuality as he was with his dream at the end of Act One. Here words spoken by the Saint in Act One acquire greater significance:

> you'd do well to be thinking on the way sin has brought blindness to the world, and to be saying a prayer for your own sakes against false prophets and heathens, and the words of women and smiths, and all knowledge would soil the soul or the body of a man (118).

Although it is not Martin's sin that has brought blindness again, he has endured experiences and acquired knowledge that tem-porarily soil his soul and body, as his next speech shows. Yet in this extremity, when all else is lost, his imagination sustains him; it creates a fierce picture which gives him some compensation and prevents his disintegration:

> And that's the last thing I'm to set my sight on in the life of the world – the villainy of a woman and the bloody strength of a man. Oh, God, pity a poor blind fellow, the way I am this day with no strength in me to do hurt to them at all. Yet if I've no strength in me at all I've a voice left for my prayers, and may God blight them this day, and my own soul the same hour with them, the way I'll see them after, Molly Byrne and Timmy the smith, the two of them, on a high bed, and they screeching in hell. . . .
>
> It'll be a grand thing that time to look on the two of them; and they twisting and roaring out, and twisting and roaring again, one day and the next day, and each day always and ever. It's not blind I'll be that time, and it won't be hell to me, I'm thinking, but the like of heaven itself; and it's fine care I'll be taking the Lord Almighty doesn't know (146).

So the act ends, with the man who had imagined, and yearned for, a world of wonder, praying strenuously for the damnation of Molly and Timmy, and of himself, and longing to spend eternity with them in hell. To him such a consummation would be heaven compared with the actuality he has found on earth.

By the opening of Act Three the agony has given place to a dull ache, to a prevailing mood of despondency. The references to the natural world, which mirror and express the dispirited mood of the blind couple, show that they feel that their surroundings are drab and unfriendly, in contrast to the opening of Act One where they enjoyed a congenial environment. Mary, blind again, entering alone, can foretell nothing but unending gloom for the rest of her life. Blindness seems much worse than it was before, and existence far harder. Only her resentment against Martin gives liveliness to her mind, and her sole source of comfort and self-respect is the image of herself as an old woman with long white hair curled over her head and brow.

Martin comes in even more dejected, grumbling: 'living people is a bad lot'; and so unhappy that the company of Mary Doul would be very welcome to him. Bitterness and loneliness are breaking him up; it is just as impossible for him to live in utter nakedness of spirit without some companion or dream, as it is impossible for the artist to be creative without some audience, whether actual or ideal. ('All art is a collaboration', Synge says.) After the amusing passage when the two recognize each other, mutual relief and traces of gladness are noticeable, although Mary, with her usual equanimity, shows this less than the excitable Martin. The process of rehabilitation begins with an exchange of banter which lifts their spirits: they have not had the pleasure of a lively wrangle for a long time. As the one stimulates the other to wholesome activity of mind and fancy, it becomes plain that they still have much in common, that their need for each other is no less. From this the pattern of the new dream begins to emerge.

Mary, more self-preoccupied, and not so profoundly disillusioned, having begun to create her new dream earlier, has it in embryo, and under the promptings of Martin, and under his obvious admiration, this dream quickly becomes complete:

> When I seen myself in them pools, I seen my hair would be grey, or white, maybe, in a short while, and I seen with it I'd a face would be a great wonder when it'll have soft, white hair falling around it, the way when I'm an old woman there won't be the like of me surely in the seven counties of the east (151).

Taken with this notion, and not knowing whether to prize more her new comeliness or her agility of mind, Martin cries out: 'You're a cute thinking woman, Mary Doul, and it's no lie.' His admiration is mingled with relief; he begins to see a way out of the impasse: a woman with such an appearance, and with such a facility of fancy and expression, would be an excellent partner; infinitely better than the icy, conceited Molly. He examines himself to see if he can find any marks of distinction on his person:

> I was thinking if I'd a bit of comfort, the like of yourself, it's not far off we'd be from the good days went before, and that'd be a wonder surely. But I'll never rest easy, thinking you're a grey beautiful woman, and myself a pitiful show (152).

As he is rubbing his chin thoughtfully the vital notion comes to him: he will grow a beard to match Mary's hair. Again Martin's resources of imagination and verbal expression play a major part; he uses them to build a comforting image of a magnificent beard. Epithet by epithet, aided by image and allusion, all borne on a

persuasive rhythm, the beard takes shape, until it becomes a kind
of emblem of distinction and wealth:

> I'll be letting my beard grow in a short while, a beautiful,
> long, white, silken, streamy beard, you wouldn't see the like
> of in the eastern world. Ah, a white beard's a grand thing for
> making the quality stop and be stretching out their hands
> with good silver and gold, and a beard's a thing you'll never
> have, so you may be holding your tongue.
> MARY (*Laughing cheerfully.*) Well, we're a great pair, surely, and
> it's great times we'll have yet, maybe, and great talking before
> we die.
> MARTIN: Great times this day, with the help of Almighty God,
> for a priest itself would believe the lies of an old man would
> have a fine white beard growing on his chin (153).

Both are thoroughly convinced, the new dream is established, and
they are now as happy as they ever were. The wheel has come full
circle, and their condition is similar to that of the opening of the
play, except that they have gained knowledge and experience of
the world which make them no longer desirous of sight.

Then, for the second time in the play, the Saint's bell is heard.
But now it is a menace, no herald of deliverance. So the blind
couple try to escape, fearing that sight will force them to be constantly aware of human mutability, and of their own defects and
those of the rest of the world, and will dissolve the comfortable
dreams with which they hope to cloak themselves from harsh
actuality:

> MARTIN: . . isn't it a poor thing to be blind when you can't
> run off itself, and you fearing to see.
> MARY (*Nearly in tears.*) It's a poor thing, God help us, and what
> good'll our grey hairs be itself, if we have our sight, the way
> we'll see them falling each day, and turning dirty in the rain?
> (155).

When they are seized and brought before the Saint, Martin, after
pleading in vain to be left alone, joins issue with him in a crucial
passage which contrasts their attitudes to actuality:

> SAINT (*Severely.*) I never heard tell of any person wouldn't have
> great joy to be looking on the earth, and the image of the
> Lord is thrown upon men.

MARTIN: Them is great sights, holy father. . . . What was it I seen when I first opened my eyes but your own bleeding feet, and they cut with the stones? That was a great sight, maybe, of the image of God. . . . And what was it I seen my last day but the villainy of hell looking out from the eyes of the girl you're coming to marry – the Lord forgive you – with Timmy the smith. That was a great sight, maybe. And wasn't it great sights I seen on the roads when the north winds would be driving, and the skies would be harsh, till you'd see the horses and the asses, and the dogs itself, maybe, with their heads hanging, and they closing their eyes (160).

The Saint is too honest to deny the truth in this; he finds comfort not so much in the everyday activities of men but rather in places with religious associations, and in the immanence of God. He seems to admit, tacitly, that actuality is as harsh as Martin alleges it to be, but his religious sense enables him to see around and beyond this present grimness to a supernatural reality which, he believes, is good and beautiful:

Did you never hear tell of the summer and the fine spring, and the places where the holy men of Ireland have built up churches to the Lord? No man isn't a madman, I'm thinking, would be talking the like of that, and wishing to be closed up and seeing no sight of the glittering seas, and the furze that is opening above, will soon have the hills shining as if it was fine creels of gold they were, rising to the sky? (161).

Martin, however, lacks this religious belief, nor does he desire it; he prefers (as a cloak against actuality) the vision which his imagination creates from the sounds and smells and rhythms of the natural world; a vision of an imaginary world (made perfect by art, in which things appear not as they are, but as they should be) far more satisfying than any actual world:

I'll say it's ourselves have finer sights than the lot of you, hearing the birds and bees humming in every weed of the ditch, or sitting abroad in the sweetness of the warmth of the night, hearing a late thrush, maybe, and the swift crying things do be racing in the air, till we do be looking up in our own minds into a grand sky, and seeing lakes, and broadening rivers, and hills are waiting for the spade and plough (161).

Nevertheless the Saint and the villagers join in trying to force sight and actuality upon the blind, and the excitement leads to a climax in which Synge again secures powerful effects by simple means. Martin's single movement that sends the can rocketing across the stage (like Mary's swipe at the climax of Act Two and Martin's turning to see Mary for the first time at the climax of Act One) is an exceedingly effective stroke. It cuts the blind off, irrevocably, from the source of sight; and it expresses with clarity and force their wholehearted decision to renounce actuality. It is a deliberate rejection, and a necessary one, for actuality had come near to killing them. Martin's great speech here indicates the need for compassion between men in their varying stances and ways of life, since we are all confronted, whether we realize it or not, with the same dread actuality:

> Go on now, holy father, for if you're a fine Saint itself, it's more sense is in a blind man, and more power, maybe, than you're thinking at all. Let you walk on now with your worn feet, and your welted knees, and your fasting, holy ways have left you with a big head on you and a thin pitiful arm. . . . For if it's a right some of you have to be working and sweating the like of Timmy the smith, and a right some of you have to be fasting and praying and talking holy talk the like of yourself, I'm thinking it's a good right ourselves have to be sitting blind, hearing a soft wind turning round the little leaves of the spring and feeling the sun, and we not tormenting our souls with the sight of the grey days, and the holy men, and the dirty feet is trampling the world (167).

The Saint and the villagers cannot accept this view, and they drive the pair out, thereby confirming in the minds of the blind the impression of the brutality of human beings. So, with their new dream secure, Mary and Martin go off in the hope that they may find a more favourable place to live in, where the unloveliness of actuality will be concealed from them, or, at least, will not be obtrusive.

It is not correct to speak of a tension between dream and actuality in the case of the villagers. For none of them comes into contact with actuality in the way that Martin, Mary and the Saint do. The villagers live entirely in the dream. Like many of us they are so immersed in the difficult task of getting a living that their eyes are normally closed to actuality. The common cares and petty interests of existence have dulled their sensibilities; the prison house has closed around them.

It is one of the functions of the artist to help people in this condition towards a richer and fuller life by rousing their minds from the lethargy of custom and by removing the 'film of familiarity and selfish solicitude', which covers the horror and glory of actuality. Martin tries to perform this function for the villagers in Act Two. But he can show them only the horror of actuality; that is all he knows, and he must be true to his vision, whether pleasant or not. The villagers act, as many of us would act in the face of such a vision; they reject it, and the author, as coming from the powers of darkness.

The villagers might have been brought into contact with some kind of reality through the Saint. He knows both the horror and the glory, and it is part of his function, presumably, to teach the truth. The Saint, however, would shield them from 'all knowledge that would soil the soul or the body of a man', he would not draw undue attention to the horror, for he believes that there is a supernatural reality, wholly good, which more than compensates for all human anguish. It is to this supreme benign power, whose glory may be seen shining through the natural world, and to the piety and the holy works of the religious orders, that the Saint would constantly direct the villagers' attention. He does not have much success in this difficult mission; he is able to convince himself, but not the others; and so although the villagers, apparently, fulfil their religious observances, the reality of the Saint's God has little effect on their minds and behaviour. The day-to-day business of living hides them from awareness of the terror of God and from knowing fully his love and mercy; it also protects them from the horror that Martin sees in life. Ironically enough, and in harmony with the main theme of the play that naked actuality is intolerable, the villagers are the most blind, and the most content.

In the scale of awareness of the tension between dream and actuality the villagers are at the bottom. Like many of us they hardly know that the tension exists, and, cloaked from actuality by routine and the concern to gain a living, they live entirely in the dream (though they would deny this and say they were sound practical men). Mary is a stage advanced beyond the villagers.

She comes into contact with actuality and it shatters her dream. She does not, however, probe further into actuality; her main concern is to build another dream, and by the end of the play she has done this. The Saint and Martin both know actuality, and a comparison between their outlooks may help finally to indicate the pattern of the play.

The Saint's view of the tension is a religious one. He acknow-ledges that there is horror in actuality, but he asserts that this is caused solely by Man's sin; and 'sin has brought blindness to the world'. In addition, then, to trying to cure physical blindness, the Saint has to try to cure two kinds of spiritual blindness: the blind-ness of the villagers and the blindness of Martin. The villagers are blind to the fact of sin, they have not yet reached the stage of being aware that actuality is horrible. They will need to be enlightened to the fact of sin and to the horror and blindness (both physical and spiritual) which sin has brought into the world, before they will feel the need for the particular kind of cloak that the Saint offers against actuality. The Saint's mission is to remove blindness and thus show the glory of God. It is particularly ironic that when he removes Martin's blindness Martin sees only horror, not glory. The reason for this, the Saint says, is that Martin is still spiritually blind. Martin's sin and blindness consist both in assuming that because he sees nothing but horror in actuality, the whole of actuality is horrible; and also in refusing to turn his attention away from the horror to the supernatural reality of God. Because of this sin physical blindness returns to Mary and Martin, the Saint believes, saying 'I'm thinking the Lord has brought you great teaching in the blinding of your eyes.' The Saint's cloak, then, against the horror of actuality is a life of religious asceticism; one must mortify the flesh, perform good works, avoid the taint of the world and seek always for the ultimate and only reality, that of God, intimations of whom may be gained through the splendour of the natural world. The essence of the Saint's attitude can be seen at the end of Act One in the advice he gives to Mary and Martin:

> May the Lord who has given you sight send a little sense into your heads, the way it won't be on your two selves you'll be looking – on two pitiful sinners of the earth – but on the splendour of God, you'll see an odd time shining through the big hills, and steep streams falling to the sea. For if it's on the like

of that you do be thinking, you'll not be minding the faces of men, but you'll be saying prayers and great praises, till you'll be living the way the great saints do be living, with little but old sacks, and skin covering their bones (126-7).

In Synge's writings values are never stated, but implied, and in *The Well of the Saints* Synge does not assert that either of the conscious attitudes to actuality is better or right. He presents the Saint's point of view fairly and vigorously, and he makes the Saint, with his simple piety and kindliness, the most sympathetic character in the play. Yet it is the tension in Martin which is given salience and which interests Synge most, for it is, in a way, his own.

Both Martin and his creator agree with those of a religious outlook in acknowledging the fact of horror but they do not agree that it is caused entirely by Man's sin; they do not know who is responsible for it, and they are unable to accept the cloak of religion against it. Martin, then (seen throughout as performing the same function in his society as the artist does in ours), represents the agnostic artist, and he is linked to Synge. But, paradoxically, he is linked to Synge the man, rather than to Synge the artist, because Act Three shows that Martin the artist's solution is radically different from the solution of Synge the artist. In other words Martin's problem is the same as Synge's, both are artists faced with the fact of human suffering; but Martin's solution in Act Three is deliberately to renounce the suffering, the horror of actuality; whereas Synge's solution, as an artist, is to embrace the whole of life, horror and glory, and by the excellence of his art to 'make', as Keats says, 'all disagreeables evaporate from their being in close relationship with Beauty and Truth'.

Look briefly at Martin's career. When blind he had two dreams that gave him pleasure and comfort in his affliction: (*a*) that he and Mary were a handsome couple; (*b*) that the world was full of wonder and delight (this being symbolized in Molly). Act One destroys dream (*a*); Act· Two destroys dream (*b*). Sickened by actuality, he rejects it, and creates, to make life tolerable, some new dreams. Martin, then, is representative of the artist who creates, fancies, dreams works of art to comfort himself. Eventually actuality shows that these dreams, works of art, are not based upon the facts of human existence. The artist, then, unable to grapple with the whole of existence, unable to create something vital and beautiful out of actuality, turns away from it, and consoles himself again with private fancies and dreams, which, while perhaps ingenious and charming, do not deal with mature issues and 'are far away from the profound and common interests of life'. Here the paradox comes in: the great artists of the world are not like the artist just described, not like Martin. The great artists in their work embrace and present actuality, the horror and the glory, creating from its essence (so intense is their imaginative insight) a harmony, works of art of beauty and significance. All are constantly haunted by 'the burthen of the mystery', all question: 'Is there any cause in nature that makes these hard hearts?', 'Why should woman suffer?', and all, through the power of the imagination, find some answer, at least in their work, if not in their lives. Some artists (such as Chaucer, Spenser, Milton, Hopkins, Eliot) are aided in finding a harmony between good and ill by a specific religious view; others (such as Wordsworth, Blake, Browning) have a more private religious view; and others (such as Keats, Rossetti, Hardy) are agnostic. Synge is in the last category, and the paradox about him is that as a man he was in exactly the same position as Martin – he found life meaningless – but as an artist he behaved quite differently from Martin. He did not turn away, he embraced actuality in his writings, and produced plays like *The Well of the Saints* of which not his most hostile critic has been able to say that it is a flight from the harsher actualities of life. The usual complaint from those who fail to see the play as a whole is that it tends to stress unduly the gloomier aspects of life. But Synge not only contemplates the horror of actuality, he presents it dramatically, and enables us to contemplate it too. Moreover we enjoy the vision, and derive from it a freshening and deepening of our sympathies and understanding, although the valuation of human existence that it implies is one that we would find painful in everyday life. Through the power of Synge's imagination, therefore, we are able to experience and enjoy something that we would normally shun. And in giving us this Synge performs one of the prime functions of the artist; for as Sir Philip Sidney says in *An Apologie for Poetrie*, echoing Aristotle's *Poetics*, 'those things which in themselves are horrible are made in poetical imagination delightful'.

Yet the very success of *The Well of the Saints* challenges, in a way, the main notion it suggests: that naked actuality is horrible, and that human beings only have a tolerable life by creating (consciously or unconsciously) some dream that will cloak them from actuality. For if Synge the artist had accepted the consequences of this notion, he would have rejected life and set about building up private dreams, and there would have been no play. Fortunately for us he seems to have realized that provided they are adult it is not so much the quality or originality of an artist's ideas that matter as his ability to communicate these ideas; ideas and feelings are only part of the raw material of his art and they must be fused with other factors. Synge's ideas, his vision, are not particularly fresh and profound (though they are tenable and occur in every generation) but this does not matter. It is not the artist's job to have rare feelings and extraordinary ideas but to use the ordinary ones and to make them rich and significant. If he is going to disturb and delight people, to give them the true, rare experience of art, he must study them and their surroundings intensely and devote himself to his craft. He must not reject life as intolerable, and cultivate private fancies. Accordingly, for the artist it is essential to immerse himself in actuality (though as a man he finds that actuality horrible); he must continually take upon himself the mystery of things, and feel the 'agony, the strife of human hearts'. Hence the unhappiness and pain that many artists undergo in their lives, and hence too the surge of ecstasy which follows the successful completion of a work of art in which something beautiful and memorable has been made out of the instability and incoherence of life. Martin, the artist, used his imagination in the end to create merely private fancies. Synge, the artist, used his imagination to grapple with the horror of actuality and formed from it a *new* actuality that is good – his writings. In life it may be impossible to blend richness and reality. Martin found it impossible, and he forsook reality and made a sort of Ivory Tower. Synge, however, succeeded in blending both richness and reality in his work.

The Playboy of the Western World

In *The Well of the Saints* we see the tension between dream and actuality with the imagination, the major force working on this tension, used by Martin to escape from it. In *The Playboy of the*

Western World we see the same tension with the imagination the major force working on it, but in this case Christy's imagination transforms the dream into actuality. If Keats's cry: 'lord, a man should have the fine point of his soul taken off to become fit for this world', may be thought of as an apt gloss on *The Well of the Saints*, another saying of his: 'The Imagination may be compared to Adam's dream – he awoke and found it truth' is well exemplified in the main theme of *The Playboy*.

The actuality in the opening of *The Playboy* is the terrified weakling, Christy. An impetus to imaginative activity on his part is given by the admiration of the villagers when they hear his tale. They present to his imagination a dream or ideal picture of himself, and his imagination becomes creative. It works upon himself, that is upon the original actuality, and as the play goes on the raw material of the Christy of the opening scene is shaped by the power of the imagination in accordance with the dream or ideal presented by the villagers, until by the end of the play Christy actually is the daring playboy that the villagers thought him to be at first. The actuality of the first scene is transformed by the dream into a new actuality, and in the end the dream and the actuality are one. Christy wakes and finds his dream truth. This is in direct contrast to the end of *The Well of the Saints* where the dream and actuality are at complete variance.

Synge starts by creating the kind of situation in which such a transformation would be most likely to take place; he presents a soil and climate most apt to welcome vigour and imagination, and to make them blossom. With the exception of Shawn and, presumably, Father Reilly, everyone living in the small, remote Mayo village is stifled by the drabness of existence and longs for action and excitement. The people are not altogether lacking in capabilities: Pegeen is pretty and spirited; there is a capacity for enjoyment in Michael James; Philly is cunning and shrewd; and Jimmy has a tender sensibility. Yet they can find no outlet for their energies, except in drinking bouts. Even these are beyond the feeble Shawn, whom Pegeen is going to marry. He is the only young man available – all the vigorous young men seem to have emigrated – and he merely moves Pegeen to tease or scold him.

Upon this inert community certain disorderly groups impinge; Pegeen declares: 'Isn't there the harvest boys with their tongues red for drink, and the ten tinkers is camped in the east glen, and the thousand militia – bad cess to them – walking idle through the land' (183). The villagers fear the savagery of these people, and yet, somehow, are attracted by it; so that, when they hear that a queer strange fellow is roaming nearby, all conclude that he is dangerous. Shawn is asked to stay to protect Pegeen, but he refuses, not so much because he is afraid of being hurt but because he is scared of a rebuke from Father Reilly if he spends any time alone with a young woman at night:

> Let me out. . . . Oh, Father Reilly, and the Saints of God, where will I hide myself today. . . . Leave me go, Michael James, leave me go, you old Pagan . . . or I'll get the curse of the priests on you, and the scarlet-coated bishops of the Court of Rome (184).

After the spectacle of a lover too fearful of upsetting his priest to look after his fiancée, Pegeen and Michael James are ripe to applaud any sign of enterprise, however unusual, and the appearance of a daring young fellow who has prevailed against the authority of his father is welcome. Thus Synge skilfully and amusingly prepares the entrance of Christy and sets him down where he is most likely to be appreciated – among people who, finding life intolerably dull, are avid for sensation.

Christy provides the sensation. Yet, entering, he seems quite incapable of doing so. But this is part of Synge's method of establishing Christy, at first, as a downtrodden, inoffensive creature, in order that his eventual transformation may be the more marked and glorious. Accordingly Christy creeps in, so tired and frightened and dirty that any people less starved of incident than the villagers would have ignored him. To them, however, he is of interest, particularly when he betrays anxiety about the police. The villagers question him, but, although he begins to feel a little flattered by being, for the first time in his life, an object of attention, he reveals nothing. His evasive answers increase their curiosity and pleasure; they sense a mystery; and when, partly to retain their attention, partly under Pegeen's skilful examination – which plays upon his pride by denying his achievement – he abruptly confesses, no one is disappointed. Their admiration is heartfelt: 'There's a daring fellow.' His first account of the deed is unadorned: 'I just riz the loy and let fall the edge of it on the ridge of his skull, and he went down at my feet like an empty sack, and never let a grunt or groan from him at all' (191). The matter-of-fact tone of this, and the gentleness of Christy's demeanour – he protests that he is 'a law-fearing man' and not 'a slaughter-boy' – impress the villagers more than a deal of boasting would have done. They are awed by the feeling that there are mysterious forces in this slight figure, and they think that this lad who speaks so humbly and reasonably of slaying his dad, and sits peacefully with his drink, 'should be a great terror when his temper's roused'. Moreover, their dislike of the police and the belief that the police would be scared of Christy are additional recommendations; and Christy soon has their approval so firmly that they readily put a favourable construction on all he says and does. Also, as Jimmy points out, the villagers need a brave man:

> Bravery's a treasure in a lonesome place, and a lad would kill his father, I'm thinking, would face a foxy divil with a pitchpike on the flags of hell. . . . Now, by the grace of God, herself will be safe this night, with a man killed his father holding danger from the door, and let you come on, Michael James, or they'll have the best stuff drunk at the wake (193–4).

The men go out, Pegeen contemptuously dismisses Shawn, and then begins to take possession of Christy and to beam on him; and the seed, in a favourable environment for the first time, begins to bud under her warmth.

Pegeen holds before him an image of 'a fine handsome fellow with a noble brow', who has the qualities of the great poets of the past, 'fine fiery fellows'. Christy's significant rejoinder (contrasting well with the rounded cadences of most speeches) conveys his delight and surprise perfectly: 'Is it me?' It is not he yet, but it will be. Christy finds some difficulty at first in recognizing himself in Pegeen's image, but every instinct urges him not to cast doubts upon it, but to believe in it and confirm it. 'Expanding with delight at the first confidential talk he has ever had with a woman' he begins to see the day on which he struck his one blow as a crucial moment in his life. Before, he had been merely existing, disdained by all, and unaware of his own powers: 'Up to the day I killed my father, there wasn't a person in Ireland knew the kind I was, and I there drinking, waking, eating, sleeping, a quiet, simple fellow with no man giving me heed' (198). In common with most of those characters in Synge who are imaginative, and like persons with a particular kind of poetic temperament, Christy found solace only in the natural world:

> I after toiling, moiling, digging, dodging from the dawn to dusk; with never a sight of joy or sport saving only when I'd be abroad in the dark night poaching rabbits on the hills . . . and there I'd be as happy as the sunshine of St Martin's Day, watching the light passing the north or the patches of fog, till I'd hear a rabbit starting to screech and I'd go running in the furze. Then, when I'd my full share, I'd come walking down where you'd see the ducks and geese stretched sleeping on the highway (199).

But he was continually beset by one horror – his father:

> He after drinking for weeks, rising up in the red dawn, or before it maybe, and going out into the yard as naked as an ash-tree in the moon of May, and shying clods against the visage of the stars till he'd put the fear of death into the banbhs and the screeching sows . . . he a man never gave peace to any, saving when he'd get two months or three, or be locked in the asylums for battering peelers or assaulting men . . . (200).

Christy's vivid picture of Mahon serves at least four purposes: it establishes Mahon as a giant whom Christy has killed, thus giving Christy a source of endless self-congratulation, and providing evidence on which his imagination can feed; it helps to make Christy's eventual transformation even more credible, since Mahon is so savage there is at least the possibility that his son will have some savagery in him; it depicts Mahon as a villain, one whom the villagers would consider deserved death, particularly in view of his lasciviousness; it helps to prepare for the eventual entrance of Mahon. The memory of the monster whom he has overcome excites Christy further: the 'tap of the loy' of some minutes previously is now a skull-splitting blow, and Christy regards himself as 'a fine lad deserves his good share of the earth . . . a seemly fellow with great strength and bravery'. Widow Quin's hammering on the door at this instant produces terror in Christy, but his collapse is only temporary. When he sees two fine women quarrelling over him his admiration for himself reaches new heights, and the dream moves another step towards actuality. Furthermore, this clash, marked by Pegeen's eloquent invective and Widow Quin's craft, makes it clear that Christy has come to the spot where there is scope and appreciation for quickness of fancy, fine talk and daring; and well might he say as he nestles in bed: 'it's great luck and company I've won me in the end of time – two fine women fighting for the likes of me – till I'm thinking this night wasn't I a foolish fellow not to kill my father in the years gone by' (207).

This mood is sustained and strengthened at the opening of Act Two. For the first time in his life Christy is enjoying himself and beginning to perceive and prize qualities in himself which he had not been conscious of before:

> Well, this'd be a fine place to be my whole life talking out with swearing Christians, in place of my old dog and cat; and I stalking around, smoking my pipe and drinking my fill, and never a day's work but drawing a cork an odd time, or wiping a glass, or rinsing out a shiny tumbler for a decent man. . . . Didn't I know rightly, I was handsome . . . and I'll be getting fine from this day, the way I'll have a soft lovely skin on me and won't be the like of the clumsy young fellows do be ploughing all times in the earth and dung (208–9).

The subsequent passage in which some village girls worship Christy as a hero has been objected to as mere padding, but it seems to me to have a function. It gets the act under way in a fresh and engaging manner, yet without startling – tension should, and does, come later; it shows how widespread is the ennui and how strong the craving for excitement in the village – Christy has become a sensation overnight – it motivates Pegeen's annoyance with Christy later in the act; and it provides good comedy. The passage also mirrors the behaviour of some people towards persons of notoriety. These girls who peep through a crack at Christy, who touch his bed with awe and try his boots on, who acclaim him with all the superlatives at their command, and who beseech him to take their offerings, have counterparts among us today. Popular journalism has given them an appetite for the lurid, and they (not unlike the crowd at a murder trial) are 'after rising early and destroying themselves running fast up the hill' to gaze on a man who has done a deed of violence.

A little later Widow Quin enters, and, after making herself very agreeable to Christy, pleases him further by asking him to relate how he did his deed. This he does, with great relish, demonstrating his actions by means of a half-eaten leg of chicken in one hand and a mug of tea in the other. When he reveals that the quarrel started on his refusal to follow his father's wishes by marrying a venomous hag, their sympathy and admiration for him are complete. Spurred on by this most amiable audience he presents the action (which now to his mind, as to theirs, is of heroic proportions) with dramatic and bloody detail: 'I hit him a blow on the ridge of his skull, laid him stretched out, and he split to the knob of his gullet. (*He raises the chicken bone to his Adam's apple*)' (215). The girls are in ecstasies at this, but Pegeen's entry ends the performance. The girls are sent packing, Widow Quin, after a brisk encounter with Pegeen, retreats, and Christy is left alone to face Pegeen's anger. The next passage is, by contrast to what has gone before, sombre, and displays a depth of feeling untouched in the play previously.

Among the impulses behind Christy's mainly instinctive desire to make himself like the image that has been presented to him, the conscious drive has been the wish to impress Pegeen. She played a major part in exciting his imagination with this image, and he wishes to prove to her (as well as to himself) that he really is the same as the image. In this shaping process he is getting into touch with actuality, and becoming aware of certain powers in his nature which were lying dormant until the force of the imagination brought them into activity. Now, faced by Pegeen's anger, Christy experiences a kind of fear and distress unknown to him before; if she withdraws her protection and inspiration he feels that he will never make the image actual, and that he will undergo pain and disappointment unexperienced previously. His character is developing rapidly, and accordingly the opportunities for happiness and sorrow, the rewards and punishments are becoming greater. He is in the middle way; he can never go back to his former undeveloped condition, and his new personality is only in the process of being formed. He still needs the right audience and the stimulus of Pegeen's admiration. In the days before his deed he welcomed solitariness; but now he dreads it; and he sets forth his fears in a precise image from Irish life:

it's a lonesome thing to be passing small towns with the lights shining sideways when the night is down, or going in strange

places with a dog noising before you and a dog noising behind,
or drawn to the cities where you'd hear a voice kissing and talking deep love in every shadow of the ditch, and you passing on
with an empty, hungry stomach failing from your heart (220–1).

Pegeen can hardly accept this; like all the villagers she treats any
admission of weakness in Christy as a mere subterfuge to cloak
some daring design; she is puzzled; but she can see that he is
genuinely in love with her, and that he is convinced of the dangers
of confiding in other women, so she becomes kinder and more
attentive than ever. She is declaring that she 'wouldn't give a
thraneen for a lad hadn't a mighty spirit in him and a gamey heart'
when Shawn rushes in.

The contrast between Shawn and Christy is marked most
effectively, when, having got rid of Pegeen by a trick, Shawn and
Widow Quin try to persuade Christy to leave. In his own community in Meath Christy was probably as weak and despised a
creature as Shawn is here, but now Christy, made masterful by
imagination, rejects Shawn's offer with scorn, and swaggers out
to try on the fine new clothes. Christy's first essay in arrogance,
fortunately against weak opposition, is overwhelmingly successful. Shawn's desperation produces one of the most amusing
speeches in the play:

> Oh, Widow Quin, what'll I be doing now? I'd inform against
> him, but he'd burst from Kilmainham and he'd be sure and
> certain to destroy me. If I wasn't so God-fearing, I'd near have
> the courage to come behind him and run a pike into his side.
> Oh, it's a hard case to be an orphan and not to have your father
> that you're used to, and you'd easy kill and make yourself a
> hero in the sight of all (226).

Amusing too is the fact that Shawn's best clothes help to make
Christy more handsome and imposing, thus impressing the
villagers further, and increasing still more Christy's self-esteem.
The fall from this height of pride is set forth with considerable
skill. Christy's rotund rhythms boasting of a blow of epic grandeur, his grandiose struts and frets and gestures, change instantly
to sharp phrases of horror and a terrified scramble into a hiding-
place, as Old Mahon appears:

CHRISTY: From this out I'll have no want of company when

all sorts is bringing me their food and clothing, the way they'd
set their eyes upon a gallant orphan cleft his father with one
blow to the breeches belt. (*He opens door, then staggers back.*)
Saints of Glory! Holy Angels from the throne of Light!
WIDOW QUIN: What ails you?
CHRISTY: It's the walking spirit of my murdered da!
WIDOW QUIN: Is it that tramper?
CHRISTY (*Wildly.*) Where'll I hide my poor body from that ghost
of hell? (228).

Christy is now more desperate than was the despised Shawn a
few moments earlier; and the comic effect of the contrast is driven
home by Old Mahon's descriptions of his son as 'a dirty stuttering
lout . . . and ugly young blackguard'.

Synge's skill is seen in contriving that Widow Quin should be
the one to meet Old Mahon and to learn the truth. Any other
character would have published the truth at once; Pegeen, for
instance, would have sent Christy off lonely on the roads or back
to subjection, and the transformation from dream to actuality
would have been incomplete. But the wily Widow Quin sees that
she may turn this knowledge to her own advantage, and she tries
to persuade Christy to give up Pegeen and to marry her. This is the
great moment of temptation and decision for Christy; acceptance
of Widow Quin's proposals would be the safe course but would
involve the surrender of his imagination, since he would have to
cut himself off from the main conscious source of his inspiration –
Pegeen – and he would no longer be able to believe in himself as a
daring young hero; the image would be shattered, and the transformation from weakling to champion playboy would not take
place. It is not suggested that Christy deliberated in his mind about
these matters – he was probably not fully aware of them, and his
choice was an intuitive one – but the whole tone and tenor of the
play gives us cause to entertain the notion that this passage is,
among other things, emblematic of the temptation, which must
often come to the emergent artist, to leave his work half-finished,
and to turn away to what appears to be ease and safety.

Christy, however, is true to his dream, and he rejects Widow
Quin's suggestions, persuading her instead to help him keep Old
Mahon out of the way:

WIDOW QUIN: If I aid you will you swear to give me a right of

way I want, and a mountainy ram, and a load of dung at
Michaelmas, the time that you'll be master here?
CHRISTY: I will, by the elements and stars of night.
WIDOW QUIN: Then we'll not say a word of the old fellow, the
way Pegeen won't know your story till the end of time (236).

Thus Christy is lifted from this trough through the power of his
imagination and the co-operation of Widow Quin; and by the end
of the act, as he leaps out to the sports, he is rehabilitated and more
eager than ever to prove to all that he is a wonder.

When we see Christy again he is at the height of his public fame
and fortune, though still protesting that all his triumphant deeds
at the sports are insignificant compared to his killing of his dad. So
great is his feeling of power and exultation that he has quite forgotten that his dad is still alive and near at hand. The love-scene
which follows shows that the transformation is approaching
completion. The man who makes love with such ardour is a
different person from the shy recluse of Meath, different from the
abject, then flattered, fugitive of Act One, and different even from
the boaster of Act Two. He actually possesses those qualities
which Pegeen and the others fancied they saw in him at first, and
there is a confident energy in his rhythms and an assured exactness
in his imagery that have not been marked in his speech before.
The passage has most of the features usually found in Synge's
dramatic poetry, and here they are wrought to a peak of splendour
and dramatic effectiveness.

An indication of Synge's quality may be gained from noting
some lines from Douglas Hyde's *Love Songs of Connacht* which
Synge probably had in mind. Hyde says: 'I had rather be beside
her on a couch, ever kissing her, than be sitting in heaven in the
chair of the Trinity.' Synge gives us: 'I squeezing kisses on your
puckered lips, till I'd feel a kind of pity for the Lord God is all
ages sitting lonesome in His golden chair . . .' (251). Synge's
choice of words is more accurate and evocative: passionate kisses
are 'squeezed' and the lips must be 'puckered'; and there is, as
Oliver Elton says, 'a melodious and passionate extravagance' –
which aptly conveys Christy's extreme joy – in Synge's transformation of the notion of lovers preferring their joys to those of
heaven. At the opening of the passage both Christy and Pegeen
are happy but shy, as if expecting a crucial declaration of their

feelings. When this is made each inspires the other to further eloquent expressions of devotion, and towards the climax the speeches (all of about the same length and with a similar rhythmic flow and cadence) give the impression of ritual, one lover praising the other in perfect measure and time. There is nothing mawkish about this duet, and consequently it is enhanced rather than damaged by the immediate contrast with another kind of richness and reality, by being ended with the entrance of Michael James 'swamped and drownded with the weight of drink'. Shawn helps him in but the mere sight of Shawn is sickening to Pegeen, and Christy chases him off. The climax of the happiness of Christy and Pegeen comes now, as Michael James gives them his blessing, in a speech which summarizes the qualities the villagers admire Christy for:

> It's the will of God, I'm thinking, that all should win an easy or a cruel end, and it's the will of God that all should rear up lengthy families for the nurture of the earth. What's a single man, I ask you, eating a bit in one house, and drinking a sup in another, and he with no place of his own, like an old braying jackass strayed upon the rocks? (*To Christy*.) It's many would be in dread to bring your like into their house for to end them, maybe, with a sudden end; but I'm a decent man of Ireland, and I liefer face the grave untimely and I seeing a score of grandsons growing up little gallant swearers by the name of God, than go peopling my bedside with puny weeds the like of what you'd breed, I'm thinking, out of Shaneen Keogh. (*He joins their hands*.) A daring fellow is the jewel of the world, and a man did split his father's middle with a single clout should have the bravery of ten, so may God and Mary and St Patrick bless you, and increase you from this mortal day (258).

The fall from this height is the most severe that Christy undergoes. The entrance of Old Mahon casts him in a few seconds from the peak of delight down to a depth of anguish and despair which makes all his former troubles mere trifles. And this time there is no one to help him. Previously when his confidence had been shaken Pegeen or Widow Quin had helped to stimulate and nourish his imagination and thus to restore his faith in himself. But now Widow Quin can do nothing, and Pegeen, very hurt and disappointed, begins to assail him, while Michael James and the crowd, feeling that they too have been cheated, join in. For some moments Christy is desperate:

> And I must go back into my torment is it, or run off like a vagabond straying through the unions with the dust of August making mudstains in the gullet of my throat; or the winds of March blowing on me till I'd take an oath I felt them making whistles of my ribs within? (261).

But he is developing every minute; the stress, the pressure, now harden not dissolve him; and the jeers of the crowd instead of breaking him (as they would have done at any time previously) make his transformation almost complete. There is a brief moment of imaginative activity, then the truth comes to him, and, as a man who has proved himself superior to all around, he speaks with authority to the crowd, now in a frenzy at the prospect of a fight: 'Shut your yelling, for if you're after making a mighty man of me this day by the power of a lie, you're setting me now to think if it's a poor thing to be lonesome it's worse, maybe, go mixing with the fools of the earth' (263). He then charges through the mob and rushes out to strike down Old Mahon.

Christy's first words on returning reveal the conscious motive behind this act, as behind all others in the play so far: 'I'm thinking, from this out, Pegeen'll be giving me praises, the same as in the hours gone by.' He is not a weakling or a charlatan, he knows now; he has beaten every man in the sports, overthrown Shawn, wooed and won Pegeen in a way that any fiery poet of the old world could hardly surpass, and he has felled his Dad. He actually is all that the villagers thought him to be, a hero; and he expects Pegeen to recognize this. But it is now Christy who is in love with a dream, and it is Pegeen who falls far short of Christy's image of her. For she herself is mainly responsible for the capture of Christy; she alone hitches the rope over his head, thereby giving Shawn his solitary moment of joy in the play – 'Come on to the peelers, till they stretch you now.'

'Me,' roars Christy, 'I'll not stir.' He then directs his last appeal to Pegeen: 'And what is it you'll say to me, and I after doing it this time in the face of all?' But she rejects him unreservedly:

> I'll say, a strange man is a marvel, with his mighty talk; but what's a squabble in your back yard, and the blow of a loy,

have taught me that there's a great gap between a gallous story and a dirty deed. (*To men.*) Take him on from this, or the lot of us will be likely put on trial for his deed today (266).

This is the bitterest blow Christy has to face, the last test and the severest, and for a moment the anguish of this disillusionment, along with the vivid imaginative apprehension of death, almost shatter his newly created personality:

> And it's yourself will send me off, to have a horny-fingered hangman hitching slip-knots at the butt of my ear. . . . Cut the rope, Pegeen, and I'll quit the lot of you, and live from this out, like the madman of Keel, eating muck and green weeds on the faces of the cliffs (267).

It seems that having come so far Christy is to fail at this last extremity; dream and actuality will disintegrate just as they were about to become one. Then (by a masterly piece of dramatic irony) Pegeen, this time against her will, saves Christy, and makes the transformation complete. Previously her admiration and affection had inspired Christy; now her coldness, her unjust taunts, move him to resolute and effective action. She calls him 'a saucy liar', and co-operates with Shawn to torture and capture him. At this Christy's spirit bends to his full height, and he becomes completely transformed:

> PEGEEN (*Blowing the fire with a bellows.*) Leave go now, young fellow, or I'll scorch your shins.
> CHRISTY: You're blowing for to torture me. (*His voice rising and growing stronger.*) That's your kind is it? Then let the lot of you be wary, for, if I've to face the gallows, I'll have a gay march down, I tell you, and shed the blood of some of you before I die (268).

Thus, at the supreme crisis, Pegeen has abandoned Christy and has joined the others against him. Their feelings for each other, which found such consummate expression in their duet only a few minutes earlier, die as Pegeen blows the fire to burn Christy, and as he, realizing the truth about himself and her, hisses out: 'That's your kind is it?' words, in their simple directness, contrasting effectively with the rich fervour of the love duet.

The making actual of the image, fullness of stature, self-realization, independence, all come together. Now Christy fears nothing;

his spirits mount as he feels his strength; he actually is the Playboy, the wonder of the west, a Samson compared with the villagers who vainly try to hold him down, and against whom he roars rich and colourful defiance:

> CHRISTY: If I can wring a neck among you, I'll have a royal judgement looking on the trembling jury in the courts of law. And won't there be crying out in Mayo the day I'm stretched upon the rope, with ladies in their silks and satins snivelling in their lacy kerchiefs, and they rhyming songs and ballads on the terror of my fate? (*He squirms round on the floor and bites Shawn's leg.*)
>
> SHAWN: My leg's bit on me. He's the like of a mad dog, I'm thinking, the way that I will surely die.
>
> CHRISTY: You will, then, the way you can shake out hell's flags of welcome for my coming in two weeks or three, for I'm thinking Satan hasn't many have killed their da in Kerry, and in Mayo too (268).

Pegeen's final act against Christy (not done without some pity) does not touch his heart, but causes him much pain, so that he kicks and flings around until he comes face to face with Old Mahon. This is a wonderful climax. Father and son, both on hands and knees, stare at each other for a moment while the truth sinks in: that Christy is now master – as his first words show: 'Are you coming to be killed a third time, or what ails you now?' The old order has gone for ever; the son is emancipated, and in the new relationship he is the dominant figure:

> CHRISTY: Go with you, is it? I will then, like a gallant captain with his heathen slave. Go on now and I'll see you from this day stewing my oatmeal and washing my spuds, for I'm master of all fights from now. (*Pushing Mahon.*) Go on, I'm saying (270).

Old Mahon's reply to this is a further example of Synge's excellence: 'Is it me?' he says, thereby echoing exactly Christy's words in Act One. At that early stage Pegeen presented to Christy the image of the daring poet she thought him to be, and which he was to become. Christy's 'Is it me?' then marked the beginning of his recognition of a new situation and the beginning of his transformation. Now at the end of the play image and actuality

are one, and the 'Is it me?' of Act One is now 'It *is* me.' Likewise
Old Mahon's 'Is it me?' marks the beginning of a new situation,
he realizes that from this out he is to be the subordinate partner.
And his feelings about this are similar to those of Christy in Act
One: surprise not unmingled with delight. For his son has made
good, he is not an idle weed, he is a true Mahon; and Old Mahon,
having had his reign, is pleased to resign his authority into such
worthy hands; Old Mahon too is at last happy. Christy's delight in
his power and distinction and his confidence in a splendid future,
do not prevent him from giving due thanks and praise: in success
he remains likable. He alone knows that Pegeen and the villagers
have, unwittingly, helped to 'make a mighty man of him by the
power of a lie', and his last words are of gratitude: 'Ten thousand
blessings upon all that's here, for you've turned me into a likely
gaffer in the end of all, the way I'll go romancing through a
romping lifetime from this hour to the dawning of the Judgement
Day' (270).

Pegeen's grief is (naturally) that she has lost Christy, the only
Playboy, and it might be said that she lost him because, at the
crucial moment, her belief in the image collapsed; ironically
enough, just at the moment when it was palpable that the image
had become actual. In those moments when Christy realized that
the image was truth, Pegeen shut her eyes to it. If Christy's
development through the play may be thought of as an illustra-
tion of Keats's observation: 'The imagination may be compared
to Adam's dream – he awoke and found it truth', Pegeen's
behaviour may be thought of as emblematic of the attitude of the
person who denies the validity of imaginative experience as a
moral agent and as an avenue to truth. She rejects Christy and
calls him 'a crazy liar' because he has been responsible for her
belief in a fiction: that Christy killed his father. She fails to see that
by means of this fiction acting upon Christy's imagination her
image of a daring poet has become truth. Christy at the end really
is the daring poet she believed him to be, and he has become that
without killing his father. But Pegeen refuses to see the new
actuality. She regards only the old fiction; she is blind to the *end*
and fails to see that the fiction was the *means* to this end; a fiction,
moreover, in which no one consciously deceived anyone else,
which brought only good, no harm. The play, then, embodies
ideas of some consequence, as Synge explains;[166] 'it is not a play

with "a purpose" in the modern sense of the word, but although parts of it are, or are meant to be, extravagant comedy, still a great deal that is in it, and a great deal more that is behind it, is perfectly serious when looked at in a certain light'.

In important respects *The Playboy of the Western World* and *The Well of the Saints* are complementary – there is sameness with difference – and both plays together present a fairly comprehensive treatment of the workings of the imagination. Both embody several degrees of blindness to, or awareness of, dream and actuality; instances of deception occur, but the conscious deception brings unhappiness when confronted with actuality (in *The Well of the Saints*), while the unconscious deception, the poetic fiction, helps to create a new and better actuality and to bring happiness (in *The Playboy*). It has been said that there is a good deal of the artist in Martin Doul; the same can be said of Christy. All that we learn of Christy, both before and after the blow, indicates that he has the powers of the artist and an outstanding ability to use words. Even Old Mahon has to admit that Christy has facility of tongue and fancy: 'a murderous gob on him ... he a lier on walls, a talker of folly ... a man you'd see stretched the half of the day in the brown ferns with his belly to the sun'; and in those solitary days in Meath Christy found solace and stay in a wise passivity, in introspection and the building of fancies, and in contact with animals and the natural world.

Appropriately enough an important characteristic of the play is a concern with matters of language. Pegeen praises Marcus Quin for his skill in telling 'stories of Holy Ireland'; and the chief delights of Jimmy's life have been 'Dan Davies's circus and the holy missioners making sermons on the villainy of man'; they speak of the 'preaching North'; there is to be 'great blabbing at the wake'; Pegeen presumes that Christy 'had much talk and streeleen' on his journey; Christy sees his father as a monster 'who'd be raging all times, the while he was waking, like a gaudy officer you'd hear swearing and cursing and damning oaths'; one of the joys Widow Quin promises Christy is to 'hear the penny poets singing in an August Fair'; Christy thinks 'this'd be a fine place to be my whole life talking out with swearing Christians'; the girls are in ecstasies at hearing Christy's 'grand story, and he tells it lovely'; Shawn is despised largely because he has no fluency of speech, he says, 'I'm a poor scholar with middling faculties to coin a lie,' and so he has to descend to telling the truth; Old Mahon is after walking long scores of miles 'winning clean beds and the fill of his belly four times in the day' merely by telling stories of how his son struck him; Old Mahon drunk was 'a terrible and fearful case . . . screeching in a straightened waistcoat, with seven doctors writing out his sayings in a printed book'; Pegeen thinks it would be a bitter thing to marry Shawn, and 'he a middling kind of scarecrow, with no savagery or fine words in him at all'; Michael James looks forward to 'seeing a score of grandsons growing up little gallant swearers'; and it is Christy's words more than anything else that win Pegeen – to her he is a coaxing fellow, he has no match for 'eloquence or talk at all', and at the height of their joy in the love-duet they think of happiness in terms of speech: they intend to talk in the spring, to coin 'funny nicknames for the stars of night' and they are delighted to know that they are speaking with love and kindness to each other – the climax of the duet is:

CHRISTY: And to think I'm long years hearing women talking that talk to all bloody fools, and this the first time I've heard the like of your voice talking sweetly for my own delight.
PEGEEN: And to think it's me is talking sweetly, and I the fright of seven townlands for my biting tongue (253).

The above quotations give some notion of the distinctive vitality of the play; it possesses a rich joy that has been rare in our drama since the early seventeenth century, and an abundance of sheer fun to which it is impossible to do justice in the course of this, or of any, exposition. Although its high worth is generally recognized, it is not so often noticed how a good deal of this magnificence comes from an exceedingly skilful use of one or two simple devices. For instance the device of dramatic contrast is used throughout with infinite variety and resource. Synge's skill in this is derived to a considerable extent from his study of earlier dramatists, especially the French, as V. S. Pritchett recognizes.[167]

To his handling of roguery, Synge brought all the subtlety he had learned from Molière . . . it stands out a mile in his handling of the dramatist's use of continual contrast, whereby almost every speech creates a new situation or farcically reverses its predecessor.

A detailed examination of *The Playboy* would show how true this is, and how there is an unbroken movement from beginning to end, in which each phrase or action blends in, or contrasts with, what has gone before or is to come. There are peaks in the play, but they are parts of a coherent structure, not isolated volcanoes. Or, to vary the metaphor, the development of Christy from weakling to hero is a wave-like movement, an undulation with steep troughs, and the last and greatest wave, lifting him from the bottom of the deepest trough, throws up the new man. At first Christy, worn and anxious, is in a trough. He is lifted from this by the admiration of Pegeen and the villagers. He falls, momentarily, into a shallow trough when Widow Quin hammers on the door, but is carried up on another wave by the sight of two handsome women fighting for his company. He is borne up higher on this wave by the hero-worship of Widow Quin and the village girls but Pegeen's anger at this topples him into a steep trough and he experiences a new depth of distress. But, by this time, under the influence of all this stimulation his imagination is becoming more powerful, and his words convince Pegeen that he is truly in love with her, and she receives him back into favour. At once he mounts higher than ever on another wave. His triumph over Shawn and his natty appearance in Shawn's clothes send him even higher, but the unexpected appearance of his father dashes him into a deep trough. Widow Quin helps him out of this, and his singular success at the sports sends him to new heights on another wave. With his love-duet with Pegeen and Michael James's consent to their marriage he soars on this wave to heights of joy undreamed of, only to fall abysmally to the extremest depth of distress when Old Mahon returns. In this final extremity there is no one to help him up: Pegeen and the villagers assail him, and all seems lost. But his imagination is now fully active and potent and his character developed remarkably. And so, stimulated further by Pegeen's hostility, he rises again, and soars up on the final wave beyond the ken of the villagers to a level where his new, superior personality will have scope for action.

To this theme and rhythm the comedy of the play is integral: one remarks, for instance, how Christy's sudden descents from the top of a wave to the bottom of a trough – which are very funny – always occur when he is boasting of his heroism in felling his dad. In fact there are few comedies so well made, few in which humour is so cunningly built into the whole situation that it is not dependent upon the talent of an outstanding comic actor, and hardly requires any 'gagging' or stage 'business' manufactured by a producer. Clearly in *The Playboy* we have the unusual phenomenon of a play which obeys the rules of twentieth-century naturalism and yet produces a fullness of effect hitherto obtained only by dramatists working in conventions more suitable for the poetic dramatist.

Alongside dramatic contrast there is much irony in the play. It is ironic that as Pegeen's admiration for Christy impelled him to make himself like the image, so her loathing at the end was a big factor in making the transformation complete. Likewise Pegeen believes in the dream, that is, she deludes herself during most of the play, but when the dream becomes actual she rejects it and takes up another delusion – that Christy is 'a crazy liar'. Ironically enough, Pegeen, the villagers in *The Playboy* and the villagers in *The Well of the Saints* are considered to be 'sensible, practical people' in contrast to the more imaginative figures who are thought to be 'queer'; yet there is no doubt that Martin and Christy have a much firmer grasp of reality than anyone else has: in all this how exact a reflection of life these plays are. It is ironic too that throughout *The Playboy* there is almost continual talk about stirring deeds and mighty sensations, things or people easily become 'wonders', everything is coloured and made to appear more startling and momentous than normal; yet really there is very little action, except for the sports (off-stage) and the scuffle at the end, and to the impartial observer all the objects used or referred to would appear most prosaic. In presenting this immense deal of talk (all of it much more than tolerable) to one poor ha'p'orth of action Synge may have intended, among other things, to have a sly grin at blather and blarney, at the Irish fondness for 'a good crack' and verbal virtuosity, at those who manipulate words for their own benefit and others' entertainment – at himself. For *The Playboy* is not devoid of the kind of wit described by T. S. Eliot, which 'involves, probably, a recognition, implicit in the expression of every experience, of other kinds of experience which are possible'.[168] *The Playboy* displays this kind of tolerance and humanity throughout; it implies a sanity and 'a darling freshness deep down things': all the references to the natural world show Nature, benign and sunny, co-operating with Man.

These are the dominant effects and tones of a serious and wholesome play which embodies a mature enjoyment of life in many aspects; it is the only work of Synge's in which mutability is not stressed; perhaps because in this play imagination has made an eternal triumph over harsh actuality and time.

CHAPTER SEVEN

Tragedies

Riders to the Sea

*R*iders to the Sea is probably one of the shortest and most concise plays in the language. In it a number of Synge's diverse experiences, along with the predominant interests and attitudes of his life and writings, are fused into a new whole, which sets forth the essence of Aran life and which is also Synge's image of Man's place in the universe.

I find difficulty in following the criticism voiced by D. Figgis[169] that the play lacks progression, is a stasis, that it is 'a slice of life set in the atmosphere of tragedy. Even as there is not water in a mist of the hills because it is all moisture, so there is not tragedy in *Riders to the Sea* because it is all tragical.' Clearly, the tragedy is centred on the figure of Maurya; she is the true tragic protagonist, and the rest of the figures have only varying degrees of partial awareness of the meaning of the whole. They have not yet attained her tragic stature and insight, nor reached that final illumination which sees life as essentially tragic, and, accepting this fact, gains thereby 'calm of mind all passion spent'. Furthermore, there are in this play both progression and also variety and contrast of texture, pace and mood. The play can be seen to fall into four movements: (*a*) (pp. 37–39½) the exposition; mood – near normal, subdued, apprehensive; method – mainly naturalistic and the particular; (*b*) (pp. 39½–42) the development; mood – more elevated, antiphony between Maurya and Bartley; method – mainly symbolic, suggesting the universal through the particular; (*c*) (pp. 43–7) a variation; mood – domestic pathos; method – mainly naturalistic and the particular, rising to (*d*) (pp. 48–end) the climax and resolution – the lament and benediction by Maurya in which the universal shines through the particular. These movements are parts of a seamless whole, and the increase or decrease of tension and significance is always the logical outcome of the circumstances.

(*a*) The play opens on a level near enough to the everyday world to persuade an audience to accept it without difficulty as a valid representation of life. The young girl, Cathleen, who deftly kneads the cake, puts it into the oven and at once begins to spin at the wheel (so hard is existence that she cannot pause for a minute), is reassuringly life-like. And the quiet entry of the younger sister, Nora, carrying the bundle, together with their simple words, completes and establishes the dramatic illusion. Their restrained tones and movements, Cathleen's sudden action of stopping the wheel and listening when Michael's name is mentioned, and the way they are startled when the door is suddenly blown open, all indicate plainly the strain and anxiety under which they labour. This is threefold: anxiety lest Maurya should hear about the bundle; anxiety lest it confirm the death of Michael; anxiety about Bartley's proposed journey. Thus the scene is set, essential information is put over economically and naturally, foreboding is aroused by the sight of the new boards, and the recurrent references to the rampant sea, and curiosity stimulated regarding the contents of the bundle, hidden unopened in the turf-loft, before Maurya enters.

(*b*) Worry is ravaging Maurya; as is shown by her querulousness, and by the way she repeats her sayings, groping for comfort: 'He won't go this day with the wind rising from the south and west. He won't go this day, for the young priest will stop him surely' (39). Young Nora, unthinking, tells her mother that the priest cannot stop Bartley and he is bent on going; and Maurya braces herself for a final struggle to keep back her last son from the sea. The rest of this movement is a battle of wills, with the mother trying desperately to break her son's resolve to carry on the ageless tradition of their kind, of wresting a living from the sea; a battle the more tense because it cannot be fought openly and directly but is carried on by nuance and suggestion – Cathleen and Nora are hardly aware that it is happening. Bartley, sad and quiet, is already a doomed man; his sisters cannot see this yet (when they are older and mothers they may), but Bartley knows it, and so does Maurya. But she cannot express this premonition directly; if she did Bartley would be bound to scoff at it as a mere fancy and be more determined to go. Maurya, in fact, is severely handicapped in this crucial struggle. If she describes the dangers of the journey fully, she will distress the girls further, perhaps

unnecessarily, and she may provoke Bartley into going in order
to show that she is wrong and that he is not a coward, particularly as other men are attempting the trip, and the priest has not
forbidden it. At the same time the nature of the people (their self-
respect and reserve) and their traditions prevent her both from
begging or ordering him not to go. And so she catches at his
every word and gesture, trying to wring from them some reason
why he should stay. This gives a kind of versicle and response
quality to the speech which is peculiarly elevated and potent,
making an incantation or ritual for approaching death, and seeming symbolical of thousands of similar scenes. Pathos is further
heightened by the way Bartley ignores his mother, and gives
directions to the girls regarding the tasks to be done about the
home, as if his absence was only to be temporary, though it is
clear to an audience that he is really departing for ever. When
Bartley takes the rope Maurya tells him to leave it because it will
be needed to bury Michael, but he replies: 'I've no halter the
way I can ride down on the mare, and I must go now quickly.
This is the one boat going for two weeks or beyond it, and the
fair will be a good fair for horses, I heard them saying below'
(40). She snatches, as is her custom, at his last words: 'It's a hard
thing they'll be saying below if the body is washed up and there's
no man in it to make the coffin, and I after giving a big price for
the finest boards you'd find in Connemara' (41). Like most primitive peoples these islanders are sticklers for custom and social
proprieties, and she stresses the importance of observing due
form, in the hope that this will make him stay: although her real
worry is not that Michael, if washed up, will not get a decent
burial, but that Bartley will go to sea. Bartley resists her, and her
tone intensifies to a searching question: 'If it was a hundred
horses, or a thousand horses, you had itself, what is the price of a
thousand horses against a son where there is one son only?' (41).
This cry, addressed to Bartley, also reverberates through our
minds; it is a prayer for a true sense of values, a refusal to weigh
one human life in the same scales as commercial gain, and a protest against conditions of life which compel men to risk their lives
constantly in order to gain a bare subsistence. Is life worth having
on such terms? It is a question which echoes through the play; but
Bartley dare not consider the question, let alone attempt to answer
it, and he goes on giving directions to the girls, ending: 'It's hard

set we'll be from this day with no one in it but one man to work.'
Once more Maurya pounces on his words, desperate now that
she is losing the struggle, and dropping all reserve, forced to make
the direct appeal: 'It's hard set we'll be surely the day you're
drowned with the rest. What way will I live and the girls with me,
and I an old woman looking for the grave?' (42). At this tense
moment there is a stage direction: '(*Bartley lays down halter, takes
off his old coat, and puts on a newer one of the same flannel.*)' Bartley in
performing these simple movements in silence – while the girls
look on doubtfully and Maurya yearns towards him in agony –
shows that he is deeply moved by his mother's appeal and distress
and is almost persuaded not to go. At last this extremely effective
moment of stillness, seeming so long, is ended as Bartley makes
some slight gesture indicating decision. Then he asks about the
boat and says, with great tragic irony, 'I'll be coming again in two
days.' Maurya knows she is defeated and breaks into lament:
'Isn't it a hard and cruel man won't hear a word from an old
woman, and she holding him from the sea?' (42). Cathleen's quick
reply to this expresses an attitude completely opposed to
Maurya's: 'It's the life of a young man to be going on the sea, and
who would listen to an old woman with one thing and she saying
it over?' (42). Cathleen's words embody the outlook of those
islanders who still have the hope that life may be bearable, even
enjoyable; she is youth, courageously and confidently facing a life
which the old woman, who has greater knowledge and experience,
and who is shattered in spirit, now wishes to reject. Maurya's
agony reaches a climax as Bartley departs: 'He is gone now, God
spare us, and we'll not see him again. He's gone now, and when
the black night is falling I'll have no son left me in the world'
(43).

(*c*) But the time has not yet come (though it will) to stress and
develop this theme. At this stage in the play some change of mood
or pace, some variation of tension, are necessary, to give relief for
highly charged emotions in both characters and audience, to forward the action and supply further essential information, particularly about the contents of the bundle, and to provide contrast with what has gone before and prepare for the ultimate
climax. The transition from elevated and symbolic gesture and
utterance to a concern with more domestic matters is brought
about with great skill by Maurya's aimless raking at the fire (how

natural and how expressive of her desolation this is) and by Cathleen's alarm about the cake:

CATHLEEN: The Son of God forgive us, Nora, we're after
forgetting his bit of bread.
NORA: And it's destroyed he'll be going till dark night, and he
after eating nothing since the sun went up (43).

At first sight their cries and their anxiety may appear to be exces-
sive; why, when there is so much distress upon the house, should
they make these outbursts about a mere matter of forgetting
bread? But closer consideration will reveal how exact is Synge's
understanding of psychology. The two girls *are* worried – about
Michael and Bartley – but they cannot show their worry, they
must put on a brave face for as long as they can; yet, at the same
time, their pent-up feelings demand some outlet, and so this flaw
in their domestic arrangements enables them to give vent to these
feelings, without disclosing that they are really alarmed, not
about the cake of bread, but about their brothers. Meanwhile
Maurya, bowed over the turf fire, is visibly distressed, and the
girls, partly in the hope that seeing Bartley again and giving him
her blessing may console Maurya, and partly in order to get rid of
her, advise Maurya to go out to the spring well. She goes out
slowly and painfully, saying, with great pathos, as she takes
Michael's stick: 'In the big world the old people do be leaving
things after them for their sons and children, but in this place it is
the young men do be leaving things behind for them that do be
old.' They at once bring out the bundle, and Nora, in a few brief
words that help to hold the play near to everyday actuality and
suggest a normal world going on all round, tells how it was found:
'There were two men, and they rowing round with the poteen
before the cocks crowed, and the oar of one of them caught the
body and they passing the black cliffs of the north' (45). The two
girls, like a person who has just received a message containing
either very good or very bad news, are both eager and reluctant
to open the bundle; yet anything is better than uncertainty, and
they try to open it. But the tension is further intensified when the
knot proves too tight and they have to find a knife and cut the
string. By such simple means does Synge get his effects. Noteworthy too is the way Nora's youth and comparative inexperience
of these crises are brought out by her artless questions: 'I've heard

tell it was a long way to Donegal' and 'And what time would a man take, and he floating?' At such moments of intense stress and uncertainty the young person's mind, as if by some natural defence mechanism, swerves away into speculation. Most felicitous of all is the way in which the domestic and the tragic are mingled; ordinary things, such as the bundle, string and knot, the knife, the flannel shirt on the hook, acquire momentous meaning, and serve to set forth and heighten the tragic emotion. In addition, there can be few more sad experiences than handling the clothes of someone dear and lately dead, and it is by Nora's recognizing her dropped stitches that the truth is brought home. At once the language lifts from the quiet, anxious phrases they have been exchanging to a more passionate, unparticularized, lament:

> CATHLEEN: Ah, Nora, isn't it a bitter thing to think of him floating that way to the far north, and no-one to keen him but the black hags that do be flying on the sea?
>
> NORA (*Swinging herself half round, and throwing out her arms on the clothes.*) And isn't it a pitiful thing when there is nothing left of a man who was a great rower and fisher but a bit of an old shirt and a plain stocking? (46–7).

But they must go on living, and the immediate task is to prevent Maurya knowing that Michael is drowned. Yet here too there is pathos in the way in which the two girls have to devise subterfuges to spare Maurya just a little sorrow and to allow her to retain her hope about Michael for a few hours longer. In fact throughout the play there is a general conspiracy for each person to hide, if not from himself, at least from all the others, the terrible truth that death is ever near and inexorable. Cathleen, though she is only twenty, is already something of an expert in such evasions, and she tells Nora to sit with her back to the light so that Maurya will not see that she has been crying.

(*d*) But when Maurya enters she is not in a condition to remark such features. She is absorbed by the vision of her dead husband and sons she has just seen; and the rest of the play is one great lament by Maurya for Bartley and Michael, for all her family, for all the islanders, for all men. In these few minutes Maurya goes through imaginatively a whole lifetime of suffering; seeing into the mystery of things she finds at the core death, but, accepting this, she comes out on the other side of grief with a kind of poise and calmness. This lament is punctuated only by the brief words of Cathleen and the islanders which serve to anchor the poetry and symbolism to normality, to blend the particular with the universal and to highlight the tragic mood; how moving are the man's words on hearing that Maurya has not thought of nails for the coffin: 'It's a great wonder she wouldn't think of the nails, and all the coffins she's seen made already.' Cathleen, at this stage, is seen to be taking on all the responsibility for keeping the home together, now that her mother is beyond it; she finds out how Bartley met his death, and arranges for his burial, Maurya being no longer interested in such details, as she becomes aware of something bigger, which includes and transcends particularities.

In presenting this climax Synge uses the two fundamental methods of the dramatist: narration and enactment on the stage, the classical method and the modern. But the narration is not merely of a particular happening, it is of what has happened, is happening, and will happen; just as the enactment is representative not of one event, but of all. Maurya's narration evokes and concentrates a whole lifetime of suffering and conflict; eight men move vividly across her imagination, and ours, all riders to the sea, which is death:

> I've had a husband, and a husband's father, and six sons in this house – six fine men, though it was a hard birth I had with every one of them and they coming to the world – and some of them were found and some of them were not found, but they're gone now the lot of them . . . (50).

The old woman's memory is better for far-off events, and it is while she is describing one of the earlier family disasters – how they brought the body in, the time Patch was drowned, when Bartley was only a baby on her knee – that the wheel comes full circle: they bring in the body of her last son. Her imagination has reduced multitude to unity, succession to an instant, her life has been made up seemingly of nothing but such scenes and she asks: 'Is it Patch or Michael, or what is it at all?' For her the sea seems almost saturated with dead men: 'There does be a power of young men floating round in the sea.' Here there is a particularly fine touch. Maurya is speaking, partly to Nora, as if to instruct and console her youngest child, and, with that knack many of us have of remembering trivial details in some moment of stress, she explains how they brought in Patch's body: 'A thing in the half of a red sail, and water dripping out of it – it was a dry day, Nora – and leaving a track to the door' (51). At this moment the islanders begin to enter, mourning, and Nora, looking out, sees the men carrying Bartley's body wrapped in a 'bit of red sail', and she cries: 'They're carrying a thing among them, and there's water dripping out of it and leaving a track by the big stones' (52). Nora is being initiated into this ritual of death. She is in the same position as her mother was many years ago; and in the future, it is implied, she will be in the position of Maurya, seeing her children brought home in this procession. It is always the same: in past, present, future, men ride down to the sea and are brought home in this way; nothing can break the cycle of 'these dying generations'.

The enactment on the stage too is the climax to Maurya's words, a concrete example to reinforce them, and also a symbolic representation of all the deaths on the island, and elsewhere. It hardly matters whether it is Patch or Michael or Bartley that is being brought home: all at some time or other find alike the inevitable end, and the one ritual we see on the stage is not only for Bartley but for all of them. Everything combines to persuade spectators that they are watching a scene of universal significance. There is no confusion, everyone knows what to do: the women enter ceremoniously, cross themselves, group near the foot of the stage, and, putting their red petticoats over their heads, begin to keen softly; the two girls quickly get the table out, then kneel at the foot; the men place the body on the table with practised ease, then take up their accustomed positions kneeling near the door; and Maurya, like a priest taking his place at the altar, bows, kneels by Bartley's head, and conducts the requiem.

Yet although Maurya uses Christian terms and symbols and sprinkles Bartley's body with Holy Water, she has come to a position where, for her, the comforts of organized religion are of no avail. The young priest had said that God would not leave her destitute with no son living, but as Maurya declares, 'It's little the like of him knows of the sea': she feels that the sea, the hunger for destruction at the heart of the universe, is too powerful for the antidotes of religion. Worn by repeated suffering and mourning, she has reached 'A condition of complete simplicity (Costing not less than everything)'; and her gesture in putting the empty

cup mouth downwards upon Bartley's body symbolizes that she
has drained life to the lees, and feels that the end is come. Hence
in her last great speeches it is not so much on the agony she has
experienced that she dwells but upon the comfort that may come
through total defeat and acquiescence; she is getting beyond personal pain:

> They're all gone now, and there isn't anything more the sea
> can do to me . . . I'll have no call now to be up crying and
> praying when the wind breaks from the south, and you can hear
> the surf is in the east, and the surf is in the west, making a great
> stir with the two noises, and they hitting one on the other. I'll
> have no call now to be going down and getting Holy Water in
> the dark nights after Samhain, and I won't care what way the
> sea is when the other women will be keening. . . . It isn't that I
> haven't prayed for you, Bartley, to the Almighty God. It isn't
> that I haven't said prayers in the dark night till you wouldn't
> know what I'd be saying; but it's a great rest I'll have now, and
> it's time surely. It's a great rest I'll have now, and great sleeping
> in the nights after Samhain, if it's only a bit of wet flour we do
> have to eat, and maybe a fish that would be stinking (53).

Maurya is finding a little peace and consolation; but for an audience this intensifies the tragedy – that in this life the only way to
get rest and comfort is through the death of loved ones, through
the exhaustion of all capacity for suffering. Yet at the end one
feels that remarkable exultation which is at the heart of real
tragedy. Having supped pain and horror to the full and known the
pitch of agony, Maurya gets beyond the world, since she no longer has any claims upon it, nor it upon her. Accordingly calm and
compassion come to her, she forgets herself and acquires humility
and charity, and in her last words uttered as she stands up alone
there is a predominant note of reconciliation and a new concern
for others:

> They're all together this time, and the end is come. May the
> Almighty God have mercy on Bartley's soul, and on Michael's
> soul, and on the souls of Sheamus and Patch, and Stephen and
> Shawn (*bending her head*); and may He have mercy on my soul,
> Nora, and on the soul of every one is left living in the world. . . .
> Michael has a clean burial in the far north, by the grace of the

Almighty God. Bartley will have a fine coffin out of the white boards, and a deep grave surely. What more can we want than that? No man at all can be living for ever, and we must be satisfied.

Integral to this is the theme of dream versus actuality. The dream is the hope that one may escape the sea; the actuality is the sea or death; though nightmare would probably be a more accurate word than dream to apply to the side of the tension opposite to the sea or death. For the hopes, the dream, of such a person as Maurya are from time to time shattered by the actuality, the sea or death. Her life is a continual alternation between hope that someone will escape the sea or death and the fear that no one will escape. Unlike the figures of *The Well of the Saints*, who are normally able to ignore harsh actuality and enjoy a tolerable life in the dream, the islanders cannot rest in the dream. The islanders' dream is constantly turning to nightmare as actuality remorselessly intrudes with the death of a dear one at sea. Nevertheless, while some men are still alive, the islanders must go on hoping, must believe in the dream. And if no deaths occur for a while, and the men are able to make a little money by their labour, the islanders can enjoy their festivals and customs and delight in some of the good things of life. But there is a further twist of pain in the fact that they can only have these material necessities of life, and a little more if lucky, through the sacrifice of men. Men must risk their lives to keep all alive; the cost in human life and suffering merely to maintain the existence of the community is enormous, but unless one wants to lie down and die without an effort, this cost must be paid. Hence arises the terrible dilemma that if a woman has, like Maurya, several men in the family, she has a good chance of always having enough to eat at least, but she has also constant anxiety about their safety, and recurrent agony as one by one the sea devours them. Without sons or men one is spared the worry but one goes short of the necessities of life; one has only 'a bit of wet flour' and 'maybe a fish that would be stinking'. Thus in *Riders to the Sea* horror comes from the fact that no one can rest in the dream; it is shattered from time to time by actuality – the sea or death. All know that the dream may only be a dream, that no-one may escape actuality, yet they must go on believing in the dream, there is nothing else short of emigration or suicide; and this constant tension between the dream (that one may escape) and the many evidences around proving that hardly anyone will escape, makes worry and restlessness endemic to life. As Synge says:[170]

> The maternal feeling is so powerful on these islands that it gives a life of torment to the women. Their sons grow up to be banished as soon as they are of age, or to live here in continual danger on the sea; their daughters go away also, or are worn out in their youth with bearing children that grow up to harass them in their own turn a little later.

The tension is always present in some degree until the time when the dream is finally extinguished. This occurs when no one has escaped, and there is no need to dream further: 'there isn't anything more the sea can do'. At this stage the tension disappears, and one sees actuality as it is – the sea or death. From the ending of this tension and from the contemplation of the actuality behind all appearances and dreams, comes a new state of calm acquiescence, humility and compassion; the mood of Maurya's last speech: 'No man at all can be living for ever, and we must be satisfied.' The horror goes out of life – one has been through the worst – but with it go both the motive and the means of life, and only rest and oblivion remain.

Yeats says:[171] 'The old woman in *The Riders to the Sea* in mourning for her six fine sons, mourns for the passing of all beauty and strength.' I think this is true. Our consideration of this play, of all Synge's writings, and of his life, gives us cause to entertain the suggestion that although Maurya is primarily both an individual – a mother living in a particular place at a particular time – and also representative of the enduring characteristics of her kind, she is also something else. She represents not only all the Aran islanders but also all humanity. She is an image of humanity facing a hostile universe, and through her Synge hints, as he does in other ways, that life is essentially tragic and the final reality is death, and that through the acceptance of this fact, along with compassion for doomed humanity, charity and peace may come.

Deirdre of the Sorrows

Although Synge's last play, *Deirdre of the Sorrows*, was written mainly during his fatal illness, and not quite finished, it is a coherent whole, and has been produced successfully on a number of occasions. Synge's dramatization of this 'lay of the Red Branch', perhaps the most moving and most popular of all Gaelic legends, does not mark a change in him as a dramatist; it is not a new departure but a development. He does not revoke the attitude antagonistic to the romanticizing of Celtic myth, expressed in his lines 'The Passing of the Shee'. While giving his regal figures richness and nobility he portrays them mainly in terms of peasant life, and avoids the shortcomings of the contemporary versions of the legend which treated Deirdre rather like Tennyson treated King Arthur. These versions (and there was a spate of them) tended to veil the stark legend in a rarefied, dream-like atmosphere, which was poetic in an unsuitable way. They are graceful closet dramas, but lacking in the tang of reality; they incline towards the Celtic Twilight, while Synge, as Una Ellis-Fermor says,[172] 'belongs, not by sentiment and wistful longing, but by the roots of his nature to the Celtic noonday which had been sweet and sane'. These facts have been recognized by commentators, and have led some to say that Synge captures and re-creates the spirit of the original legend. I fail to see how it is possible (or desirable) for even the greatest genius to re-capture the spirit of any past age. Synge's version, with its beauty and astringency, is probably nearest to the spirit of the original, but one of its main distinctions is that it appeals not only to the cultivated few interested in this kind of play, but also to the wider audience normally indifferent to poetic drama; this, Yeats's version, despite its merits, hardly does, and 'A.E.' 's deplorable version never does.

Deirdre of the Sorrows is one with the rest of Synge's writings, and in it the main characteristics of Synge as a dramatist can be seen clearly: the use and transformation of material from Irish life and legend; the tension between two inimical ways of life, between the dream and the actuality; the influence of the natural world upon character; and the awareness of mutability. For example, the first act of *Deirdre of the Sorrows* sets forth a situation basically similar to that in Synge's first published play, *The Shadow of the Glen*. There is the same tension between two differing ways of life, and the same ending with an instinctive defiance of wealth and power and a movement of the younger, imaginative people towards a new life. There are strong affinities between Nora and

Deirdre, between Dan and Conchubor, and to a lesser degree between Tramp and Naisi. There is the same incompatibility between Deirdre and Conchubor as there is between Nora and Dan, life for Deirdre with Conchubor would be as intolerable as it has become for Nora with Dan; and both Deirdre and Nora have to decide whether or not to defy the man who provides material security but nothing else. From this impasse Naisi and Tramp provide the way out, with the difference that the Tramp has to offer their course to Nora, while Naisi has to be helped to see their course by Deirdre. In making this choice it is the awareness of the inevitability of decay and death that is the salient factor in both plays: better to risk all in the hope of enjoying some love and happiness than to moulder away in Dan's cottage or in Conchubor's palace. The influence of the natural world on character is important in both plays, and both women dread the surroundings associated with the older men: Nora dreads the glens around Dan's farm, and Deirdre dreads the great, bare palace Conchubor has prepared for her. The difference is that in the beginning Deirdre is in her right environment in the natural world (from which Conchubor wishes to take her) while this is the kind of environment which Nora and Tramp seek.

The conflict between Deirdre and Conchubor is foreshadowed in the opening words of the play. Old Woman reproves Lavarcham for not preventing Deirdre from straying on the hills, but Lavarcham knows that it is both wrong and impossible to restrain the abundant and intuitive enjoyment of life which is in Deirdre, and that, even if there were no prophecy, Conchubor's attempt to do so would bring only trouble. Old Woman, who inclines towards Conchubor (as Lavarcham inclines towards Deirdre) cannot understand this:

> Shouldn't she be well pleased getting the like of Conchubor, and he middling settled in years itself? I don't know what he wanted putting her this wild place to be breaking her in, or putting myself to be roasting her supper and she with no patience for her food at all (276).

Old Woman's use of the words 'breaking her in' is interesting, for that is what Conchubor is trying to do, to bind to himself a joy. The tragedy is that Conchubor fails to see that to break Deirdre in, to make her suitable for palace life with its tainted opulence and intrigue, is to destroy her. Blake's words are apposite to the play:

> He who binds to himself a joy
> Does the winged life destroy;
> He who kisses joy as it flies
> Lives in eternity's sunrise.

Lavarcham partly understands this, and she tries to show Conchubor how inherently unsuitable for him Deirdre is, by indicating that Deirdre ignores the rich ornaments which Conchubor sends her, and prefers her own native crafts: 'She does be all times straying round picking flowers or nuts, or sticks itself; but so long as she's gathering new life I've a right not to heed her, I'm thinking, and she taking her will.' But the sort of new life Deirdre is gathering is not what Conchubor desires or can understand. He wants her to be wise and busy in the ways of his world, but Lavarcham again points out that Deirdre is having an education as appropriate for her nature as the training which Conchubor wants to force on her is hostile to it:

> she's little call to mind an old woman when she has the birds to school her, and the pools in the rivers where she goes bathing in the sun. I'll tell you if you seen her that time, with her white skin, and her red lips, and the blue water with the ferns about her, you'd know, maybe, and you greedy itself, it wasn't for the like of you she was born at all (279–80).

This engaging picture, with its fresh primary colours, has an effect which Lavarcham did not intend. It naturally stimulates Conchubor's greed: 'It's little I heed for what she was born; she'll be my comrade, surely.' Conchubor is as dead to the intuitive life and the natural world as was Dan who dismissed it all as blather. He refuses to try to understand Deirdre, and in attempting for the sake of his own desire to force her from a wholesome way of life into an alien one he is responsible for the tragedy.

The extreme incompatibility between Deirdre and Conchubor is established at their first meeting: Deirdre's poor clothes and instinctive grace and dignity contrast with Conchubor's rich adornments and his coarse, uneasy manner, and this contrast is underlined by their bringings: Conchubor has rings and jewels from Emain Macha, while Deirdre has 'A bag of nuts, and twigs

for our fires at the dawn of day'. This, and Deirdre's quiet defiance: 'I have no wish to be a queen,' annoy Conchubor and bring
to the surface the insensitivity and arrogance which he was trying
to conceal under a cajoling manner:

> And it's that way you're picking up the manners will fit you to
> be Queen of Ulster? . . . You'd wish to be dressing in your duns
> and grey, and you herding your geese or driving your calves to
> their shed – like the common lot scattered in the glens (281–2).

By such means is the opposition between Deirdre and Conchubor
stressed as Conchubor strives to win her by bluster, flattery,
warnings, promises of wealth and protection, and, eventually,
when all these have failed in turn, by force. Deirdre however is
firm. She is even adroit enough to mark the contrast between
Conchubor and the man she would like, 'a mate who'd be her
likeness'; and, incidentally, to prepare for the entrance of Naisi
and for her feelings for him. Conchubor's attempt to counter the
grace of Naisi by promises of further expensive gifts is futile. In
addition, his warnings of great troubles are foretold if Deirdre has
any connexion with Naisi, his assurances that he will protect her,
and his final plea that he needs her gaiety, affection and solace to
enable him to bear the heavy responsibilities of kingship, are all
equally vain. But when Conchubor, speaking no longer as a lover
but as a ruler, declares that it is his pleasure to have her, and that
he will take her away to Emain in two days, Deirdre is alarmed:

> I'd liefer stay this place, Conchubor. Leave me this place,
> where I'm well used to the tracks and pathways and the people
> of the glens. . . . It's for this life I'm born surely. . . . You don't
> know me and you'd have little joy taking me (284).

But, Conchubor, triumphant that at last he has moved her, ignores
this appeal and refuses to consider her reluctance as anything more
than coyness: 'Young girls are slow always; it is their lovers must
say the word.'
    After Conchubor and Fergus have gone Deirdre is *terrified with
the reality that is before her* as the stage direction indicates. Here the
predominant theme of the play, developing perfectly out of the
opening theme, begins to be heard. Reality is death. Existence
with Conchubor would crush all that is precious in Deirdre's
nature, and physical death would probably follow. For a moment

she can see no way of avoiding it; Lavarcham says no one can go against the High King, and she must come to terms with him. Then in this extremity she looks out of the window as if seeking solace from the natural world, and in a flash it comes to her: the floods and storm will drive Naisi and his brothers to her hut; she will defy Conchubor, and try to kiss 'the joy as it flies'. In this moment of insight she grasps the truth: death must come to everyone; better then to defy it, to risk all in attempting to gain the kind of life and love which she and Naisi may enjoy together, and which alone makes life precious, than to moulder away in Conchubor's palace.

Her immediate endeavour is to make Naisi see this truth; and she causes the hut to be decorated with Conchubor's rich hangings and she dresses herself in the robes, in order to help Naisi to realize that she is both a woman and a queen, who will 'have the right of a queen who is master' to take her own choice and make a 'stir to the edges of the seas'. Rich life is surging in her, and as Lavarcham recognizes, 'she's a good right' to have her pleasure, for 'When all's said, it's her like will be the master till the end of time.' Naisi, when he enters, is in a similar mood, exuberant with well-being, despite the storm:

> At your age you should know there are nights when a king like Conchubor would spit upon his arm ring, and queens will stick out their tongues at the rising moon. We're that way this night, and it's not wine we're asking only. Where is the young girl told us we might shelter here? (293).

When we, and Naisi, saw Deirdre last she was a queen dressed as a country-girl, now on re-appearing she is fully a queen. Naisi is clearly in love with her, but he controls his feelings and keeps a formal distance, because he believes she is promised to the High King, and he does not want to cause trouble. Consequently, Deirdre, seating herself in a high chair, as on a throne, has to take the initiative in wooing. This is done delicately and naturally; and at length she is able to carry the truth alive into his heart:

> It's a sweet life you and I could have, Naisi. . . . It should be a sweet thing to have what is best and richest if it's for a short space only. . . . You must not go, Naisi, and leave me to the High King, a man is ageing in his dun, with his crowds round

him, and his silver and gold. . . . I will not live to be shut up in Emain, and wouldn't we do well paying, Naisi, with silence and a near death. . . . I'm a long while in the woods with my own self, and I'm in little dread of death, and it earned with riches would make the sun red with envy, and he going up the heavens; and the moon pale and lonesome, and she wasting away. . . . Isn't it a small thing is foretold about the ruin of our-selves, Naisi, when all men have age coming and great ruin in the end? (297–8).

Naisi feels the truth of this, and at once makes his noble and generous decision, promising, not, as Conchubor did, wealth and 'a place is safe and splendid', but love in communion with the natural world:

Then we'll go away; it isn't I will give your like to Conchubor, not if the grave was dug to be my lodging when a week was by. . . . The stars are out Deirdre, and let you come with me quickly, for it is the stars will be our lamps many nights and we abroad in Alban, and taking our journeys among the little islands in the sea. There has never been the like of the joy we'll have Deirdre, you and I, having our fill of love at the evening and the morning till the sun is high.

The resemblance between this speech and the last speech of the Tramp in *The Shadow of the Glen* is striking; and Deirdre and Naisi, like Nora and Tramp, go off at the end of the act towards a new life. Thus Synge felicitously introduces his main theme – death the ultimate actuality, and love the dream that alone can deride death and make life worthwhile – using this theme to motivate the lovers' actions, to express the deep and genuine nature of their feelings, and to prepare for subsequent events.

That Deirdre and Naisi do find love and joy and a satisfying personal relationship together is made clear by Act Two. But it is also made clear that in the nature of things this relationship, though the most valuable that human beings can enjoy, is not per-fect and not immutable. All must fade and die. This is the main theme of the act and the chief motive for the return of the lovers to Emain. The act takes place seven years later in Alban, and opens at the point where the relationship, having reached its peak, is about to decline. Deirdre speaks lightheartedly enough to Lavarcham at first, but during their discussion of Conchubor's plans it becomes apparent that this gaiety is only Deirdre's habitual mask. Underneath there is anxiety and a complete absence of hope. Happy as she has been, she knows that there is no escaping the inevitable end; though she has been successful in concealing her dread from Naisi and his brothers who think she is never anything but gay:

> There's little power to stop what's coming . . . it's this day I'm dreading seven years, and I fine nights watching the heifers walking to the haggard with long shadows on the grass; or the time I've been stretched in the sunshine, when I've heard Ainnle and Ardan stepping lightly, and they saying: Was there ever the like of Deirdre for a happy and sleepy queen? . . . I've dread going or staying, Lavarcham. It's lonesome this place, having happiness like ours, till I'm asking each day will this day match yesterday, and will tomorrow take a good place beside the same day in the year that's gone, and wondering all times is it a game worth playing, living on until you're dried and old, and our joy is gone for ever (304–5).

This truth of the relentlessness of decay and death is the main theme of the play but it is stressed particularly in this act since it is to be the motive for the return of the lovers and must be convincing. Accordingly each character in turn (except Lavarcham) brings out this truth until Deirdre and Naisi consciously recognize it, admit it to each other, and decide to face death together rather than moulder away.

That singular figure Owen, whose function is that of stressing facts which other characters either overlook or dread to utter, recognizes this truth, and forces it upon Deirdre. Thoughts and feelings which have been gathering in Deirdre for some time he puts into words and she is unable to contradict him, not even when he places the choice starkly before her, indicating that either way the end is the same – death:

> Well, go, take your choice. Stay here and rot with Naisi or go to Conchubor in Emain. Conchubor's a wrinkled fool with a swelling belly on him, and eyes falling downward from his shining crown; Naisi should be stale and weary . . . I tell you, you'll have great sport one day seeing Naisi getting a harshness in his two sheep's eyes and he looking on yourself . . . (308).

And the fault, it is implied, is really no one's; it is there in the
nature of existence, and a relationship so unusually felicitous as
that of Deirdre and Naisi cannot alter the fact that: 'Queens get
old, Deirdre, with their white and long arms going from them,
and their back's hooping. I tell you it's a poor thing to see a
queen's nose reaching down to scrape her chin' (308). The only
way to defeat decay is to end life and love when they are starting
to decline: 'I'll give you a riddle, Deirdre: Why isn't my father
as ugly and old as Conchubor? You've no answer? . . . It's because Naisi killed him. . . . Think of that and you awake at
night, hearing Naisi snoring . . .' (309).

Fergus in his attempts to persuade the two to return, plays upon
the exiled Irishman's well-known yearning to return to his native
land:

> When I was a young man we'd have given a lifetime to be in
> Ireland a score of weeks; and to this day the old men have
> nothing so heavy as knowing it's in a short while they'll lose
> the high skies are over Ireland, and the lonesome mornings
> with the birds crying on the bogs. Let you come this day, for
> there's no place but Ireland where the Gael can have peace
> always (309–10).

But when this does not succeed he too begins to stress the fact
that age and decay will warp love: 'You'll not be young always. . . .
It's little joy wandering till age is on you. . . .' Then to Naisi
alone: 'You'd do well to come back . . . and not be lingering until
the day that you'll grow weary, and hurt Deirdre showing her the
hardness will grow up within your eyes . . .' (311). Because these
words echo and focus his own scattered feelings Naisi is drawn
by them, and, unaware that Deirdre can overhear him, he begins
to confess to Fergus (just as Deirdre had confessed to Lavarcham at the opening of the act) that he too has the dread that their
love is bound to fade: 'I'll not tell you a lie. There have been days
a while past when I've been throwing a line for salmon or watching for the run of hares, that I've a dread upon me a day'd come
I'd weary of her voice . . . and Deirdre'd see I'd wearied' (312).
But Naisi in thinking that this dread can be overcome, and they
can continue to be happy differs from Deirdre: he has no Owen to
confirm and emphasize the truth which he has just realized. And
so assuming that Deirdre is completely happy and has no fears,

and that he can conceal his dread from her, he dismisses these notions of getting old and weary and losing his delight in Deirdre as dreams only. Deirdre however knows that they are not dreams but the actuality breaking in to end their dream of love. She knows that there is no place to stay always, and her simple words express movingly the terrible grief which breaks her heart:

> There's no safe place, Naisi, on the ridge of the world. . . . It's this hour we're between the daytime and a night where there is sleep for ever, and isn't it a better thing to be following on to a near death, than to be bending the head down, and dragging with the feet, and seeing one day a blight showing upon love where it is sweet and tender? (315).

This is the beginning of twilight, the brightness of their seven years is passing irrevocably, and they are for the dark. Better not to endure years of it but to forestall death by a swift and clean end; or, in the unlikely event of Conchubor's not practising some treachery, to devote oneself to the duties of some high position in the state:

> There are as many ways to wither love as there are stars in a night of Samhain; but there is no way to keep life, or love with it, a short space only. . . . It's for that there's nothing lonesome like a love is watching out the time most lovers do be sleeping. . . . It's for that we're setting out for Emain Macha when the tide turns on the sand. . . . We're seven years without roughness or growing weary; seven years so sweet and shining, the gods would be hard set to give us seven days the like of them. It's for that we're going to Emain, where there'll be a rest for ever, or a place for forgetting, in great crowds and they making a stir.

Once again Naisi, tender and unselfish, is helped to see the truth by Deirdre; he says: 'You're right, maybe. It should be a poor thing to see great lovers and they sleepy and old. . . . We'll go, surely, in place of keeping a watch on a love had no match and it wasting away' (316).

The reluctance of Ainnle and Ardan to go back, and Owen's violence and suicide when he hears the news, make it clear that Conchubor intends treachery, and that the two are going to their death; this is underlined by the stage direction: '(*They are all subdued like men at a queen's wake.*)' The shadow of death begins to

distort, and the quarrel between Naisi and his brothers is an adum-
bration of the quarrel which later severs Deirdre and Naisi at the
grave's edge. Here however Deirdre interposes, and after she has
given reasons for their return in such a way as to prevent Lavarcham, Ainnle and Ardan from worrying about the real reasons,
the melancholy pilgrimage is begun.

Thus Synge makes a marked change in the motive for the
lovers' return. The traditional motive – the one used by every
writer on the subject except Synge – was that Conchubor, urging
that the country needed them now he was growing old, offered
them a high position by his side and complete pardon, if they
returned, and Fergus guaranteed all this. In Synge's version Conchubor makes these offers, and Fergus backs them, but the lovers
are not deceived, and their suspicions of treachery are confirmed
by Owen. Nevertheless they go back because they have learned
that the ultimate actuality is death, and that love is a dream, and
they prefer to end the dream and life cleanly rather than drag on
deteriorating. For them, as for Donne in his 'A Lecture upon the
Shadow':

> *Love is a growing, or full constant light;*
> *And his first minute, after noon, is night.*

Events at the end of Act Two indicate that Deirdre, and Naisi
and his brothers, are going back to their death, and this impression
is strengthened by the opening of Act Three. Conchubor is
prowling about the tent waiting for Deirdre, rather like he did
seven years previously in the hut on Slieve Fuadh. He is much
older, less confident, more irritable and bitter, and hungrier than
ever for Deirdre. His examination of the opening at the back
making sure it is closed suggests that he has something prepared
there, and the news that Fergus has been stopped in the north,
and Deirdre and Naisi and his brothers are coming alone, make it
certain that they are moving into a trap. Lavarcham, entering,
knows this, and once more, as in Act One, she pleads with Conchubor to spare Deirdre, stressing again the inherent unsuitability
of Deirdre for Conchubor. But Conchubor is now desperate; all
his wealth and power have left him unsatisfied, he feels that
Deirdre comprises what is most precious in life, and he is ready
to go to any lengths, 'to destroy mankind and skin the gods' to
possess her, before it is too late.

One knows however that Conchubor will never have Deirdre alive, and so her end, along with that of Naisi and his brothers, is inevitable. But for an audience to await an inevitable end for nearly all the last act of a play is not normally good drama. To provide and maintain interest and tension, to give variety of pace and mood, it is necessary to introduce some illusion of hope, some chance that the victims may escape their doom, so that when at last the catastrophe does come it may be startling (though inevitable) and not just the end of an obvious progression to death. And so Synge, by a master-stroke, improves on the traditional ending and on that provided by Ferguson, Yeats and 'A.E.' by introducing two 'turns' of the action which increase excitement, blend and contrast emotion, and fill out and deepen characters, making them both more human and more tragic. Synge's catastrophe is not merely inevitable; it is both inevitable and unexpected, and in this it accords with the suggestions of Aristotle in his *Poetics* for the best kind of tragic plot and catastrophe, and also with the observations of T. S. Eliot:[173] 'the audience should be kept in the constant expectation that something is going to happen and when it does happen, it should be different, but not too different, from what the audience has been led to expect'.

The first unexpected 'turn' occurs with Deirdre's almost successful attempt to make peace between Conchubor and Naisi. Deirdre and Naisi enter, weary from their long journey, and not knowing death is so near. The pathos of their situation is heightened by their remarks (so like the chatter of a married couple who have come into a new lodging) about the domestic arrangements. Their examination of the rugs and hangings leads naturally to their discovery of the grave, just as Deirdre is playfully deploring Conchubor's bachelor untidiness and complimenting herself on keeping their tent in better order than this. In the exchanges which follow, Naisi's motive in behaving harshly to Deirdre is to persuade her not to die with him, but to make terms with Conchubor and save her life. Deirdre however is inflexible: 'I'll die with you, Naisi. I'd not have come from Alban but I knew I'd be along with you in Emain, and you living or dead. . . . Yet this night it's strange and distant talk you're making only' (331). Naisi's reply foreshadows the second unexpected 'turn' – the quarrel between the lovers: 'There's nothing, surely, the like of a new grave of open earth for putting a great space between two

friends that love' (331). Deirdre looks forward too, but to the
triumph of their end: 'If there isn't, it's that grave when it's
closed will make us one for ever, and we two lovers have had
great space without weariness or growing old or any sadness of
the mind' (331). Conchubor comes to look on Deirdre, and she,
aware of her power over him, restrains Naisi from attacking him,
and tries to make peace. Her plea is the now well-known one of
Synge: the equality of all men in the face of the great common-
places of life, and of death – the reality, and the need therefore for
compassion between men: 'so near that grave we seem three
lonesome people, and by a new made grave there's no man will
keep brooding on a woman's lips, or on the man he hates'. Beside
this common inheritance our differences appear trifling and men
should bear with each other. These are the first sweet and friendly
words Conchubor has heard from Deirdre, and he responds not
ungenerously. Naisi follows suit, and peace is almost gained when
the shouts of Ainnle and Ardan assailed by Conchubor's men,
shatter it. Death is stronger than peace or anything:

> CONCHUBOR: I was near won this night, but death's between
> us now. (*He goes out.*) (333)

This episode varies movement and emotion – the shining space
makes the ensuing darkness more pitiful and fearful – it emphasizes that death which overcomes Conchubor's readiness to
do what he could to please Deirdre is alone omnipotent, and it
carries on the portraiture of Conchubor as a man not altogether
lacking in good qualities.

The second 'turn' of the action – the sudden and unexpected
quarrel of Deirdre and Naisi – follows immediately and is well
motivated. Deirdre and Naisi have partly prepared themselves for
death, but when it comes, with the noise of battle outside, they
are thrown off their balance. Deirdre, with the instinctive action
of a trapped being to save herself and her mate, clings to Naisi,
beseeching him not to leave her broken and alone; while Naisi,
his instincts as a warrior to aid his brothers in their extremity
overcoming all else, throws her aside. Hence the quarrel, which,
contrasting with the scene of near-reconciliation just before, increases pathos, and makes the catastrophe more profound. It also
shows Synge's integrity – his refusal to temper the blow however
unpalatable it may be – and his knowledge of the realities of

human behaviour as distinct from the postures of romantic final
partings. In addition the quarrel is emblematic of the fact that in
'a little while' Deirdre and Naisi would 'have lived too long',
their love would be bound to decline; and the quarrel is a fore-
runner of others which might follow if they missed 'the safety
of the grave'.

This misunderstanding is not unlike the misunderstanding between Antony and Cleopatra, except that they were reconciled in
the flesh before Antony's death. Deirdre and Naisi are denied
this, but, it is hinted, they, like Antony and Cleopatra, become
one after death; and *Deirdre* ends, as does *Antony and Cleopatra*,
with the tragic lament of a queen whose life has become one of
the great legends of the world. There are certain resemblances
between the two women: Deirdre's aim is to express her grief,
to praise her lover and prepare to meet him, and to prevent
the worldly conqueror from cheating her of death and re-union
with her beloved. Like Cleopatra too, Deirdre, great tragic queen
as she is, is at the same time a 'lass unparallel'd', and firmly linked
with 'the maid that milks And does the meanest chares'. And also,
like Cleopatra, Deirdre in her final speeches, has 'immortal longings', she is getting beyond this world, and the aspirations and
rivalries of its powers are seen to be the inanities of an 'ass un-
policied'. Deirdre cries out to Conchubor: 'in this place you are an
old man and a fool only', and when Fergus opposes Conchubor
she calls: 'draw back a little with the squabbling of fools when I
am broken up with misery'. Here she, like Lavarcham earlier, de-
livers her prediction regarding the fate of Emain and its people:

> I see the flames of Emain starting upward in the dark night;
> and because of me there will be weasels and wild cats crying on
> a lonely wall where there were queens and armies and red gold,
> the way there will be a story told of a ruined city and a raving
> king and a woman will be young for ever (343).

Then, by a natural association of ideas, she glances briefly back to
her happy days, giving a picture of them which contrasts movingly
with her present distress, heightening both experiences and im-
plying, by means of the pathetic fallacy, that all nature will mourn
for the lovers:

> I see the trees naked and bare, and the moon shining. Little

moon, little moon of Alban, it's lonesome you'll be this night,
and tomorrow night, and long nights after, and you pacing the
woods beyond Glen Laoi, looking every place for Deirdre and
Naisi, the two lovers who slept so sweetly with each other
(344).

The closing of this play is perhaps the finest thing Synge ever
wrote. Here his technique and his exuberance of phrase and fancy,
are purified and perfected, and directed to one end; each word,
each gesture is functional and serious. The speech defies analysis
in the last resort but it clearly owes a good deal to the wonderful
rhythmic flow and to great fastidiousness in the choice of words;
they are mainly homely and monosyllabic, with nouns and verbs
doing most of the work, and adjectives and adverbs used very
sparingly. It is based upon the fundamental artistic principle of
sameness with difference; in this case, the repetition, with variation and development, of words, rhythms and feelings:

> Let us throw down clay on my three comrades. Let us cover up
> Naisi along with Ainnle and Ardan, they that were the pride of
> Emain. There is Naisi was the best of three, the choicest of the
> choice of many. It was a clean death was your share, Naisi; and
> it is not I will quit your head, when it's many a dark night
> among the snipe and plover that you and I were whispering
> together. It is not I will quit your head, Naisi, when it's many
> a night we saw the stars among the clear trees of Glen da
> Ruadh, or the moon pausing to rest her on the edges of the
> hills (340).

Here one repetition (with variation and development) grows out
of a former one in a wave-like movement which constitutes a
most moving pattern to express the simple ideas. The last speeches
of Deirdre have the nobility and inevitability of great ritual; they
are a beautiful lament, applicable to all generations, for the love
and joy is continually leaving the world, and yet, at the same time,
they are quite apt for the particular figures and dramatic situation.
Synge's speech has been spoken of as approximating to some of
the great monodies in the Bible, and here it does so triumphantly;
being however an individual utterance and not pastiche. One remarks how plain and concrete the words are, how felicitously
the negative is used, what distinction is conferred by one or two

exact, widely comprehensible images, and how the rhythm moulds the whole into pure and enduring dramatic speech:

> DEIRDRE (*In a high and quiet tone.*) I have put away sorrow like a shoe that is worn out and muddy, for it is I have had a life that will be envied by great companies. It was not by a low birth I made kings uneasy, and they sitting in the halls of Emain. It was not a low thing to be chosen by Conchubor, who was wise, and Naisi had no match for bravery. It is not a small thing to be rid of grey hairs, and the loosening of the teeth. (*With a sort of triumph.*) It was the choice of lives we had in the clear woods, and in the grave we're safe, surely. . . . It was sorrows were foretold, but great joys were my share always; yet it is a cold place I must go to be with you, Naisi; and it's cold your arms will be this night that were warm about my neck so often . . . it's a pitiful thing, Conchubor, you have done this night in Emain; yet a thing will be a joy and triumph to the ends of life and time (344).

This ending gives that rare and precious kind of elevation and rapture in tragic experience that we normally get only at the end of plays such as *Othello* and *Antony and Cleopatra*. This comes, partly, from the fact that Deirdre herself experiences a sort of ecstasy in the realization that Naisi and she have had the best life and it 'will be a joy and triumph to the ends of time'. Like Maurya at the end, Deirdre has got beyond personal sorrow; the cry of 'old, old' which echoed through Act Two is here resolved into exaltation; and now the notion of youth escaping decay is predominant, as Una Ellis-Fermor says:[174]

> Synge's climax is a paean of triumph, where love and immortality break through the grave and death, as in the fourth movement of Brahms' first symphony. Deirdre's keen over Naisi before she kills herself is a song of life, not of death.

The reason for this may be made clear if we examine the whole of the play in relation to the prevailing theme of all Synge's writings: here the dream is love and the actuality death. Deirdre has had a kind of Wordsworthian upbringing in communion with nature, and when we first meet her she is by no means fully conscious of actuality or dream; though she has had some instinctive premonitions, for she says: 'There are lonesome days and bad nights in this place like another' (actuality), and she has been attracted by Naisi (dream). Deirdre is first confronted with actuality in the shape of Conchubor: marriage with him, she realizes intuitively, will mean death. Her feelings for Naisi, and his for her, offer an avenue of escape from this actuality; and the two elope, hoping that love will be an actuality at least as strong as death. For seven years they enjoy love and are happy. Then since Man, however great and good, is not perfect; since all must decay:

> *Since brass, nor stone, nor earth, nor boundless sea,*
> *But sad mortality o'ersways their power,*

dread enters into their love and it shows signs of decline. They realize (and this is where Deirdre's heart breaks) 'There's no safe place on the ridge of the world . . . no way to keep life or love for more than a short space only.' They understand that death is the only actuality, and love a dream; and so they go back to Emain to face death rather than endure the agony of living with a love or dream that they know must fade. But just before she dies Deirdre sees all – actuality and dream – clearly and accurately, and is accordingly happy and triumphant. She knows that her seven years with Naisi are something priceless and rare, something which Conchubor would give his all to possess, but which neither he nor any figure in the play will ever attain. She knows also that their death will forestall decay and prevent the perfection of the dream becoming marred, so that they will be a wonder to all people till 'the ends of life and time'. Once one has enjoyed the dream of love, life becomes unbearable when it begins to fade, and then – if one is denied the opportunity of serving one's fellow men – there is nothing left but to seek the safety of the grave and find quiet consummation there.

Thus Synge has again made an important and characteristic change in the presentation of an ageless story. He has broadened and deepened his theme by shifting the emphasis from the destructiveness of an individual ruler to the destructiveness of Time. The tragedy is not so much that people like Deirdre and Naisi are crushed by powerful men like Conchubor, but that all earthly beauty, youth and love decay and die.

The position of Conchubor and Lavarcham in this pattern is worth remarking. In the traditional legend and in the versions of Yeats and 'A.E.', Conchubor is little more than a despot who desires Deirdre, whose baffled feelings turn to hatred when the lovers elope, and who eventually brings about their death by treachery. Hardly any insight into his nature, into his needs and motives, is given; he is a dark force which crushes the lovers, rather than an individual. Synge's Conchubor however is not static, he develops through the action, and he too learns, through suffering, the truth that safety and splendour are not enough without love. He comes to realize the inadequacy of his belief set forth in Act One: 'What we all need is a place is safe and splendid', and to feel the truth in Act Three: 'There's one sorrow has no end surely – that's being old and lonesome'. The marked difference in the attitudes embodied in these two quotations is a measure of Conchubor's progression towards true awareness. Synge, then, makes his Conchubor more human and interesting, and much more meaningful.

Conchubor has never doubted that material stability and magnificence are the chief desirable aims in life; but, having gained them, he still feels an emptiness, and finds that happiness eludes him. He senses, accurately enough, that Deirdre enjoys what he lacks, and he supposes, inaccurately, that marriage with her will give him what he wants. Deirdre, with all she represents, is a mystery to him and an irresistible fascination. She is a living challenge to all his most cherished beliefs: she is not safe nor has she material splendour, yet there is a beauty and joy in her life that he has never seen before, and that he longs for. But being ignorant of her nature he despises the environment and the activities of which she is fond and which have helped to make her what she is, and he assumes that she will be even lovelier in his palace. He assures himself and Deirdre that he is 'safe and splendid' but despair is near his heart often, and occasionally it is revealed; as when he gives his reasons for wanting to marry Deirdre: to have a young lovely creature, innocent of worldly matters, who will divert him: 'The like of me has a store of knowledge that's a weight and terror. It's for that we do choose out the like of yourself that are young and glad only. . . . I'm thinking you are gay and lively each day in the year?' (283). Worldly power and pride, ignorance, fear and sterility are continually associated with him:

How would I be happy seeing age coming on me each year, when the dry leaves are blowing back and forward at the gate

of Emain. . . . I'm sick and weary thinking of the day you'll
be brought down to me, and seeing you walking into my big
empty halls. I've made all sure to have you, and yet all said
there's a fear in the back of my mind I'd miss you and have
great troubles in the end (283–5).

He is an understandable and recognizable – and occasionally
pathetic – figure, although not a likeable one. His yearning for
what he cannot have is intensified by the last act to agony; he
knows that he has missed something of the greatest value, that

> *Kingdoms are clay: our dungy earth alike*
> *Feeds beast as man: the nobleness of life*
> *Is to do thus,*

that is, as Antony and Cleopatra show, to love. Such noble doing
has not been for him and he feels that he is with all his wealth
'more needy than the thieves of Meath'. He is suffering continually from the pain of loneliness and age, and the words 'old',
'desolate', 'pity', recur in his speeches. A hunger for pity and
affection racks him and blots out all other considerations; he no
longer hates Naisi, and has him removed only because he stood in
the way of his gaining the solace of Deirdre: 'I know well pity's
cruel, when it was my pity for my own self destroyed Naisi.' And
he is well pleased Deirdre has 'a store of pity for the three that
were (her) friends in Alban'. But more than anything he wants her
pity for himself: 'It isn't long till a day'll come when you begin
pitying a man is old and desolate, and High King also.' For he
feels that he has such a share of troubles 'it would be a good bargain if (he) were in the grave, and Deirdre crying over (him) and
it was Naisi who was old and desolate'.

To this pass has the arrogant king of Act One come: he knows
that there is such a thing as the heart, that its affections are priceless, and that 'There's one sorrow has no end surely – that's being
old and lonesome.' And so '(*with extraordinary pleading*)' he makes
his final attempt to win Deirdre and gain a crumb of what she has
given Naisi, to gain a few months in his old age of the happiness
which Naisi enjoyed for seven years in his prime. Yet he has not
learned his lesson thoroughly; he will not accept the fact that
'there's things a King can't have' and in this extremity he reveals

his own bankruptcy and his ignorance of Deirdre by still trying to
win her with splendour and safety:

> Let you not break the thing I've set my life on, and you giving
> yourself up to your sorrow when it's joy and sorrow do burn
> out like straw blazing in an east wind. . . . But you and I will
> have a little peace in Emain, with harps playing, and old men
> telling stories at the fall of night. I've let build rooms for our
> two selves, Deirdre, with red gold upon the walls and ceilings
> that are set with bronze. There was never a queen in the east
> had a house the like of your house, that's waiting for yourself
> in Emain (337).

Immediately upon this a Soldier runs in crying: 'Emain is in
flames. Fergus has come back, and is setting fire to the world.
Come up, Conchubor, or your state will be destroyed' (337).
This is an excellent dramatic moment, tense with excitement and
irony; it also represents the extinction of all Conchubor's power
and underlines his basic impotence. Yet so frenzied is he with
desire, pain and frustration, that he is comparatively unmoved
by the destruction of his capital: 'Come forward and leave Naisi
the way I've left charred timber and a smell of burning in Emain
Macha, and a heap of rubbish in the storehouse of many crowns'
(341). He is quite ready to abandon his kingdom – it means no
more to him than Naisi's body – so long as he can have Deirdre;
he is concentrated on one resolve: 'not to lose the thing (he's)
bought with sorrow and the deaths of many'. Here the word
'bought' is significant: even now he has not got rid of the notion
that such relationships may be bought if one pays a high enough
price for them – and he is willing to pay, literally, everything.
He hurls defiance at Fergus, pathetic, in its contradiction: 'Fergus
cannot stop me. I am more powerful than he is, though I am
defeated and old.' And he is ready to take on the whole world:

> CONCHUBOR (*Wildly*.) When I've killed Naisi and his brothers
> is there any man that I will spare? And is it you will stand
> against me, Fergus, when it's seven years you've seen me
> getting my death with rage in Emain? (343).

Finally, when Deirdre is dead, he knows that all is lost irrevocably; his 'own heart is gone within' him; and he is led out, a broken
old man.

Far from being a bleak, aloof tyrant, Conchubor is a credible and human figure of some complexity, caught between several contending passions. Thus his treachery does not revolt us and make us hate him entirely, for we are aware of the terrible hunger which impelled him to act so, and we extend to him something of the pity which we extend to Macbeth and Othello when they commit similar deeds. We realize too that in bringing about the deaths of Deirdre and Naisi Conchubor is, unknowingly, doing them a good turn – by preserving them from declining love and from decay. In a way he is a tragic figure; or rather, it is *his* tragedy that with all his suffering and scheming he never attains the tragic plane and never experiences exaltation, however brief; wretchedness, desolation and drouth alone are his. In contrast with Deirdre and Naisi and all they represent – the power of love – he is a destructive force – not least to himself.

In his *Deirdre* Yeats observed the Unities and used a chorus of beautiful women musicians for the purposes of retrospective narration. Synge sensed that this neo-classic method was not suitable for the twentieth-century stage (that he was correct is indicated by his own practice and by T. S. Eliot's remarks on his own experiments in *Murder in the Cathedral* and *The Family Reunion*). And his 'chorus', in the persons of Old Woman and Lavarcham, is integrated with the action. He follows Ibsen in contriving that the information which it is essential for the audience to have at the beginning of the play comes out naturally and economically through the conversation of Lavarcham and Old Woman; and so credibility is established. One or both of these characters is present at the beginning of each act to start it off at a level near enough to normality for an audience to accept it as plausible. In addition, Lavarcham and Old Woman who, among other things, represent the mass of ordinary folk watching the action, help particularly to give substance to the play, to link it with everyday reality.

Lavarcham's part is vital to the whole; and here again Synge develops his source and adds complexity and significance to his theme. In the legend, and in Ferguson and 'A.E.' (Yeats leaves her out), Lavarcham is the faithful nurse of Deirdre who accompanies her in all her joy and adversity and who buries her in the end. But Synge, in addition to giving Lavarcham these functions, also makes her a character in the fullest sense, and assigns to her an important part in the pattern of the play.

To make this clear we must consider the figure of Owen. His character is only sketched but the outlines are firm and his function is fairly well marked. In some respects he resembles the Fool in *King Lear*. In one section of his book, *Shakespeare's Doctrine of Nature*, J. F. Danby sets forth the dilemma of the Fool who sees everything as 'handy-dandy'. The Fool suffers because his reason urges him to side with the Sisters–Edmund faction, while his intuitions compel him to follow Lear. In the same way Owen's reason demonstrates that he is a fool to bother about Deirdre; he should side with Conchubor and revenge himself upon Naisi (who killed his father); and he cries (with a glance at Helen and Troy) 'Was there ever a man crossed nine waves after a fool's wife and he not away in his head?' Nevertheless his intuitions are stronger than his reason; he loves Deirdre, and he is the first man to die because of her; like the Fool too, Owen is intelligent, and his understanding of the situation in Act Two is more immediate and cogent than that of anyone else. So, because some of the others think he is crazy, and because his passion for Deirdre makes him reckless, he is able to utter truths with a trenchancy that others cannot or dare not attain. Thus one of Owen's functions is to impress decisively upon Deirdre the fact, which she is secretly becoming aware of, that even queens grow old, that youth and beauty must decline, and love decline along with it. Another of his functions is, by his words, actions and by his suicide when he hears that the lovers are returning to make it clear to an audience that the lovers are going to their deaths, and also to stress the fact that they are going back to avoid waning love and decay. Furthermore he provides a kind of grim comic relief, which gives contrast and solidity to the whole; and although there is never any real danger of over-facility of pathos and sweetness in the play, the presence of the enigmatic and grotesque Owen adds welcome irony and astringency. Finally it is Owen's function to communicate some important information about Lavarcham. He says:

> It's Naisi, Naisi, is it? Then, I tell you, you'll have great sport one day seeing Naisi getting a harshness in his two sheep's eyes and he looking on yourself. Would you credit it, my father used to be in the broom and heather kissing Lavarcham, with a little bird chirping out above their heads, and now she'd scare a raven from a carcase on a hill. (*With a sad cry that brings dignity*

into his voice.) Queens get old, Deirdre, with their white and long arms going from them, and their backs hooping. I tell you it's a poor thing to see a queen's nose reaching down to scrape her chin. . . . I'll give you a riddle, Deirdre: Why isn't my father as ugly and old as Conchubor? You've no answer? . . . It's because Naisi killed him . . . (308–9).

This speech swiftly places before Deirdre's imagination an example of the favour to which she must come if she lives on. She reads Owen's riddle and her determination not to endure declining youth and love is strengthened further. For Owen's words demonstrate that Lavarcham was once, like Deirdre, beautiful; but that when her lover was killed, she did not join him in the grave but chose to live on. Thus, for Deirdre – and for an audience – Lavarcham is a living example of the pass to which Deirdre will come if she elects to survive Naisi. This is Lavarcham's important function in the play.

She was once in the same position as Deirdre, but she made the other choice – life instead of death; and seeing her we know that Deirdre made the right choice. Existence for Lavarcham has been miserable, and she is the most unhappy person in the play. Even Conchubor has, at least, the hope that his schemes will gain him what he wants in the end. But Lavarcham never has any real hope; she knows that Deirdre and all are doomed, yet she refuses to accept this fact; there is some restless principle in her which will not abandon life, and which impels her to go on existing and striving, although she knows in her heart that she will be defeated. Consequently she is always torn between, on the one hand, pain and helplessness when she acknowledges the facts, and, on the other hand, anxiety and restlessness – which have made her 'a great wonder for jogging back and forward through the world' – when she denies the facts and attempts the impossible task of changing them. Whenever she is on the stage she is pleading with someone to change a course of action, and each time she is refused. Defeated, she draws back hopelessly with a cry like 'Then the gods have pity on us all'; only to be jolted out of this apathy by another apparent, but vain, opportunity to alter events. Her love for Deirdre, far from being a source of joy and comfort for her, is the cause of pain and worry (in this she resembles Maurya in *Riders to the Sea*) for she knows that Deirdre is doomed,

yet she cannot do anything else but try to save her. Lavarcham is
the only character not to stress the fact of mutability, and she
opposes Deirdre's contention that it is hardly worth living when
'you're dried and old, and joy is gone for ever':

> If it's that ails you, I tell you there's little hurt getting old,
> though young girls and poets do be storming at the shapes of
> age. (*Passionately*.) There's little hurt getting old, saving when
> you're looking back, the way I'm looking this day, and seeing
> the young you have a love for breaking up their hearts with
> folly (305).

What pathos and irony there are in the way Lavarcham unwittingly
reveals the flaw in her case and proves Deirdre right with the
phrase beginning: 'saving when you're looking back . . .'; for
that is just what life will become in old age, 'plague and torment',
a nightmare after the dream of love has faded. Lavarcham's
existence is proof that life, once youth and love are gone, is nightmare, yet she clings to it, and tries to persuade others to do the
same. She asserts, against all evidence and instinct, that life may
be happy without love, that life may be tolerable if one comes to
terms with it; and at each disaster, although she has always to
accept harsher terms, she tries to salve something from the
wreckage. Towards the end when Naisi is dead and Deirdre is
broken with grief by the grave, Lavarcham still refuses to deny
that life may be worthwhile for Deirdre, and she urges her
passionately to go on living:

> There's a score of woman's years in store for you . . . come till I
> find you a sunny place where you'll be a great wonder they'll
> call the queen of sorrows; and you'll begin taking a pride to be
> sitting up pausing and dreaming when the summer comes. . . .
> Rise up Deirdre and come to Fergus . . . (339–41).

Finally when Deirdre is dead, this instinct to preserve life in any
conditions is directed towards aiding the failing Conchubor: so
great is Lavarcham's desire to maintain life that she will try to save
the man who she thinks is responsible for the tragedy: 'I have
a little hut where you can rest, Conchubor; there is a great dew
falling.'

As we look at Lavarcham, in whom heroism, cowardice and
pathos are so singularly mingled, we know that the existence

which she endures is most certainly not the life for one who has known what Deirdre has known. Lavarcham and Conchubor are the best proof of the wisdom and rightness of the life and death of Deirdre and Naisi. Life for the old has been a long nightmare; for the young a brief, exquisite dream. They have tried to bind to themselves a joy, and have destroyed it: the young kissed it as it flew, and they live in eternity's sunrise.

CHAPTER EIGHT

Concluding

In this book an attempt has been made to expound and examine the main theme of all Synge's work, and, at the same time, to indicate some of his qualities as a writer. The extent of success or failure in the attempt is by now marked, but probably something should be said in conclusion about the more important implications of some of the points raised.

It is worth noting how closely bound into one main theme are the three elements of tension between dream and actuality, interaction between Man and the natural world, and awareness of mutability. All the sympathetic figures in Synge's plays are driven by an impossible dream; each, with a single-minded, intense, almost child-like longing to become 'a wonder' is continually reaching out for a finer and fuller life. Imagination is creative in each of them, and it gives them a vision of some good beyond the poverty or drabness or terror which surround them; towards that vision, that dream, they strive. Yet they are nearly always frustrated. Only in *The Playboy* does the power of the imagination make dream and actuality one, and accordingly this play is the richest and most joyous that Synge wrote. *The Tinker's Wedding* too is largely happy, because Sarah's dream is of something worse than her normal life and she gets rid of it in the end and returns thankfully to her proper station. But in *The Shadow of the Glen*, although it is clearly implied that Nora's choice was the right one, it is not asserted that she and the Tramp attain what they seek, and in the other plays and in the prose works and the poetry the dream is invariably overcome by actuality. Hence the tragic undertones, the sombreness and the awareness of mutability pervading Synge's work.

The reason for this defeat of dream and spirit by the inhumanity of the universe and time is that all Synge's figures are very closely linked to the world around them. There is little that is ideal or transcendent in their dreams, they have no religious vision of a new Jerusalem nor any political vision of an earthly Utopia; they are truly children of Nature and the love and happiness and beauty of which they dream is in terms of this world, and particularly of the natural world, here and now; their paradise is the continuation in unchanging fullness of joys they have experienced partially and momentarily in this life. But Nature is not God; she may lead to God and she is a source of loveliness and solace for human beings but she is also harsh and ugly, and Synge's figures in staking all on her are bound to lose in the end: Hugh I'A. Fausset[175] puts it well:

> His people are not sophisticated enough to experience any subtle moral entanglements. They have the ideal beauty and wisdom of the earth, but it is upon the facts of earth that they are broken; they stand, as it were, for the grace of Nature, and like Nature's own flowers they are mangled and tossed aside, but not before they have expressed the tragedy of illusions shattered by realism, of beauty buried in the mire from which it aspired. Like Nature, therefore, they are both romantic and realistic: they have her dignity, but they are also conscious of her degradation. She instructs them only to destroy her pupils.

Synge speaks for his dramatic figures as well as for himself in those moments of revelation in his prose works when the tension between dream and actuality in conjunction with the natural world produces a mood 'in which we realize with infinite distress the short moment we have left us to experience all the wonder and beauty of the world'. Martin Doul too speaks for all:

> It is a bad black day when I was roused up and found I was the like of the little children do be listening to the stories of an old woman, and do be dreaming after in the dark night that it's in grand houses of gold they are, with speckled horses to ride, and do be waking again, in a short while, and they destroyed with the cold, and the thatch dripping, maybe, and the starved ass braying in the yard (137).

The fact that a number of Celtic writers – among them Martyn in his prose play, *The Heather Field* – have dealt with the theme of dream versus actuality, though by no means as profoundly and comprehensively as Synge deals with it, has led some critics to regard it as mainly, if not exclusively, a characteristic of the Celt;

Howe,[176] discussing the views of Matthew Arnold and Ernest Renan on this, says:

> Both alike have found the cue and motive in the Celt to be his need of illusion. He is, says Arnold, a sentimentalist – 'always ready to react against the despotism of fact'. If he gets drunk, says Renan – and goes on to add that he does so very often – his drunkenness 'is due to this invincible need of illusion'.

The Celt may be more prone to this tension than most other peoples, but it seems to me to be an essential feature of the human condition, and to find expression in different forms in many places; in our literature alone the conflict between the world as it is and the aspiring mind, the 'devotion to something afar from the sphere of our sorrow' is by no means confined to Marlowe and Shelley.

Synge does not see how this tension can be resolved in every-day life, nor does he lead us away from it to a transcendent reality; Una Ellis-Fermor says:[177]

> He shapes a fragment of life, man's and nature's intermingled, a fragment charged with passions that beat against fate, and, giving it clear form leaves it isolated . . . there is no relating of the world of men with any wider, less tangible metaphysical universe.

Although it is probably true that the work of the greatest artists has metaphysical and religious implications, the lack of such implications is not to be thought of necessarily as a flaw in Synge as an artist; it suggests that he is not among the greatest and that there may be limitations in his outlook as a man, but it does nothing more. Synge believed that the orthodox religious views were no longer tenable, and he felt that there were two vital factors only to hold on to: the supreme power of the imagination and the mysterious influence of the natural world; he says in his Notebooks:[178]

> The religious art is a thing of the past only – a vain and foolish regret – and its place has been taken by our quite modern feeling for the beauty and mystery of nature, an emotion that has gradually risen up as religion in the dogmatic sense has gradually died. Our pilgrimages are not to Canterbury or Jerusalem, but to Killarney, Cumberland and the Alps. In my

plays and topographical books I have tried to give humanity and this mysterious external world.

In this he resembles the great Romantics, though he does not share the view that God, though transcendent, also pervades the natural world, nor does he think of the imagination as an avenue of approach to some ultimate 'Truth' or as giving access to a unifying or controlling 'Spirit of the Universe'. The link with Wordsworth is noticeable, particularly as Synge said that 'he preferred Wordsworth to any other English poets . . . he was more at one with nature . . . there was a purity and simplicity about Wordsworth's poetry that appealed to him strongly'.[179] Thus in his belief in the great powers of the imagination and of the natural world, and also, as we have seen, in his critical outlook, Synge is near the great Romantics.

In other respects as a dramatist he is related to the Jacobeans; as Una Ellis-Fermor shows:[180]

Synge often leads us back in thought to the Jacobeans and even those of us who often recognize this kinship wonder at times precisely where it lies. Yet we need hardly do so. For he has something of their knowledge of the inevitable, though hidden, movements of the spirit in the supreme moments of tragic experience. He, who knew so much of the fundamental loneliness of human life, who lived so constantly with death at his elbow, shared their knowledge of the searching interplay of death and life. 'I am in the way to study a long silence. To prate were idle.' The same power to condense thought and passion into all but silent and inarticulate vision that gave them their mastery over tragic event is his also. And he too can show, in these brief sentences spoken at the height of tragic revelation, depth below depth of knowledge. There are few words in twentieth-century drama that bring the same shock of conviction as Deirdre's or Maurya's in the face of death. Synge's is a profound knowledge, the knowledge of the freedom that comes from the parting of the last of the bonds of life: 'They're all gone now. And there isn't anything more the sea can do to me.' This is the grief 'that cuts the heart-strings', freeing the spirit from the claims of the world; Cleopatra, Imogen, Cornelia, the Duchess of Malfi and Calantha are among those who share it.

With regard to comedy too, Synge's realism and mordant humour, his powers of construction and of gorgeous invective, the appetite for sensuous enjoyment and the vigour possessed by his characters, remind one of Ben Jonson, a dramatist he admired greatly. In placing Synge near such eminent company I do not feel that too much is being claimed for him, since, although on the surface his scope may appear to be restricted, the fact is that he is dealing in a fresh and profound way with the enduring concerns of mankind; his figures though precise in their setting are never confined to it; Una Ellis-Fermor again puts it well:[181]

> The drama of Synge is severely, almost deliberately limited. In comedy he writes only of one kind of man, the peasant of the east or the west of Ireland. Yet he chooses so unerringly what is fundamental in the manners and motives of his people that his comedies, though local, are universal, though national, international.

Since the passing of the great Elizabethan tradition of poetic drama the main problem for the potential serious dramatist has been to obtain both verisimilitude and universal significance in terms of dramatic naturalism. In the nineteenth century the plays written in imitation of the Elizabethans were, apart from any other failings, clearly lacking in verisimilitude; and those prose plays which did approximate to life were merely of ephemeral interest. Ibsen found a solution to the problem, at least for himself, but his followers, adopting his techniques though lacking his genius, wrote competent, lifelike plays void for the most part of those poetic undertones, that extra dimension, which make a play rich and meaningful for succeeding generations.

It is Synge's major achievement that he too found a solution to this problem: he unerringly avoided both the snare of following the Elizabethans, and the snare of copying Ibsen; and he wrote good poetic drama within the severe limits of naturalism; he was the first to do this in English for about two hundred years, and no more than two or three dramatists have done it since. Moreover Synge is one of the few poetic dramatists of any age who can today compete successfully with the conventional prose play. The appeal of Synge's poetic plays, unlike the appeal of much twentieth-century verse drama, is not limited to a specialized audience in a particular frame of mind, but it extends also to that wider public which T. S. Eliot and Christopher Fry are trying, with some success, to reach: the normal modern agnostic audience, brought up on Milne, Coward, Lonsdale and Maugham, which is inclined to be ignorant or prejudiced with regard to poetry.

Synge was aided in combining poetic richness and vitality with reality by the qualities of Irish peasant speech, and many critics have praised his dramatic speech as his greatest distinction. But two critics see it as a limitation:

> There remains the speech of the plays – the most evident of their beauties, and the chief, perhaps, of their disabilities; if our concern be the ready absorption of these plays into the common heritage of the English-speaking theatre. For their speech is not the English spoken in England.[182]

Howe wrote this in 1911; and today we can see that he was wrong; for even if we lay aside the question as to how far dramatic speech should be a close imitation of the speech of the people watching the play, we are still left with the fact that the plays of Synge, along with the plays of one or two modern American and Irish dramatists, and along with a number of American films, all using speech which is not the English spoken in England, have been found enjoyable and meaningful by English people and are presumably part of their heritage. But perhaps Howe is doubting whether Synge's speech can ever create a fresh and important development in English drama and serve as a model and inspiration for future poetic dramatists. If so he is on firmer ground.

T. S. Eliot considering the question of language for the person who wants to write poetic drama today, after noting that Synge based the language of his poetic plays upon the speech of the country people of Ireland, says: 'The language of Synge is not available except for plays set among that same people.'[183] This is true; furthermore Synge's language is hardly available even for such plays because the speech of the rural Irish people, though it remains more vivacious than normal English, is not what it was in Synge's day, and because, as the floundering of Synge's imitators quickly showed, Synge's language seems peculiar to himself and tends to become corrupted or intractable in other hands. But although it is useless to pretend that Synge can offer assistance in solving one of the most urgent problems of the contemporary poetic dramatist – that of speech – it is wrong to conclude therefore that his intrinsic merit as a dramatist is impaired. Arnold doubted whether our greatest dramatist has been a good influence on succeeding writers, and Eliot certainly, and Fry apparently, seek to avoid any echo of Shakespeare in their dramatic language, but this does not detract in any way from Shakespeare's greatness. It just means that some good writers are of no help to their successors at certain points in time, and that in our day Synge's idiom, and Elizabethan blank-verse – along with such things as Congreve's prose – give no positive assistance to the practitioner of poetic drama. Yet this does not lessen our enjoyment or our valuation of Synge, of the Elizabethans and of Congreve, in themselves. Moreover Synge's plays are not poetic merely in language; they are poetic in their total structure and design, and each play as a whole is a coherent and memorable image of some fundamental aspect of life. While presenting definite and recognizable situations vividly and precisely the plays have a vitality and significance far beyond any particular situation or relation; they operate, like all good poetic drama, on more than one level of meaning at once, and show, as Una Ellis-Fermor says, 'depth below depth of knowledge'. They are, finally, examples of that supreme faculty, indispensable to a poet, and which, no matter what literary form it may take, alone distinguishes him as such – the imagination, revealing itself 'in the balance or reconcilement of opposite or discordant qualities: of sameness with difference; of the general with the concrete; the idea with the image; the individual with the representative; and a more than usual state of emotion with more than usual order.'[184]

Notes

1 *The Irish Dramatic Movement* (1939), p. xi.
2 There were hundreds of articles, book reviews, lectures, etc. M. Bourgeois, with remarkable diligence, lists them in his *John Millington Synge and the Irish Theatre* (1913), pp. 265–96.
3 op. cit. p. 63.
4 op. cit. pp. 239 and 247.
5 *Englische Studien*, Band 45, pp. 272–92.
6 Lady Gregory, *Our Irish Theatre* (1913), p. 187. Bourgeois says that 'Synge's work was appreciated in America long before it was appreciated either in England or in Ireland'. op. cit. p. 240.
7 p. 195.
8 *John M. Synge* (1915), a special Cuala Press edition. Masefield wrote an article on Synge for the *Dictionary of National Biography*, Second Supplement, vol. iii, pp. 468–71 (1912).
9 op. cit. p. 12.
10 op. cit. p. 18.
11 op. cit. p. 10.
12 *Fortnightly Review* (1924).
13 p. 151.
14 pp. 94–7.
15 *Some Impressions of my Elders* (1922), p. 201.
16 op. cit. pp. 116, 198–200.
17 *How to Write a Play* (1928), p. 22.
18 ibid. p. 20.
19 ibid. pp. 68–72, 77–80.
20 *The Road Round Ireland* (1926), p. 370.
21 op. cit. p. 373.
22 p. 11.
23 ibid. p. 39.
24 p. 114.
25 p. 184.
26 pp. 32 and 36.
27 op. cit. p. xi.
28 p. 16.
29 *Politics and Letters*, no. 4 (1948), pp. 5–12.
30 p. 57.
31 ibid. p. 56.

32 *Politics and Letters*, no. 4 (1948), p. 133.

33 ibid. p. 132.

34 *Envoy*, vol. 3, no. 11 (Oct. 1950), pp. 44–51.

35 'Yeats, Synge and the Abbey Theatre', art. in *Studies*, vol. XLI (1952), pp. 333–40.

36 p. 154.

37 e.g. C. F. McKinley, *John Millington Synge* (1951), Ph.D., Trinity College, Dublin;

     G. D. P. Allt, *The Anglo-Irish Literary Movement in Relation to its Antecedents* (1953), Ph.D., Cambridge;

     M. Brady, *John Millington Synge, the Dramatic Artist* (1953), M.A., National University, Ireland;

     J. L. Sorg, *Synge and Shakespeare* (1954), B.Litt., Trinity College, Dublin.

38 op. cit. p. 154.

39 *Irish Writing*, no. 18 (March 1952), pp. 39–42.

40 *University Review*, vol. 1, no. 5 (Summer 1955), pp. 52–8.

41 *Irish Writing*, no. 30 (March 1955), pp. 56–62.

42 Quoted in Cavenagh, op. cit. p. 94.

43 op. cit. pp. 199–200.

44 *The Contemporary Drama of Ireland* (1918), p. 102.

45 Quoted in Greene and Stephens, op. cit. p. 245.

46 ibid. p. 248.

47 Quoted in Lady Gregory, *Our Irish Theatre* (1913), p. 300.

48 art. cit. in *Irish Writing* (March 1952), pp. 39–42.

49 W. B. Yeats, 'J. M. Synge and the Ireland of his Time' in *Essays* (1924), p. 405.

50 See Greene and Stephens, op. cit. pp. 86, 265 and 182.

51 *Essays*, p. 362.

52 'The Irish Dramatic Movement' in *Plays and Controversies* (1923), p. 159.

53 *Essays*, p. 388.

54 pp. 352 and 369–73.

55 ibid. pp. 208 and 474.

56 T. O Crohan, *The Islandman* (1929), translated, with an introduction, by Robin Flower;

     M. O'Sullivan, *Twenty Years A-Growing* (1933);

     Synge in part of *In Wicklow, West Kerry and Connemara* and O Crohan and O'Sullivan were all describing the same place, West Kerry and the Blasket Islands, at the same time, between 1900 and 1912, and their accounts agree fully.

57 *J. M. Synge's Work as a Contribution to Irish Folk-Lore and to the Psychology of Primitive Tribes* (1932), p. 45.

58 op. cit. p. 246.

59 art. cit.
60 op. cit. p. 164.
61 *Ireland's Literary Renaissance* (1916), pp. 399 and 320.
62 Greene and Stephens, op. cit. p. 302.
63 Boyd, *Ireland's Literary Renaissance*, pp. 88–9.
64 *Love Songs of Connacht* (1893), pp. 9 and 127.
65 *Plays and Controversies*, pp. 28–30.
66 *Cuchulain of Muirthemne* (1902) and *Gods and Fighting Men* (1904),
   translations of the two great bodies of saga material surrounding Cuchulain and Finn.
67 *Our Irish Theatre*, p. 124.
68 Boyd, *Ireland's Literary Renaissance*, p. 75 seq., and Colum, art.
   'Dr Hyde of Eire' in *Commonweal*, XXX (1939), p. 147.
69 art. 'An Epic of Ulster', in *The Speaker* (London, 7 June 1902),
   pp. 284–5.
70 *The Irish Theatre* (1939), p. 59.
71 pp. 136–9.
72 Reid, op. cit. p. 194.
73 Boyd, *Ireland's Literary Renaissance*, p. 348, and Malone, *The Irish
   Drama* (1929), pp. 163–4.
74 *Synge and Anglo-Irish Literature* (1931), pp. 95–9.
75 Greene and Stephens, op. cit. pp. 102–6, quote letters sent to
   Synge from his friends on the Aran Islands, which show how
   firmly based on peasant speech Synge's idiom was, and Greene
   concludes that if 'some of Synge's critics who described his
   language as bogus could have read' these they 'would have
   realized that except for the linguistic refinement that goes into
   any work of art, Synge's characters speak a language which must
   have been very close to that used by the islanders'.
76 ibid. p. 65.
77 *Selected Essays* (1932), p. 46.
78 In a letter to *The Irish Times*, 13 February 1905.
79 O'Connor, art. cit.
80 op. cit. p. 22.
81 *The Contemporary Drama of Ireland*, pp. 104–5.
82 op. cit. pp. 81–2.
83 art. cit.
84 *On Poetry and Poets* (1957), p. 261.
85 op. cit. p. 318.
86 *Plays and Controversies*, p. 57.
87 *Essays*, pp. 331, 391 and 401; and *Plays and Controversies*, pp. 61
   and 97.
88 *Autobiographies* (1955), p. 219.
89 *Hail and Farewell, Ave* (1911), p. 334.

90 Yeats, *Plays and Controversies*, p. 56.
91 *Plays and Controversies*, pp. 45, 50, 103, 113 and 151; and *Essays*, p. 421.
92 *Essays*, pp. 493 and 326.
93 ibid. p. 493.
94 *Plays and Controversies*, p. 146.
95 *Essays*, p. 494.
96 ibid. p. 399.
97 ibid. p. 400.
98 *Plays and Controversies*, p. 81.
99 *Autobiographies*, pp. 486–7.
100 *Plays and Controversies*, p. 200.
101 ibid. p. 51.
102 ibid. p. 155.
103 *Essays*, p. 337.
104 ibid. p. 281.
105 *Autobiographies*, p. 279.
106 *Plays and Controversies*, p. 12.
107 *Autobiographies*, p. 283.
108 *Plays and Controversies*, pp. 190–1.
109 ibid. p. 119.
110 *Essays*, pp. 339–41 and 414.
111 *Plays and Controversies*, p. 120.
112 'The Old Stone Cross', *Poems*, p. 365.
113 *Essays*, p. 373.
114 ibid. p. 263.
115 *Plays and Controversies*, pp. 29–30 and 119–20.
116 ibid. pp. 32, 121–3 and 157–8.
117 *Essays*, p. 369.
118 *Autobiographies*, pp. 493–4.
119 ibid. p. 520.
120 *Essays*, p. 384.
121 ibid. p. 418.
122 ibid. p. 423.
123 *Plays and Controversies*, p. 141.
124 Una Ellis-Fermor, op. cit. p. 61.
125 R. Williams, op. cit. p. 162.
126 *Essays*, pp. 375–6, 407 and 415–16.
127 *Autobiographies*, pp. 509–12.
128 *Essays*, pp. 382 and 420.
129 *Autobiographies*, p. 457.
130 *Essays*, pp. 379–80.
131 *Plays and Controversies*, p. 212.
132 R. Williams, op. cit. p. 205.

133 *On Poetry and Poets*, pp. 261-2.
134 From Synge's Notebooks, quoted in *Plays* (1932), p. iv.
135 ibid. p. v.
136 Notebooks, quoted in Greene and Stephens, op. cit. p. 93.
137 ibid. pp. 229-30.
138 ibid. p. 130.
139 op. cit. p. 39.
140 Quoted in Greene and Stephens, op. cit. pp. 262-3.
141 ibid. p. 259.
142 ibid. pp. 157-8.
143 Preface to *The Tinker's Wedding*.
144 ibid.
145 Preface to *The Playboy*.
146 *Plays*, p. vi.
147 Preface to *The Tinker's Wedding*.
148 *A Defence of Poetry*.
149 *Biographia Literaria*, chap. 14.
150 Preface to *The Playboy*.
151 'In Memory of Major Robert Gregory', *Poems*, p. 148.
152 *Essays*, p. 370.
153 op. cit. p. 114.
154 op. cit. p. 54.
155 op. cit. p. 233.
156 Preface to *Poems and Translations*.
157 ibid.
158 op. cit. p. 125.
159 *In Wicklow, West Kerry and Connemara*, p. 13.
160 op. cit. pp. 123-6.
161 op. cit. p. 182.
162 *Plays*, p. vii.
163 p. 90.
164 *Essays*, p. 420.
165 *Biographia Literaria*, chap. 14.
166 In a letter, quoted by Bourgeois, op. cit. p. 208.
167 *In My Good Books* (1942), p. 157.
168 *Selected Essays*, p. 303.
169 *Studies and Appreciations*, p. 42.
170 *The Aran Islands*, pp. 111-12.
171 *Essays*, p. 383.
172 op. cit. p. 165.
173 *On Poetry and Poets*, p. 85.
174 op. cit. p. 184.
175 'Synge and Tragedy', art. in *The Fortnightly Review* (1924), p. 266.
176 op. cit. p. 189.

177 op. cit. p. 185.

178 *Plays*, p. iii.

179 From reminiscences about Synge by C. H. H. in the *Irish Statesman* of 5 July 1924. Sir Walter Raleigh once said, not, presumably, with complete seriousness, 'that *The Shadow of the Glen* was what Wordsworth had for a lifetime tried to do and failed'. Strong, op. cit. p. 29.

180 op. cit. pp. 185–6.

181 op. cit. p. 184.

182 Howe, op. cit. p. 151.

183 *On Poetry and Poets*, p. 77.

184 Coleridge, *Biographia Literaria*, chap. 14.

Bibliography

References in this book are to the editions specified below.
Figures in brackets after quotations in this book refer to the editions of Synge's works specified below.

JOHN M. SYNGE. *Plays*, 1932. Allen & Unwin (London).
    The Aran Islands, 1912. Maunsel (Dublin).
    In Wicklow, West Kerry and Connemara, 1911. Maunsel (Dublin).
    Poems and Translations, 1950. Allen & Unwin (London).

'A.E.' (George William Russell). *Deirdre*, 1907. Macmillan (London).

F. BICKLEY. *J. M. Synge and the Irish Dramatic Movement*, 1912. Constable (London).

M. BOURGEOIS. *John Millington Synge and the Irish Theatre*, 1913. Constable (London).

E. A. BOYD. *Ireland's Literary Renaissance*, 1916. Maunsel (Dublin).
    The Contemporary Drama of Ireland, 1918. Talbot Press (Dublin).

D. BYRNE. *The Story of Ireland's National Theatre*, 1929. Talbot Press (Dublin).

P. COLUM. *The Road Round Ireland*, 1926. Macmillan (New York).

D. CORKERY. *Synge and Anglo-Irish Literature*, 1931. Longmans (London).

T. S. ELIOT. *On Poetry and Poets*, 1957. Faber & Faber (London).
    Selected Essays, 1932. Faber & Faber (London).

U. ELLIS-FERMOR. *The Irish Dramatic Movement*, 1939. (2nd ed. 1954.) Methuen (London).

O. ELTON. *Modern Studies*, 1907. Edward Arnold (London).

W. EMPSON. *Seven Types of Ambiguity*, 1947. Chatto & Windus (London).

ST JOHN ERVINE. *Some Impressions of My Elders*, 1922. Macmillan (New York).
    How to Write a Play, 1928. Allen & Unwin (London).

A. D. ESTILL. *The Sources of Synge*, 1939. University of Pennsylvania (Pennsylvania).

G. FAY. *The Abbey Theatre*, 1958. Hollis & Carter (London).

S. FERGUSON. *Lays of the Red Branch*, 1897. T. Fisher Unwin (London).

D. FIGGIS. *Studies and Appreciations*, 1912. Dent (London).

R. E. W. FLOWER. *The Irish Tradition*, 1947. Clarendon Press (Oxford).

D. H. GREENE and E. M. STEPHENS. *J. M. Synge*, 1959. Macmillan (New York).

LADY GREGORY. *Our Irish Theatre*, 1913. Putnam (London).
    Journals, 1946. Putnam (London).

S. GYWNN. *Irish Literature and Drama*, 1936. Nelson (London).

J. J. HOGAN. *The English Language in Ireland*, 1927. Educational Co. of Ireland (Dublin).

H. HOWARTH. *The Irish Writers 1880–1940*, 1958. Rockliff (London).

P. P. HOWE. *J. M. Synge*, 1912. Martin Secker (London).

D. HYDE. *Three Sorrows of Storytelling*, 1895. T. Fisher Unwin (London).
    Love Songs of Connacht, 1893. (4th ed. 1905.) T. Fisher Unwin (London).

S. JAMESON. *Modern Drama in Europe*, 1920. Collins (London).

P. KAVANAGH. *The Irish Theatre*, 1946. Kerryman Ltd (Tralee).
    The Story of the Abbey Theatre, 1950. The Devin-Adair Company (New York).

H. A. LAW. *Anglo-Irish Literature*, 1926. Talbot Press (Dublin).

R. LYND. *Old and New Masters*, 1919. T. Fisher Unwin (London).

A. E. MALONE. *The Irish Drama*, 1929. Constable (London).

S. MACKENNA. *Journal and Letters*, 1936. Constable (London).

M. MACLIAMMOIR. *Theatre in Ireland*, 1950. Colm O Lochlainn (Dublin).

J. MASEFIELD. *John M. Synge*, 1915. Cuala Press (Dundrum).

G. MOORE. *Hail and Farewell*, 1911–14. Heinemann (London).

T. O CROHAN. *The Islandman*, 1943. Penguin Books (London).

M. O'SULLIVAN. *Twenty Years A-Growing*, 1938. Penguin Books (London).

R. PEACOCK. *The Poet in the Theatre*, 1946. Routledge & Kegan Paul (London).

V. S. PRITCHETT. *In My Good Books*, 1942. Chatto & Windus (London).

F. REID. *W. B. Yeats*, 1915. Martin Secker (London).

L. ROBINSON. Editor of *The Irish Theatre*, 1939. Macmillan (London).
    Ireland's Abbey Theatre, 1951. Sidgwick & Jackson (London).

J. SETTERQUIST. *Ibsen and the Beginnings of Anglo-Irish Drama: J. M. Synge*, 1951. Hodges, Figgis & Co. (Dublin).

L. A. G. STRONG. *John Millington Synge*, 1941. Allen & Unwin (London).

S. SYNGE. *Letters to My Daughter*, 1932. Talbot Press (Dublin).

E. R. TAYLOR. *The Modern Irish Writers*, 1954. University of Kansas Press (Lawrence, U.S.A.).

C. WEYGANDT. *Irish Plays and Playwrights*, 1913. Constable (London).

R. WILLIAMS. *Drama from Ibsen to Eliot*, 1952. Chatto & Windus (London).

W. B. YEATS. *Plays and Controversies*, 1923. Macmillan (London).
    Essays, 1924. Macmillan (London).
    Collected Poems, 1950. Macmillan (London).
    Collected Plays, 1952. Macmillan (London).
    Autobiographies, 1955. Macmillan (London).

Articles

T. R. BARNES. 'Yeats, Synge, Ibsen and Strindberg' in *Scrutiny*, V,
    1936.
D. DAVIE. 'The Poetic Diction of Synge' in *The Dublin Magazine*,
    XXVII, 1952.
D. DONOGHUE. 'Too Immoral for Dublin: Synge's *The Tinker's Wed-
    ding*' in *Irish Writing*, 30, 1955.
    'Synge: *Riders to the Sea;* a Study' in *University Review*,
    vol. 1, no. 5, 1955.
HUGH I'A. FAUSSET. 'Synge and Tragedy' in *The Fortnightly Review*,
    1924.
GRATTAN FREYER. 'The Little World of J. M. Synge' in *Politics and
    Letters*, 4, 1948.
D. H. GREENE. '*The Tinker's Wedding*: A Revaluation' in *P.M.L.A.*,
    LXII, 1947.
A. G. VAN HAMEL. 'On Anglo-Irish Syntax' in *Englische Studien*, Band,
    45, 1912.
R. MACHUGH. 'Yeats, Synge and the Abbey Theatre' in *Studies*, XLI,
    1952.
A. C. O'CONNOR. 'Synge and National Drama' in *UNITAS*, 1954.
OWEN QUINN. 'No Garland for John Synge' in *Envoy*, vol. 3, no. 11,
    1950.
I. D. SUSS. 'The Playboy Riots', in *Irish Writing*, 18, 1952.
H. O. WHITE. 'John Millington Synge' in *Irish Writing*, 9, 1949.

Index